By Way of Accident

By Way of Accident

THE TRUE STORIES BEHIND
THE DISCOVERY OF EGYPT'S
GREATEST MONUMENTS

———

Ahmed Abul Ella

U.S. Copyright Registration Number 1-234-567-891
WGAW Registered 1234567

Published by:

☐

Publisher name
Publisher address

10 9 8 7 6 5 4 3 2 1

First Edition © 2014 Ahmed Abul Ella

Hardcover ISBN: _____
Softcover ISBN: _____
Ebook ISBN: 978-0-9881892-2-5

All rights reserved. No part of this publication may be reproduced, stored in a retrieval system, or transmitted in any form or by any means, electronic, mechanical, photocopying, recording, scanning, or otherwise, except as permitted under Sections 107 or 108 of the 1976 United States Copyright Act, without either the prior written permission of the publisher, or authorization through payment of the appropriate per-copy fee to the Copyright Clearance Center, 222 Rosewood Drive, Danvers, MA 01923, 978-750-8400. Requests to the publisher for permission should be addressed to Email@Address.com

ISBN-13: 9781523608850
ISBN-10: 1523608854

Acknowledgements

A DEBT OF GRATITUDE MUST be paid to Dr. Zahi Hawass for his support of my project and me. All the time he gave me during the final stages of my research, his advice, guidance and contributions without a doubt have made my book better for readers. His infectious enthusiasm and willingness to write the foreword to the book is certainly indisputable proof that true scientists and giants of Egyptology are caring and willing to help young researchers and beginner authors in the field of Egyptology.

I was personally surprised to see Zahi Hawass reading every page, taking notes and discussing many points within the chapters. He even generously provided me with books, articles and archeological published papers to enhance my background knowledge and enabled me to cover my stories from all sides.

I would like to extend my gratitude and sincere appreciation to Dr. Mohamed Ismail from Egypt's Department of Antiquities for all his hard work and untiring efforts reviewing my research with its historically- and archeologically-related data. His true knowledge and scientific perspective have improved my research to become readable, authentic stories.

In addition, I would like to take the opportunity to thank my friends Amr El Helly and Mohamed Ossama from Egypt for reading my draft several times and writing critical notes about some of the stories within the chapters. Their knowledge and observation put my research on the right track. For their support, advice and unconditional friendship, I want to tell them thank you.

From England, I want to thank my friends and great researchers as well, Simon Cox and Susan Davies. Their words in the early years of my research in 2006 have enlightened me greatly, and to them I want to say that we will write a great book together sometime to celebrate the long years of friendship and research.

From the United States, my appreciation and gratitude must go to David Pike, my friend whose love of Ancient Egypt is empowering even to me as an Egyptian. Also, thanks to Kelli Daley, Patty Esparza, Connie Smyer and Frances Niles for all their help and efforts in reading some of my early papers and drafts. Their constant encouragement and compliments have always pushed my projects and me forward.

Last, but not least, I would like to thank my family in Egypt for allowing me to be away from them for many days and nights traveling in Egypt and abroad or just sitting in my office reading and writing. To them, I say thank you.

Table of Contents

Acknowledgements··v
Chronology of Egypt···xi
Foreword by Dr. Zahi Hawass··xiii
Introduction···xxv

Chapter 1	**Rosetta Stone**··	1
	Egypt before the French Expedition······················	*1*
	Birth of Egypt Mania····································	*6*
	Historic Background·····································	*8*
	Discovery Story···	*11*
Chapter 2	**Tomb of Seti I, Valley of the Kings**···············	**15**
	Egypt after the French Campaign and the Rule of	
	Muhammad Ali Pasha······································	*15*
	Rise of Egyptology and Politics··························	*17*
	Discovery Story···	*20*
Chapter 3	**Serapeum at Saqqara**···	·**31**
	The Cult of the Sacred Bulls····························	*34*
	Memphis···	*34*
	Discovery Story···	·*37*
	Egypt and France: A Special Relationship················	·*39*
Chapter 4	**Royal Mummies, Deir El Bahari Cache**·············	**43**
	Historic Background·····································	·*46*
	Discovery Story···	·*47*

Chapter 5	**Naucratis, the Greek town in the Delta**	**57**
	Flinders Petrie	*61*
	Historic Background	*62*
	Discovery Story	*64*
Chapter 6	**Amarna Letters**	**69**
	Historic Background	*73*
	Discovery Story	*77*
Chapter 7	**Tomb of the Horse**	**83**
	Howard Carter	*86*
	Historic Background	*88*
	Discovery Story	*91*
Chapter 8	**Catacombs of Kom el Shoqafa**	**97**
	The Old Town	*100*
	Discovery Story	*104*
Chapter 9	**Tebtunis Papyrus**	**115**
	Historic Background	*117*
	Discovery Story	*120*
Chapter 10	**Chapel of Hathor, Mistress of the West**	**137**
	Religious Background	*138*
	Edward Neville 1844–1926	*143*
	Discovery Story	*144*
Chapter 11	**Tomb of Tutankhamun**	**149**
	Discovery Story	*156*
	After the Discovery	*161*
Chapter 12	**Tomb of Queen Hetebheres in Giza**	**165**
	Historical Background	*169*
	George Reisner tried to solve the puzzle	*171*
	Discovery Story	*174*
Chapter 13	**Royal Tombs of Tanis**	**181**
	Historical Background	*184*
	Tanis	*186*
	Discovery Story	*188*

Chapter 14	**Nag Hammadi Manuscripts** ·	**195**
	Historical Background ·	*197*
	Discovery Story ·	*200*
Chapter 15	**Solar Boat** ·	**207**
	The Religious Significance of the Funeral Boats	
	in Ancient Egypt ·	*210*
	Discovery Story ·	*211*
Chapter 16	**Sunken Monuments of Alexandria** · · · · · · · · · · · · · · · · ·	**219**
	The History of Ancient Alexandria ·	*222*
	Discovering the Sunken City—Early Beginning · · · · · · · · ·	*224*
	Discovery Story ·	*226*
Chapter 17	**Colossus of Queen Meritamun** ·	**233**
	Akhmim ·	*236*
	Discovery Story ·	*239*
Chapter 18	**Luxor Temple Cache** ·	**245**
	Historic Background ·	*249*
	Discovery Story ·	*253*
Chapter 19	**Workers Village at Giza** ·	**257**
	Historic Background ·	*260*
	Discovery Story ·	*263*
Chapter 20	**Valley of the Golden Mummies at Bahariya** · · · · · · · · ·	**269**
	Historic Background ·	*270*
	Discovery Story ·	*274*
	Epilogue ·	**281**
	Bibliography ·	**287**

Chronology of Egypt

Pre-dynastic Era	5000 BC–4000 BC
Early Dynastic Era, the Rise of the Pharaohs	3200 BC
Old Kingdom, the Pyramid Age	2700 BC–2300 BC
First Intermediate Period	2200 BC–2000 BC
Middle Kingdom	2000 BC–1800 BC
Second Intermediate Period (the Hyksos Period)	1800 BC–1550 BC
New Kingdom, the Imperial Age	1550 BC–1050 BC
Third Intermediate Period	1050 BC–750 BC
Late Period	750 BC–330 BC
Greek-Ptolemaic Period	330 BC–30 BC
Roman Period	30 BC–400 AD
Byzantine Period (the spread of Christianity)	400–641
Arab conquest (the spread of Islam)	641
Arab Islamic State in Egypt	641–868
Tulunide and Ikhshedites Kingdom	868–968
Fatimid Kingdom (the establishment of Cairo)	969–1170
Ayubide Kingdom	1170–1248
Mameluke Kingdom I	1260–1382
Mameluke Kingdom II	1382–1517
Ottoman Conquest	1517–1798
French Expedition of Napoleon	1798–1801
Muhammad Ali Pasha Kingdom	1804–1952
British Occupation	1882–1956
Egypt the Republic	1953–Present

Foreword by Dr. Zahi Hawass

THERE ARE MANY ARCHEOLOGICAL DISCOVERIES that have happened by mere accident. There are fewer discoveries that have actually occurred after careful collection of archeological clues and linguistic proof confirming their existence. Excavations sometimes start and end finding the targeted monument and affirmation of all collected data and sometimes helplessly wind up with nothing at all.

The author in this research, Ahmed Abul Ella, has skillfully managed to present a nice collection of stories and tales about these archeological discoveries that mainly occurred mainly through accidents.

Here, I would like to present the author, as I know him well, to the readers. He works as a tour guide; he is known in his field, travels throughout Egypt and presents to us very useful and nicely written stories. He chose "accidental discoveries" and all the stories behind them to reflect the world of Egyptology in a most captivating, interesting and resourceful style.

Since we are talking about accidental archeological discoveries, I must admit that I have a number of true stories about many discoveries I have made during my lifelong career as an archeologist. Some happened in my early years and some much later. In Giza, I found a small three-sided pyramid behind the Great Pyramid of Khufu. Not far from it, I found the remains of a valley temple and the mortuary temple of Khufu's pyramid in Giza.

All my life in excavation, I was quite certain of one fact. Most 19th century archeologists used to deposit all their debris from digs on top of other forgotten but equally important archeological sites. Therefore, I sometimes focused my efforts on digging out the debris of previously excavated sites, looking carefully in the sand and revealing its secrets. In this regard, I remember after returning from the United States with my PhD degree, with my colleague Mahmoud Afifi, I began to clean, restore and publish information about the Tomb of *ne sout nefr*, west of the Great Pyramid of Khufu. To achieve this mission, we had to remove a huge amount of sand and debris remaining from the time of George Reisner, the famous American archeologist who worked in Giza in the 1920s and Herrman Jonker, the German archeologist who excavated the site after Reisner. The surprise was to find a huge cemetery dating back to the age of the pyramids where we found two new magnificent tombs, one for the dwarf *per ni ankhu* and his unique gray granite statue, currently on display in the Museum of Egyptian Antiquities in Cairo. The second tomb was of the priest *kay* and his daughter who was buried next to him in a smaller tomb. We also found a superb statue of *kay*, which is one of the marvels of Old Kingdom non-royal art.

Another accidental discovery happened to me while working in 1988 near the pyramid of Teti, the 6th Dynasty pharaoh in Saqqara. I found a small forgotten pyramid belonging to an unknown queen but the excavation around the pyramid of Teti and its cemetery was very fruitful as I rediscovered the subsidiary pyramid of Queen *khuit*, the discovery proved that Queen *khuit* was the principal wife of King Teti. In addition, we found a whole cemetery from the New Kingdom. As the excavation proceeded, I spotted a huge heap of sand very close to where we were working. I spoke with Mr. Abdel-Hakim Karar, the chief archeologist on site, and I told him about what lay in this heap of sand. I was quite certain that we would find something beneath. We hired Mohamed Moselhy, the loader driver, to remove all of the debris so we could start the work. It took us three entire months, but it was worth waiting for because not long after we started we found a small hidden pyramid foundation. Only five meters remain from its original 15-meter height. It was sealed with gigantic granite blocks and at the end, inside the burial chamber we found the granite sarcophagus where the remains of the queen's mummy still exist.

Another great accidental discovery occurred in the area of Abu Sir, south of the Giza pyramids. The hero of this story was the same driver, Mohamed

Moselhy, who was born not far from the second pyramid of Khafra in Giza. Mohamed is a great lover of Egyptian monuments and works for Egypt's Department of Antiquities as our loader driver.

We were getting ready to start excavations in the area of Abu Sir, so I sent him over to the site to start clearing sand and debris around the causeway of Sahure pyramid. To prepare the area to receive tourist groups, for many weeks Mohamed would go to Abu Sir every day. One day, in the fine sands of Abu Sir, his loader hit a huge hard limestone block. He left his truck and examined the stone. He found inscriptions covering its surface. His intuition told him it was important. Immediately, he came to my office in Giza and told me about his discovery with some photographs he took. After examining the pictures, I found in one of them the scene of a group of workers dragging a pyramidion (little pyramid) on a wooden sledge and the hieroglyphic text above the scene indicated that the pyramidion was plated with white and yellow gold. It was to be placed on top of the pyramid of Sahure.

Another scene showed musicians and royal dancers in rejoice celebrating the accomplishment of the royal project, which confirmed the idea that all Egyptians celebrate such national events along with the king and his courtiers.

One other scene we found was the picture of a very unhealthy group of people, in obvious famine and starvation. The text above the scene explained who they were. A group of Bedouin intruders was arrested at the eastern gates of Egypt trying to attack a trade caravan coming into Egypt from Syria and Palestine (toward the Sinai Desert). They were brought to be judged right next to the pharaoh's pyramid. This scene is similar to the one found on the walls of Unas pyramid from Saqqara, and because it was not inscribed, it made many Egyptologists believe that there was a famine in Egypt during the Old Kingdom.

The author of this book has mentioned in his research two profound discoveries as accidental ones. One is the Tomb of Tutankhamen discovered by Howard Carter in 1922 in the Valley of the Kings, west of modern-day Luxor. The second one is the workmen's cemetery that I discovered in Giza in the early 1990s. It is important to mention here that both discoveries have clear elements of accident but at the same time, much scientific research was involved in the actual archeological survey in both cases.

As for the Tomb of Tutankhamen, Carter was searching for the mystery king for almost four years. Following strong indications of the tomb's existence inside the Valley of the Kings, especially after the finding of the embalming material caches that belonged to the boy king not far from the heart of the valley, and finding many royal objects in the valley that carry the name Tutankhamen, this was enough for Howard Carter to search enthusiastically in the valley and to look for a source of finance to pursue his dreams. When Carter met with Lord Carnarvon, he asked for sponsorship of the fifth year of work in the valley to search for the lost mysterious Pharaoh Tutankhamen. At first, Carnarvon refused to embark on this adventure. However, Carter was determined to continue no matter what and was going to continue the digs on his own (without support). Finally, Carnarvon agreed to sponsor the fifth year of excavations in the Valley of the Kings.

November 4, 1922, when Carter was excavating the mud brick workers' huts near the Tomb of Ramses VI, there was a boy (probably named Hussien Abd El Rasoul) who brought water to workers in pottery jars. He was trying to place a large pottery jar between stones so it could remain cool under the ground. The boy had to make a surface dig to adjust his jar. At that moment, he found the flat natural stone step that leads down toward the tomb. He simply ran toward the tent where Carter was sitting and told him about his finding.

Can we call it an accidental discovery? We'll leave you to decide.

The second discovery is the Giza pyramids workmen's cemetery, which achieved worldwide positive acclaim among the professionals and laypersons since it was the first time to find definitive clues that shed light on the workers who built the Great Pyramid. The story of this great find dates back to the period 1984–1987 when I was studying at Pennsylvania University, in my Master's and PhD programs, about the Giza cemetery and the cult of its pharaohs as part of a much larger study of all available archeological evidence that might support my dissertation. I discussed the possibility of finding the tombs of the builders of these great pyramids, and I clearly pointed out the possible location where we should look and excavate under the sand for the places where they used to live and the tombs where they are

By Way of Accident

buried. In my published PhD dissertation, I made it clear the area was south of the Wall of the Crow, the limestone giant block wall that used to separate the royal cemetery from the workers village. In the middle of it, we find the only gate where each day workers would enter the royal cemetery and return to their dorms after work. In 1987, I returned to Egypt as the Director of the Giza Plateau and immediately we started excavating the area south of this large stone wall (the Wall of the Crow).

I found an area full of human bones, which indicated burial grounds and tombs not far away, and I found an abundance of wheat seeds, which confirmed the existence of lodgings and homes for these workers. The work stopped in May the same year and resumed in September with a pleasant surprise to all of my team. Only six meters away from the site that we had excavated earlier, a horseback rider fell from her horse. She was a tourist (American most probably) and the accident where she fell revealed the remains of a very old mud brick wall beneath the sand.

Sheikh Mohamed Abdel Razik, the head guard of the area, came to my office at noon that hot summer day to tell me about the horse, the tourist and the mud brick wall that was found. At once, I commissioned Mansour Boriak to work with me to survey the location and soon developed a team of 15 people from archeologists, engineers, and surveyors to restorers. The work of my team was published in four different books and 22 scientific articles detailing all the discovered tombs in the area in the workers upper cemetery and the lower one. Later, another area was discovered with tombs dating back to the times of King Khufu himself (4th Dynasty). The tombs were fairly large and dedicated to the workers' chief connected with smaller tombs and underground deep shafts inside it. We found pottery jars for beer and some signs of human bones. This discovery reflected the administrative order among the workers community and how they were divided and grouped with names and tasks. We find indications of that inside the Great Pyramid of Khufu in the upper relief chambers and the famous graffiti written with red colored ink with the name of the group that cut or built the room (friends of Khufu).

Can we also call this discovery an accidental one?

Now, I would like to share with readers my notes and comments on some of the accidental discoveries mentioned in this book, starting with the Rosetta Stone, the famous Egyptian piece in the British Museum. When I launched an international campaign to retrieve the stone to Egypt from the British Museum, it was housed in a small side room in the Egyptian section of the museum. Under tremendous media pressure, the stone has gained enormous publicity and has become one of the most iconic pieces in the British Museum in a way that forced the museum curators to relocate it to a much better spot, central and well illuminated. My campaign concentrated on all Egyptian artifacts that were plundered from Egypt throughout the nineteenth and twentieth centuries. Many of these iconic artifacts were illegally taken out of the country such as the head of Queen Nefertiti.

It is important to know that the Egyptian Museum in Cairo holds a number of other stones and texts similar to, yet less important than the famous Rosetta Stone. In the Tell Basta site, the Egyptian and the German archeological joint team in 2004 found a piece of very similar stone with hieroglyphic text, Demotic and Old Greek inscribed on its surface. The object, dated back to 238 BC, is a royal decree from the times of King Ptolemy III honoring his daughter, Princess Berenice. The text is considered by scholars to be the oldest existing triple language text from Ancient Egypt.

The second important text in the Cairo Museum is the one known as the Memphis Decree, from the times of Ptolemy IV, written just a few years before the third and most famous one, the Canopus Decree from the times of Ptolemy V around 196 BC that is known worldwide as the Rosetta Stone.

The Decree of Canopus includes much larger text and hieroglyphic lines but certainly was not the only one we found. As I said earlier, the Cairo Museum houses several texts and stones all from the times of early Ptolemaic rulers who were issuing royal decrees and edicts to celebrate certain political and religious occasions and some of these texts have survived. The discovery of such texts came from various areas in Egypt. The Tanis text in 1866, the ruins of Kom El Hesn in Delta 1881 (26 hieroglyphic lines, 2 Demotic and 64 Old Greek) and the recently discovered one in the Sohag area in Upper Egypt in 2002 with 21 hieroglyphic lines, 17 Demotic and at the bottom of the stone there is a small unfinished text that says it will be completed with Greek translation.

I remember I had sent a letter to the authorities of museums in Germany to ask for the return of the head of Queen Nefertiti. After I had left office as head of the Egypt Department of Antiquities, the subject was neglected and the whole campaign stopped and dropped the issue entirely. (The 2011 Arab Spring Revolution began and I could not have the opportunity to follow the request, and also to start a campaign regarding other artifacts.)

The other discovery I would like to shed light on is the Tomb of Pharaoh Seti I, in the Valley of the Kings. In 1960, Sheikh Ali Abdel Rasoul (the descendant of the famous Abdel Rasoul family who originally found the royal mummies caches near the Temple of Queen Hatshepsut in 1871) was part of a team excavating inside the Tomb of Seti to explore the lower deep shaft beneath the floor of the final burial chamber of the tomb. Sheikh Ali strongly believed that at the end of the long mysterious shaft lay the true hidden pharaoh's burial chamber. All we needed to do was dig all the way to the end of it but because it was extremely long and narrow it was dangerous to continue the work in the 1960s.

In 1974, I met with Sheikh Ali when I worked in the Valley of the Kings as an inspector. He told me the story of the shaft and the possible hidden tomb at the end of it. He even took me to the tomb, explained his theory and urged me to start digging the shaft. He predicted that if I were to do so, I would be famous and would find the true Tomb of Seti I with hope that his legacy would be remembered. In 2002, I became the Secretary General of the Supreme Council of Egypt Antiquities and in my first visit to the Valley of the Kings, I entered the Tomb of Seti, checked the shaft myself and found the difficulties faced Sheikh Ali back in the 1960s. Not until 2007 did an Egyptian team of archeologists form to examine the shaft and start the exploration. I led the work with Tarek El Awadi, Mustafa Abdel Shakour and engineer Ayman Hamed. The work began by securing the actual body of the shaft with steel and wood beams and providing a walkway with a handrail and (decovill) cars on rails to transport dirt and rubble from excavations easily and save time and effort.

Below 150 meters deep, we reached the limestone core of the Theban mountain but had not reached the shale layer yet (the geological formation of the Theban Hills contains limestone and a thick layer of shale beneath it, which is responsible for damaging most of the lower parts of the tombs in the valley when it rains and water floods the tombs gateways). At this deep level, we found marks on the rocks explaining how the walls were being prepared for decoration and a small Hieratic text indicating some measurements of the shafts doors.

We succeeded in reaching 174.5 meters deep in the shaft where we found it blocked and dead-ended with a few unfinished steps cut into stone, which indicated that work in the shaft stopped right there maybe when workers received the news about the sudden death of the pharaoh who ruled for almost 12 years. So maybe Seti I did not have the time to finish his dream about hiding his true burial at the bottom of the secret shaft and his son and successor Ramses II, who ruled for more than 60 years, may have had the chance to achieve his secret burial tomb. The Tomb of Ramses II was not fully cleared and excavated yet.

Now, we go to the desert of Saqqara and the giant Serapeum, the burial ground of the sacred Apis bulls and a number of royal family members in Ancient Egypt (Prince *khaimwas*, son of Ramses II). My story about this unique place started in 1984 when the labyrinth of underground corridors and burial vaults began to crumble and its ceiling started to crack and fall apart, until engineer Hassan Fahmy from the Center for Antiquities Engineering offered a complete plan to save the falling walls of Serapeum. He suggested building steel supporting beams to all of the underground vaults that house the granite sarcophagus of Apis bull mummies in order to hold the ceiling and walls. However, the project was declined without any other alternative plans to restore the Serapeum. This unbelievable situation remained suspended with more damage every day to the Serapeum until I came to office in 2002 as head of the Supreme Council of Antiquities and decided to face the problem together with archeologists and restorers.

I called for a meeting of experts from Egypt and abroad to find the best way to tackle this vexing problem that had been occurring since 1984. I offered the restoration project from Hassan Fahmy and told everyone in the room, *"If you don't agree on this salvage project, you immediately have to offer another one to save the Serapeum."* I managed to convince the crowds of the importance of this salvage project, and we started the restoration with engineer Ibrahim Mehleb, the head of the Arab Contractors Company then (now he is the prime minister of Egypt), who led the team of restorers. The work proceeded inside the giant Serapeum and we nearly finished the entire south wing and even scheduled to open it for visitors by 2011. However, the January 25, 2011 Revolution halted everything, and the opening was postponed until 2013, when it was open for visitors without the slightest mention of the names behind its restoration.

Now, we go up the Nile to Luxor, where the royal mummies cache were found in 1871 by the local family of Abdel Rasoul who used to live in the village of Qurna very close to many tombs and the houses literally built on top of tombs. This particular discovery has confused us for many years, as people who wrote about it were uncertain of the actual year of the discovery. Some suggest 1871 and others think 1875. However, what the author said is right; the year of the discovery was 1871. There is another issue regarding the family members of Abdel Rasoul and their names Ahmed, Mohamed or Abdel Rahman, and which one truly led the police to the location of the cave where the royal mummies were buried for over 300 years.

I went to the royal mummies cache myself one day during my long lasting search for the mummy of Queen Hatshepsut. Every time I went, I used to wonder how the family of Abdel Rasoul would come to the cache area back in the 1870s without the modern equipment we use now. It's a really difficult and dangerous task. However, a modern medical examination of all of the royal mummies has recently taken place. I wrote a book in cooperation with Sahar Salem, Professor of Radiology at the faculty of Medicine Cairo University, about the results of CAT scans and DNA laboratory testing on all of the mummies found.

Here it is important to mention yet another accidental discovery in the Valley of the Kings related to another collection of royal mummies, the discovery made by Victor Loret in 1899 inside the Tomb of Amunhotep II. Behind one of the painted and decorated walls, Loret found a hidden room with mummies. Howard Carter was then the chief inspector of Luxor's West Bank archeological area. He used his authority and moved all of the mummies to the then newly opened Egyptian museum. Only three mysterious mummies were left inside the tomb. The mummies were known by the titles "the old lady," "the young lady" and "the child mummy" until they were recently examined using modern CAT scan and DNA laboratory techniques that we have in the Cairo Egyptian Museum in association with Cairo University Medical School. The research finally revealed the identity of the two women. The elder woman now has been identified as Queen Tiye and the young woman has been identified as the mother of Tutankhamen and the daughter of Queen Tiye and King Amunhotep III, which means that Pharaoh Akhenaten did actually marry his own sister.

The two female mummies were moved to the Egyptian Museum in Cairo, but the mummy of the mystery child is still in the tomb today.

Since we are talking about Queen Tiye and Amunhotep III, we eventually must mention their son and heir Akhenaten who lived most of his life as a king in his new capital in Middle Egypt, Akhetaten, nowadays El Amarna, where much has been discovered in its ruins, the famed Amarna letters story that the author recorded being one of the greatest finds in the area.

The place was ignored for many decades until recently when development finally came to the famous site. A well-paved web of roads connects the main sites to one another, especially the tombs including the far away royal tomb and ancient sites of Akhenaten's palaces. All of it is now easy to visit by car or bus. We (Egypt's Department of Antiquities) has built a high-quality visitor center by the Nile side to serve all visitors entering the area. Again, everything stopped because of the revolution in 2011. But the bad news we keep receiving from the area about local farmers violating the archeological sites and the excavation area is quite shocking; we have lost much land in the area because of that in the last three years.

We go back again to the north, in the Giza area. The discovery of Queen Hetepheres tomb very close to the Great Pyramid of Khufu is considered one of the most important finds in Giza and the Old Kingdom. I examined the tomb and its relics with my friend and colleague Mark Lehner and we came to the same conclusion that Queen Hetepheres must be buried in Giza in the small subsidiary pyramid known as GIA. However, later on and during the First Intermediate Period of Ancient Egypt's history, the cemetery of Giza was plundered by tomb raiders and looters, so the priests who still respected the family and lineage of Khufu moved all of the queen's personal funeral artifacts from the original unsafe tomb to a nearby deep shaft without the mummy, which most probably was lost and damaged by grave robbers.

It is important to remember here the great efforts of Ahmed Yousef, the man who worked with George Reisner in the 1920s and restored the tomb's wooden artifacts. This great man worked in restoration for more than fifty years and George Reisner was unable to take any of the discovered artifacts to Boston because the agreement between the Egyptian government and American expedition of Harvard/Boston did not allow any splitting or sharing of finds. However, the Egyptian government had offered the statue of "*ankhkhaf,*" the architect of the second pyramid of Giza (Khafre's pyramid) as a personal gift for all the years Reisner spent in Egypt working and exploring. The statue is now in the Boston Museum of Fine Arts along with a replica of all of the discovered artifacts from the tomb of the queen. (*ankhkhaf,* his name recently was found written in a papyrus found near the Red Sea which confirmed that *ankhkhaf* completed the building of the great pyramid of Khufu.)

Also in Giza, and far from the Tomb of Queen Hetepheres, the author has dedicated one chapter to the discovery of Khufu's wooden boat. After a long and deep study of funeral boats in Ancient Egypt, I found out the true meaning and religious function of this boat found near the pyramids. The boat is not funereal. Rather, it was a solar boat to enable the spirit of the king to travel in the afterlife on a two-day journey with the Sun God Ra, the journey of the day and the journey of the night. I published a book in Arabic about the Great Pyramid and its surroundings and explained my theory about the religious symbolism of the boat in various papers and research including my PhD about the kings of the Giza Plateau.

The author has nicely retold the story of the boat discovery and explained the role of Kamal El Malaakh and how he shared the making of this astounding discovery with archeologist Mohamed Zaki Nour, the Director of the Giza archeological area at the time.

Finally, I will finish with the story of the greatest statue of a queen from Ancient Egypt, and simply the finest female figure from the 19th Dynasty and Ramses II period, the statue of *Meritamun*. I remember my first time I visited the statue after its discovery. It was almost sunset, and I felt a shivering sensation when I looked at her face, a strange feeling of serendipity and life coming out of the face. In 2002, I decided to explore the area near the statue further knowing the fact that many temples used to be in the area of Akhmim from the time of the New Kingdom all dedicated to the local God Min, the ancient deity of fertility. In addition, we read from early Arab visitors and travelers their records about the area of Akhmim's ruins and how they described large temples in the area as big as Karnak in Luxor.

I remember we faced many problems regarding the local Islamic cemetery and how it was literally built on the ancient ruins of the temple. I spoke with the minister of culture, and we secured 180 million Egyptian pounds for the Governor of Sohag to relocate the cemetery away from the archeological site that we wanted to continue excavating. A new cemetery was built, but the old one is still in place today.

These are a few stories I wanted to share in this interesting book. I think readers and Egyptology enthusiasts will find it very useful and entertaining in many ways. It has the excitement of exploration and the adventure of learning the secrets of the pharaohs.

Zahi Hawass
2015

Introduction

SINCE MY EARLY YEARS OF working as a tour guide, taking people around Egypt and explaining the meanings behind the Ancient Egyptian monuments, the idea for this book never left my mind, and throughout my 20 years in Egyptology, the more I read, the more I realized the importance of the subject.

Escorting visitors to temples and tombs has opened my eyes to the interesting stories that lie behind most of the big discoveries in Egypt of the past 200 years. This is where I began collecting all the untold stories and the forgotten details residing not only in the diaries of our great, and occasionally famous, archeologists but sometimes remaining only in the memories of the workers and teams who actually made the discovery. Therefore, I embarked on a quest of discovery, searching for those stories.

Egypt, so old and so full of important archeological sites, is considered the largest archeological open-air museum in the world, with extremely well-preserved monuments that date back as far as 5000 BC. To find a story about a truly accidental major discovery along the Nile is not a difficult task; there exist countless history books, scholarly articles, archeologists' diaries and Egyptology forums around the world that refer to unrecorded incidents of discovery. The desert and oceans of sand of Egypt, however, have revealed their great hidden secrets cautiously and slowly—piece by tiny piece.

Thanks to the difficult—and sometimes dangerous—work of archeologists, we have a deeper understanding and more precise concept of Ancient

Egypt, gained through their sincere efforts and ruthless digs that have helped fuel the mania for Ancient Egyptian artifacts, but which have also contributed profoundly to answering the most difficult and complicated questions that challenge our minds:

- Who are we?
- Where do we come from?
- Where are we going?

The study of Ancient Egypt is of great importance and is unmistakably valued in the fields of the humanities and spirituality.

During the long road toward discovering and understanding the secrets of Ancient Egypt, there have been great events, curious incidents and comical moments, all of which have helped to mold the modern history of Egypt, and in turn, the history of the modern world.

Accidental discoveries, the theme of this book, have occurred in tandem with the political and social development of Egypt during the past 200 years. The three principal objectives of this book are: 1) to unveil the hidden connections and strong links among the true stories behind the major archeological discoveries in Egypt spanning the time period from the 19th century, to the French expedition into Egypt, to present day; 2) to examine the relationship between these discoveries and the sudden opening of Egyptian society to the modern western world; and 3) to explore how the study of Ancient Egypt became a bridge to enlightenment.

It is very common in the field of Egyptology to repeat the same old saying, that "Egyptology is a purely western/European science." That saying goes back to the days of Napoleon's plundering of Egypt in 1798. The question that I always ask myself is where we modern Egyptians fit into the study of Egyptology. Exploring this particular question was another reason for me to write this book.

Recently, we have seen the rise of a new generation of Egyptian archeologists who are not only attempting to contribute to this great science, but to remodel it with a uniquely Egyptian fingerprint. This new line of Egyptologists is rising to the challenge straightforwardly to face some of the historical conflicts and old-fashioned, stereotypical notions about Ancient Egypt, including misconceptions about:

- The existence of slavery in Ancient Egypt
- Who actually built the pyramids?
- Who was the pharaoh of the Exodus?

These and many other topics that could make a long list of complicated subjects have sparked acrimonious debates that arose in cultured western society during the 19th and 20th centuries.

The first generation of Egyptian Egyptologists following the days of Ahmed Pasha Kamal in the late 19th century was unable to conclusively answer every question they faced, especially on those subjects related to Egyptology and religion.

Today, however, Egypt possesses a new generation of well-educated Egyptologists and scientists, who have recently been able to demonstrate and to bravely express their ideas in answering these controversial and volatile questions. The leader of this generation is Selim Hassan; in his footsteps came Ahmed Okasha and Abd El Aziz Saleh, and today we have Ali Radawan and finally, Zahi Hawass.

I started researching the background material for this book in the mid-1990s. My stepping off point was the gathering of all the accidental discoveries in Egypt from 1798 through 1998, encompassing 200 years of exploration, debate and developments.

However, to be honest with my readers and myself, I knew that the stories of major discoveries in Egypt could easily be found in bookshops and university libraries around the world, and in a vast array of languages. From the onset, I could not ignore the fact that readers in general may not be anxiously awaiting yet another book that tells the stories of known discoveries—information that regularly hits the news channels or makes its way onto the front pages of the press—especially a book written by an ordinary person from Egypt.

However, what played in my mind most often was the idea that accident had a major role in many discoveries, and in many cases the only role—this was my starting point and the true kickoff to writing this book.

My research journey has spanned ten years, exploring the diaries of archeologists, old books and professional digging reports, and has concluded with a very long list of discoveries that have involved an accident or some elements of accident. I then began to compare notes on all my resources, including living eyewitnesses, if available, or their families. The majority of workers at archeological sites are hired, local workers, and there are some well-known families who have been doing this type of job for many generations, gaining both fame and respect. This book will mention a number of these families who retain pride in their ancestors who were part of some of the greatest discoveries of the last 200 years. It was a genuine pleasure and privilege for me to meet these families and talk with them about their fathers or grandfathers, the memory of whom is normally celebrated with a black and white photograph hung in the central room of the house.

I enjoyed hearing their original version of the truth, and their deep sense of pride. I very much liked the way they consider their fathers and grandfathers the true heroes of Egyptology. It has been solely through their hard work and long experience that archeologists have been able to achieve their goals. I also felt, however, the bitterness of the truth—that no one knows about these true heroes, nor do they care. The contributions of humble workers have historically been obscured behind the names of famous, and often foreign, archeologists, who have been afforded the credit and everything that comes with it, while these workers and their families gain nothing but the honor of a black and white picture on the wall.

This book will try to shed light on these families and honor the true heroes of the major discoveries in Egyptology. My list initially exceeded 40 stories; after many rounds of discussion with friends and my editor, we decided to limit ourselves to the 20 most interesting stories to share in this book.

These stories appear in true historical order, in a narrative style that allows me to cover as wide an area and as many fields as possible and at the same time to introduce the evolution of Egyptian society over the past 200 years.

As my research plan unfolded and I began writing, I found myself obliged to address the most important questions we ask now in modern Egyptian society, including:

- Did the French Expedition of 1798 have, on balance, a detrimental or positive influence on the preservation of Ancient Egyptian history and artifacts?
- What was the relationship of Muhammad Ali and his ruling family to Egyptology?
- What links existed between Egyptology and colonialism?
- How has archeology affected the development of tourism in the 19th and 20th centuries?
- How has Egyptology informed the modern Egyptian enlightenment movement?

I hope this book will be able to answer these questions in the course of analyzing and synthesizing the events and changes that have taken place during the past 200 years.

The book is divided into chapters, in which a particular accidental discovery will be the main theme of each chapter, but around which there has been a chance to inject all kinds of debate and discussion that may be of special interest.

My team and I have tried our best to ensure that all information, including the names of places and people, is accurate and precise whenever possible. Any and all personal opinions expressed in this book about social or political events are solely my own, representing only my own views.

At the same time, I know how tedious some scientific treatises on Egyptology can be. I wanted this book to be light and told in a narrative, storytelling style. Thus, information flows in each chapter while blending with the central theme. *By Way of Accident* is neither a history book nor an essay on Egyptology. Rather, it is a collection of true short stories about important events in Egypt over the last 200 years. Regardless, our love of Ancient Egypt's captivating charm will endure, as will our bond to its spiritual magic.

Ahmed
The Nile, on a Dahabia
2015

Note:
The research was completely finished, and the draft of this book was ready by the end of 2008. It took me two more years to rearrange some of the chapters and review others. It was ready for publishing in Arabic in 2011 but the spark of the Arab Spring in Egypt and many other countries, with the many consequences of the revolution, postponed the entire project.

Note:
All the names mentioned in this book either Arabic or Ancient Egyptian in origin may have various ways of spelling, and the same name in the book may appear with different spelling due to the way it was written in the various references and books. For example, the name Amun may appear as Amen, or as part of a pharaoh's name like Tutankhamen or Tutankhamun. Similarly, the name Amunhotep may be written Amenhotep. More modern Arabic names like Abd El Rasoul, Ali Gebara, Mustafa Agha, Zaki Nour and Kamal El Malakh may all appear in other spelling forms due to the translation of the name as it sounds in the original language. I have written other names of Ancient Egyptian origin, like *Thani*, *jedptah*, *hetebheres* phonetically and shown them in italic style, and these can all be written in various ways.

CHAPTER 1

Rosetta Stone

EGYPT BEFORE THE FRENCH EXPEDITION

IN 1517, EGYPT EXPERIENCED AN event that changed the face of life for the country. The Mamluk Kingdom collapsed under enormous pressure from the Ottoman Empire and its advancing armies who laid claim to all the lands that were known as the Kingdom of the Mamluks in Syria, Palestine, Egypt and parts of the Arabian Desert.

For 300 years, the Ottoman Turks ruled Egypt, and the powerful Ottoman soldiers, wearing their signature dark red fezzes, controlled the land of the Nile. At that time, the so-called Islamic Army of the Ottomans found no serious resistance in Egypt since the attacking troops were also Muslims. The Ottomans were praying to the same god and praising the same prophet, so naïve Egyptians did not consider them as dangerous invaders and impulsive intruders. Some Egyptians actually saw the Ottoman troops as the modern saviors of Islamic society, capable of leading them toward modernity and conquering the world by raising the green flag of Islam.

The hope for salvation by the Ottomans was all a fantasy, the dreams of the poor, the weak and devastated people who lived along the Nile in the later days of the Mamluks. (This Turkmen clan had ruled from 1250 AD until the Turkish invasion in 1517.) It is obvious now that the Egyptians put too much hope in the Ottoman Kingdom because the invaders had an entirely different agenda.

During the later days of the Mamluks, 1450–1517, the glowing lights of the greatest trade kingdom in the world had started to fade. Pressure was great throughout Europe, particularly in Portugal and Spain, to avoid the heavy taxes required to move goods from Asia to Europe through Egypt and other Mamluk ports and trade stations, such as Aleppo. It was a powerful regional kingdom with a land force and great navy that controlled most of the eastern Mediterranean waters.

The Spanish and the Portuguese not only explored the new world on the other side of the Atlantic, they also attacked every ship and every trade caravan that chose to do business with the Mamluks. It was an economic war, peaking with the Naval Battle of Dio in 1509 between the Portuguese and the Mamluks in the waters of the Indian Ocean. These were wars of survival; eventually the world map changed and along with it the trade routes. The Mamluks and their allies no longer controlled the heart of the old world. Western Europe became the new financial business center of the modern world and with the changes in the map, the rules of the game changed. As we see, trapped by history, Egypt transformed from a powerful state (rich rulers of very poor people) to a collapsing regime running from its inevitable destiny.

Therefore, the Mamluk Kingdom collapsed economically before collapsing politically. It was financial death before cultural and social death—the known world had changed from the way it had been run forever. The Ottomans on the other side of the Mediterranean were watching the whole show and waiting for the right moment to jump like a panther on the falling kingdom. The year 1517 was the perfect moment for them but certainly not for Egypt.

After the dust and noise from galloping horses, clashing swords and fighting armies settled, the Turks established a new system to rule Egypt as part of the Ottoman Empire. They liked Egypt very much for its Nile and fertile fields and most importantly for its poor, suppressed and accepting peasant population. The Turks realized how efficient the Mamluks had been in their way of ruling the Egyptians. The Mamluks collected taxes continuously and created new taxes to wrest more money from the vast Egyptian population who were then mostly farmers (nearly 85%). The genius Mamluk warlords and emirs were able to support their army and navy while building lavish and elaborate mosques around Cairo, mosques that exceeded the size and beauty of the great cathedrals of Europe. (The best example in Cairo, the Sultan Hassan Mosque, was built in 1356.)

The new Turkish rulers made a deal with the former Mamluk rulers. Together, they collaborated to govern this land and its historically oppressed people. Being smart survivors, the Mamluks realized that this was no longer their day, and that they would be forced to serve a new master in order to survive. Therefore, the wealth and all of the resources of Egypt were divided between the new Ottoman rulers and their Mamluk representatives. Eventually, all of Egypt was required to pay double to satisfy the two masters together.

The Turkish Governor of Egypt now reported directly to the Sultan in Istanbul, who required that Egypt send ships every season loaded with food and grain from the Nile Valley to the capital of the empire. Once again, Egypt became the breadbasket for the Turks, as it had been for the Romans.

Egypt relapsed into a long, fruitless dark age. In a way, Egypt entered the Dark Ages almost at the same time that everyone else came out of them.

During these years, Europe headed toward modernity and revolutions in art, industry and human rights.

However, this book is not about judging the Turkish period in Egypt (1517–1798) or even explaining how the Turkish Kingdom contributed to Egypt and its people during those three centuries. I'm not questioning the social and cultural development during this long period and whether it moved Egypt forward or it closed all windows of opportunity in science, knowledge and research as some people may argue. My argument is simply based on a fact that the 300 years of the Turkish era of Egypt are literally the most important and critical years in the history of the modern world in general, and the effect of that on Egypt was far greater and deeper than we may think. Perhaps it is the reason why Egypt now stands where it is in the world, economically and politically.

I believe it is all connected. After 300 years of isolation, Napoleon Bonaparte arrived to wake Egypt from its long, deep and far-from-sweet dreams. In the summer of 1798, it all began.

Napoleon said:

"There is no country in the world where the government controls more closely, by the means of the Nile, the life of people. Under a good administration the Nile gains the desert; under a bad administration the desert gains the Nile."

It was July 1, 1798, west of Alexandria where white sandy beaches run for thousands of miles toward the Libyan border across the vast desert of Alamein and the great sand sea.

Winds were blowing hard, and waves were strong and very rough. Under such bad conditions, Napoleon ordered his leading ship, L'Orient, to begin landing all troops ashore. Forty thousand soldiers started the French adventure in Egypt in these most inhospitable conditions on a wild beach outside the city they had romantically dreamed of—Alexandria.

Chaos and confusion overwhelmed the French troops, with everyone rushing toward the shore in small boats. They jumped from the mother ships toward the great mysterious country that lay behind the sandy beaches protected by savage sea currents and perplexing waves. This rough landing lasted a few nights, and finally the leader managed to reorganize his tired and worn out army once again.

The nightmare of those days and nights spent landing ashore dominated the atmosphere, and many who were there later recalled it was truly an adventure, right from the very first moment. This is officially how the French military expedition to Egypt began under the notorious leader and France's fearless image—Napoleon Bonaparte. Only 28 years old and already famous in Europe after his resounding victories in Austria, Italy and elsewhere, his reputation preceded him long before he touched ground in Egypt.

The French campaign in Egypt was the beginning of the end of an era and the spark of a new beginning of an entirely new age. The French raid was the official declaration of the decline and weakness of the Turkish Kingdom and the beginning of a new political system for Egypt and its surroundings.

The French army marched slowly toward Cairo. They faced the Mamluk troops in various battles along the way, but the main one was the battle at the pyramids. The French subsequently entered the city of Cairo, thereby controlling the northern part of the country. Napoleon established his headquarters in Cairo and established the Research Institute Center of Egypt near his residence, where accompanying scientists could freely record all of their finds in Egypt.

A few weeks later, the turmoil in Egypt began to calm, and Napoleon organized his expedition again, refocusing efforts on political issues and cultural aspects. As part of his plan, he successfully managed to engage with the Azhar scientists and religious scholars, then the most powerful, educated and respected leaders in Cairo. In addition, Napoleon allowed his accompanying team of French scientists to focus their efforts on research missions and exploration of Egypt in all aspects. In fact, the 166 scientists who came to Egypt with Napoleon had a great effect on Egypt's future and its relationship with the world afterward. Put simply, the efforts of these scientists essentially changed the face of life in Egypt and set a path to a new future. It was a major transition for Egypt.

Descrip de le Egypt was the book written about Egypt by these French scientists, and it was the first truly complete work about this ancient country, in every field, covering all aspects of life in Egypt in nine volumes. Here we must highlight the exceptional efforts and contribution of the great artist Denon, who was one of the scientists on the team who traveled to the south of Egypt with the army of General Desiree, at the time chasing the Mamluks and the army of Murad Bey. Murad Bey was the last of the great Mamluk leaders and warlords in Egypt, and Denon's notes included observations on all the archeological sites visited during the great chase throughout the southern Nile Valley. To an Egyptologist, it is of great value.

It was detailed, accurate and supported by wax copies he had made of the wall scenes in temples and tombs. These great wax copies helped to ignite the French mania for everything from Ancient Egypt, a mania that spread throughout Europe.

The Egyptian collection of lithographs, wax copies and artworks were shown later in Paris, and captivated the hearts and minds of artists and wealthy families who wished to collect ancient art pieces from the land of the pharaohs. This opened a new page in an old history book, a page tying Egypt to the modern world.

Birth of Egypt Mania

It is important to note that the French scientists accompanying Napoleon enthusiastically gathered the largest possible collection of Egyptian artifacts and ancient pieces during the three years of the French campaign in Egypt. This essential Egyptian material was crucial for future research and the study of Ancient Egypt that later would become Egyptology.

For the French to be able to understand the origin and the foundations of the Ancient Egyptian civilization that fascinated their imagination, it was important to come to terms with understanding the ancient inscriptions on the walls of temples and tombs and on papyrus sheets. Without being able to read or decipher the Ancient Egyptian symbols and signs, we can say without exaggeration that it was going to be almost impossible to comprehend and analyze the Ancient Egyptian religion and the basic cult system that unified the Egyptians for several millennia. The development of writing and a sign system is considered by many Egyptologists to be the single most important element the Ancient Egyptian civilization contributed to the human race. Beginning as early as 4000 BC, by the power of the written word, Ancient Egypt helped shape the spiritual world in ancient times and inspired many nations and societies by interacting through their written language.

The ability to express oneself in written words and to immortalize oneself through text is the radiant concept that governed the Ancient Egyptian mind, which the French scientists and Napoleon realized. It was a key concept in all monuments they examined during their campaign, and they learned that they needed to find the key to this ancient wisdom. This was the key to open the book of secrets and to learn the meaning of the signs and symbols.

The French soldiers' discovery of the black stone known as the Rosetta Stone was a lifeline to these scientists. It was an intriguing guide to deciphering the Ancient Egyptian symbols and the interesting usage of picture language and revealed the confusing differences between what is a phonogram and what is a pictogram in all of the texts we see.

The discovery of that black stone happened at the right time for Egypt and for Europe as well. Egypt finally decided to disclose all of her secrets and lift up her veils. In Europe, the fever of breaking this mystery called the civilization of the pharaohs was almost a public demand, and it brought Egypt back to its rightful place in the middle of the civilized world.

A lucky turn of the spade here plays a major role in moving the wheels of history toward the remarkable discovery of that insignificant looking black stone. It was actually lying ignored and shattered on the seldom-used beaches of the Egyptian Mediterranean near a small town called Rosetta, strategically located at the point where the western branch Nile meets the sea.

What a strange coincidence! The key to the room of all secrets, the Rosetta Stone, was found in a town benefiting from the fresh waters of the Nile and the salt waters of the Mediterranean. What a masterful choice fate had made. An amazing location, where the two great civilizations decided to meet—the

Nile and the Mediterranean—was where Ancient Egypt finally met modern and promising Europe.

Historic Background

When Egypt entered its final days of glory and the twilight of the rule of the pharaohs, new political and social circumstances arose and forced Egypt toward decay and loss of its power and traditional control over the Ancient Near East. For thousands of years, Egypt had been a principal military force within all of the surrounding countries. With increased frequency though, Egypt began to suffer from waves of attacks from all sides. The first to arrive were the Hyksos (1700 BC) who put Egypt under the power of occupying forces of alien rulers, although this distressed situation never totally wiped out the economic and trade strength that Egypt had gained throughout the ages. Its central location in the ancient world encouraged many peoples to move and live in Egypt along the Nile, seeking favorable trade exchanges. This included the Persians, Lydians, Carians, Greeks, Ionians and many others who immigrated to Egypt and settled in special trade colonies, mainly in the northern Delta. Seeking welfare and prosperity through the various jobs available, they found employment in trade, maritime businesses and mercenary armies. Little by little, the demographic picture of Egypt around 600 BC changed along with linguistic changes. Many new words were introduced into Egypt's everyday language. Starting in the 26th Dynasty, the Greek language was one of the commonly used street languages in Egypt, especially in the northern Mediterranean areas. The historic animosity between the Egyptians and the Persians, as well as between the Greeks and the Persians, helped to unite both the nations of Egypt and Greece against their common enemy. This bond helps explain why Alexander the Great was so well received and greatly welcomed by all Egyptians, common people as well as temples priests, when he invaded Egypt. They viewed him as a savior from Persian tyranny and their cruel governors of Egypt at the time. The enemy of my enemy is my friend.

The good relationship between the Egyptians and the Greeks remained strong even during the times of Ptolemy, who ruled Egypt from Alexandria after the times of Alexander the Great. The early Ptolemaic rulers worked hard to build bridges with all Egyptians, especially with the ancient cults who worshiped the old gods and religion. They showed great respect as they honored the old practices and traditions of Egypt until the time of Ptolemy IV.

The situation under Ptolemy IV's occupation was poor, as he disgraced Egyptian religious practices and seemed to ignore the critical political situation and the increase of nationalistic Egyptian movements. These movements called for liberation from the rule of the Greek Ptolemy IV in Alexandria, and several battles and small wars occurred. There were great disturbances throughout Egypt, notably the battle of Rafah in 217 BC in northern Sinai. In the battle of Rafah, the Egyptians defeated the Greek army of Ptolemy IV, and this small victory in Sinai ignited revolutions throughout Egypt against the Greek occupation. After these uprisings, nationalistic feelings returned to Egyptians, and the Upper Egyptians in the south managed to cut off their section of the Nile Valley from the north and declared an independent state in the south of Egypt. The southern capital was the ancient city of Thebes, and at its northern border was the city of Abydos, where the Temple of Seti I is located.

Ptolemy IV tried his best to regain control over the south of Egypt. However, while he was alive he was never able to unite Egypt again. His son and heir, Ptolemy V (205–180 BC), succeeded his father when he was just a little boy of six years. His official Egyptian coronation had to wait eight more years until he turned 14 and was legally able to rule his kingdom. In 196 BC, great festivals took place throughout Egypt to celebrate the coronation of the young king/pharaoh and his ascendance to the throne. It was summertime, but the river Nile was not promising any beneficial flood for the season. This meant Egypt was heading toward a catastrophe with the shadow of a national famine looming over the lands.

During the reign of Ptolemy V, reunification battles continued, and his armies were able to defeat the independent kingdoms in Upper Egypt and Nubia. The national congress of priests was then in the city Canopus, by the western branch of the Nile that flows into the Mediterranean. The priests seized the opportunity and sent their congratulatory letter to the young Pharaoh Ptolemy V. A special decree was written on stone for that purpose, recording the king's names and titles and all of his great virtues and personal talents.

They celebrated his new orders to minimize or cancel all taxes on Egyptian temples, as well as his declaration to restore and rebuild what had been destroyed in the temples during the wars. They also confirmed his great offers, gifts and respect to all Egyptian gods and his exceptional ability to subdue all criminals and crush all revolutions in the lands of Egypt.

The priests commented positively on the special new tax-free laws the king declared just for the priests. The priests were very grateful and pleased with the new situation. The stone noted that the priests of Egypt had decided to erect a statue to the divine King/Pharaoh Ptolemy V as the savior of Egypt. Copies of the statue were to be placed in special chapels near the great statues of the gods and goddesses in all Egyptian temples. The statue of the young king would be carried along with other statues in significant celebrations. Moreover, the king's chapel was to be decorated differently, with special ornamentations and the double crown of Egypt as an emblem on the pharaoh's head.

The priests specified that the celebration of the king's birthday be held each year on the 30th day of the month Mesra while another celebration dedicated to the king's coronation would be held yearly on the 17th of the month Babeh.

It was required that the king be celebrated annually over the first five days of the month Thot and that his honorary titles (several new ones had been coined) including "the good king that shines on earth" be added. The priests also allowed the commoners to borrow the small, portable king's chapel and his statues for private worship at home.

All of these detailed orders and public announcements were engraved on a black basalt stone, precisely dated on the 4th day from the Greek month Xandikos (April), which coincided with the 18th day of the Egyptian month Amshir in the 9th year of the reign of King Ptolemy V. The priests dated the declaration with the first year of the high priest, "Itus - son of Itus," who was the high priest of all great cemeteries of the deified Ptolemaic kings. (The Greeks in Alexandria under the Ptolemaic rulers dated their chronicles by using the name of the great funeral high priest who was in charge of the Tomb of Alexander the Great. The designated priest actually took the position for one year only, and another priest took over after him and so on.)

The Rosetta Stone was engraved in all common scripts used in Egypt at that time. The first part of the letter was written in hieroglyphic script; the middle part of the letter in Demotic script; and finally at the bottom of the stone in Greek letters. The priests ordered several copies of that letter/stone to be placed outside temple gates regardless of their location or what services they offered. The stones were also to be carried beside the deified pharaoh/king statues in big celebrations all over Egypt. Therefore, we now think that several copies of what we now call the Rosetta Stone were made, but sadly, none have ever been found except a very small part of one other, badly damaged, that was discovered in the city of Damanhur, a major town in the northeastern part of the Nile Delta. The Damanhur artifact is now in the Egyptian Museum, and it is interesting to find that it contains the upper part of the original text that has been lost from the more famous Rosetta Stone in the British Museum. Luckily, the Rosetta Stone, one of the other copies, made its way to one of the very small Egyptian temples near the town of Rosetta, where it was found.

Discovery Story

When the French expedition of Napoleon entered Egypt in 1798, France was facing a tough military conflict with the British Empire. At the same time, there was another type of confrontation, an undercurrent, taking place between the two superpowers. It was mainly about who would be able to spread their culture to the new and modern world and the colonies. For this reason, France realized in Egypt a great goal to control the great ancient monuments and to possess the initiative of exploring the mysterious ancient civilization. France considered it a singular achievement that brought glory to France. Therefore, the French concentrated their earnest efforts not only on exploring Egyptian ruins, but also on understanding the magical scripts of the Ancient Egyptian language.

During its short stay in Egypt, the French expedition managed to collect a large number of Egyptian artifacts and papyrus sheets to study with the hopes that they would reveal their mysteries. Therefore, the scientific committee in Cairo was keen to study all texts and art pieces they received, almost on a daily basis. The committee also gave clear instructions to the French soldiers and officers to collect whatever they could carry and send it all along to Cairo.

When Napoleon Bonaparte was making his final preparations to invade Syria and Palestine in 1799, there was fear that the British navy and the Ottomans would attack the Egyptian Mediterranean shores and all the fortifications along the coasts where the French army was stationed, watching the British patrol ships.

On one of those days, the French officer François Javier Pochaard, a 29-year-old engineer, received orders to reinforce one of the coastal forts in Rosetta, located near the Nile's final flow to the Mediterranean. This old castle/fort had been originally built in the days of the Mamluk Sultan Qaitbay sometime around 1475. The French army in Egypt decided to use this old castle and started a great reconstruction of its walls and towers. Officer Pochaard hired a construction contractor named Dotbole. He and his team started by rebuilding the northern walls and towers of the fort that faced the sea. They next began rebuilding other castle sections to be used as army barracks.

On July 19, 1799, one of the soldiers working on the site found a large black stone in the middle of the fort. The construction team realized after cleaning the stone with water that it had some engravings with old mysterious writing on it, and the soldiers immediately told Officer Pochaard about what they had found. He realized right away how important such a find would be, with its ancient texts, and how desirable it would be to the scientific committee in Cairo.

Pochaard took the stone and kept it under his own personal protection. One month later on August 19, he wrote a special letter to the scientific committee in Cairo. On September 15, the famous newspaper *Corrier de Egypte* (Issue 37) announced the discovery of the Rosetta Stone. They wrote this article about it:

> "*Rosetta: On the 2nd of Froctidore in the 7th year, amongst construction work, while rebuilding the old fort of Rosetta on the western side of the Nile, the French citizen Dotbole and his working team found a*

magnificent black stone that was very smooth and very hard if beaten, 36 inches high, 28 inches wide and 9-10 inches thick. On one of its two faces, which are nicely and neatly polished, we see three different inscriptions engraved in three different sets of parallel lines.

The upper set of lines written is in hieroglyphics. The second set of lines is written in letters thought to be Syriacic, and the third set of lines, the lower, written in Greek letters.

A small part of the Greek text was translated by the orders of General Menou. This stone is a remarkable opportunity to study the hieroglyphic letters; moreover, it may allow finding the key to its secrets."

Because of this great discovery, Pochaard was promoted to a higher rank in the French army. Later, he expressed his sadness and regret at having been part of Napoleon's army and expedition to the east, and he died in 1819. However, the stone opened the door to deciphering the Ancient Egyptian language by Champollion on September 14, 1822. Champollion, who never actually saw the stone with his own eyes until 1824 when he visited the British Museum, used a special rubber copy of the stone for his research made for him by the scientific committee in 1799.

As we learn, a mere accident played a major part in this discovery. Without it, the Ancient Egyptian civilization and its language might have remained a puzzle for several decades to come.

After the French expedition ultimately left Egypt in great defeat and with an especially humiliating agreement with the British navy in the Mediterranean, the French headed back to France on British ships. The British navy admiral, General Hutchinson, persisted in a strange manner to attempt to take the Rosetta Stone from the hands of the French soldiers before they boarded the ships. Although he knew nothing of the real value of the Rosetta Stone at that time, he insisted that the small black stone should be part of the spoils of war the French had lost. Everything the French had taken from Egypt had to be handed over to the British. Those who did not own gave to those who did not deserve.

This is how the Rosetta Stone made its passage across the sea to the British capital of London. Through a deal and agreement between France and

England, the stone went to reside in the British Museum, never to see home again. Currently, there are exceptional efforts being made by the Egyptian government to retrieve the Rosetta Stone from the British Museum but it's very complicated. The British authorities consider the Rosetta Stone to be one of the iconic pieces in the British Museum, and they will not relinquish it. They claim they never took it from Egypt in the first place. They assert that they took it as a spoil of war from the French army. It is truly a complex matter.

Before we drop the curtain on this exciting story, I would like to shed some light on the important results of the French campaign in Egypt. This campaign awakened Egypt after a long sleep with some unpleasant surprises. Egypt realized that she was far behind the then contemporary world and that the train of modernity (the industrial revolution in England, the artistic revolution in Italy and the human rights revolution in France) had left the station.

Egypt still had a lot to learn because for 300 years it had not believed in science and knowledge. Its people barely knew how the modern world operated, and they knew nothing about recent machines.

The only education available to Egyptians at that time was religious education at Azhar schools (the oldest schools in Cairo for Islamic and religious studies dating to the 10th century AD).

The French arrival in Egypt was a shock to many Egyptians. It was an equal shock to Napoleon when he saw how far behind Egypt was.

I personally think the Rosetta Stone not only allowed the decoding of the Ancient Egyptian language, but its discovery was a fundamental moment in Egyptian modern history and a breakthrough to a new age. It left Egypt trying relentlessly to catch up after years of ignorance and years of sleeping under the Turkish fez. The truth is Napoleon and the French campaign opened the door to Egypt to allow the world's new scientific advances to enter the land of the Nile.

Ironically, the short period the French campaign stayed in Egypt, a mere three years or a little more, left a significant influence on Egypt and changed the face of life for Egyptians.

CHAPTER 2

Tomb of Seti I, Valley of the Kings

Egypt after the French Campaign and the Rule of Muhammad Ali Pasha

The Ottoman sultan in Istanbul sent Muhammad Ali, a young military general, to Egypt to lead the people and govern the country after the French campaign's defeat and the evacuation of French troops from the country in

1801 on British boats. These years were considered critical for Egypt and the Near East, as the Ottoman sultan wanted to regain control of Egypt. Taxes were collected annually from Egypt, one of the most important sources of income for the Ottoman Empire. The main role of Muhammad Ali Pasha was to resume the flow of taxes and crops from the fertile soil of the Nile Valley, and his goal was clear and specific: to place Egypt firmly in the fold of the Ottoman Empire.

Muhammad Ali largely succeeded with his leadership of the country for several years, but other factors should be mentioned.

- The leaders of the Egyptian people and their religious establishment (senior clerics at Al-Azhar institutions) were sick and tired of the Ottoman rule and the high taxes they imposed on the people via their agents, the Mamluks.
- There was an opportunity for Muhammad Ali to separate Egypt from Ottoman rule with the assistance of senior statesmen in Egypt who preferred an independent ruler of Egypt and not a prefect of the Ottoman sultan.

Conditions were ripe for Muhammad Ali Pasha to lead Egypt, separately and independently, as a new ruler and founder of a dynasty that would last for nearly a century and a half, until 1952, ending with the reign of King Farouk, the last branch of the Ali family tree in Egypt.

It is fair to say that Muhammad Ali was the man of the era and a true hero in the literal sense of the word, as the builder of modern Egypt. In his time, he was concerned with bridging the significant gap between Egypt and Europe by focusing efforts on the development of agriculture, industry and training of the army. He was also very interested in education and sending groups of students abroad to receive modern education in European countries thereby bringing European expertise to Egypt for development work in various fields.

Under the reign of Muhammad Ali, Egypt knocked at the gates of Europe and tried to catch up to the speeding train of civilization and modernity. To help achieve his goals, it was necessary for the pasha to keep the doors open for the European missions in Egypt and to permit foreign embassies to open in Egypt to facilitate travel and trade with those countries. Moreover, he granted special privileges to the British and French ambassadors because they were the two most important players in the political arena at the time. He orchestrated special bonds that guaranteed him support from England and France. Because of his considerations, they afforded him cover and protection during the process of separation from the authority of the Ottoman sultan in Istanbul and the subsequent complications with Turkey that might arise afterwards.

Muhammad Ali was a very shrewd politician and knew that if he was under the protection of powerful European countries the Ottoman sultan could not break him. Thus, Egypt entered the 19th century with many aspirations, challenges, and a new phase of "playing with the big boys."

Rise of Egyptology and Politics

In the game of politics and regional balances in the early 19th century, Muhammad Ali Pasha, with his depth of vision, realized that the Ottoman state was inevitably going to fall and that vast territories from its empire would gradually be severed and distributed between the new emerging powers (England and France). In turn, the budding powers were attempting to extend their influence throughout the Ottoman Empire and were closely watching events on the ground in the heart of Ottoman land, a land that included Egypt, Sham countries (Syria, Lebanon, Israel, Jordan, and Cyprus) and Al Jazeera (the Arabian Peninsula). Understanding the importance of this geographic location, they readied themselves for seizure.

All of these ideas and more were in the mind of the promising and ambitious new leader, Muhammad Ali. At the same time, it was part of England and France's strategy, as world powers, to encourage Governor Muhammad Ali to move on with the process of separation from the Turkish body. Disengaging from the Ottoman house was nothing but the first step toward wounding the sagging body of the old Turkish Empire in the Middle East (a British term coined during colonial times). It was the first stage of many toward bold intervention and self-control of the region. Muhammad Ali was the perfect choice to implement such schemes and declarations of war on the Ottoman Empire, by proxy.

For Muhammad Ali to gain independence for Egypt and found the dynasty that bore his name for nearly a century and a half, he had to ride the wave of colonialism in the Near East, on the ruins of the Ottoman Empire, "the old man dying." Muhammad Ali Pasha's early years up to 1820 saw continuously heated confrontations with the Ottoman Sultan in Istanbul, with the help of the two most explicit powers in the political arena. His declaration of war (Egypt vs. Turkey) signaled Turkish weakness and the spark of rising Egypt; consequently, Muhammad Ali played an important role in ending the influence of the Turks in the southern and eastern Mediterranean.

As I said before, he introduced Egypt to the era of modernization and development and to the scientific advances of Europe. England and France played the role of older brothers and protectors of their future partner Muhammad Ali and offered him the security needed to become King of Egypt and Sudan.

Under these circumstances, and after the discovery of the Rosetta Stone and the start of its deciphering by scientists in England and later in France by Champollion, Europe became increasingly aware of the value of Ancient Egypt and its cultural richness. Europe also recognized the importance of collecting as many artifacts as possible in the shortest period of time, understanding that the pieces, valueless and of unknown origin at the time of discovery, might gain significance beyond their historic value after the decoding of the Ancient Egyptian symbols.

After the French campaign had begun in Egypt, the process of compilation of artifacts, wax copying and shipping to European ports on the Mediterranean went unimpeded, but rigorousness of activity increased during the rule of Muhammad Ali Pasha, who understood exactly what the Europeans wanted from him. He was, therefore, able to justify the "right price" for these privileges.

In this way Egyptian antiquities, which were accumulated along the banks of the Nile and on the edge of the desert became political markers. In the first half of the 19th century, the arrangement took a specific shape with France and England providing political and military protection with supplies, training, and full international cover for the State of Muhammad Ali throughout the separation process. In return, France and England were afforded special privileges to access all Egyptian antiquities sites and to exhume and ship out whatever they liked, along with many other commercial privileges.

Not to misunderstand the events or make judgments prematurely, these concessions were not the only price paid for political cover and international support for Muhammad Ali Pasha. There were many objectives behind these deals, most important of all to finish the Ottoman Empire once and for all.

In this era, a fast and interesting process began of obtaining privileges from Muhammad Ali Pasha in the form of a written statement from the king identifying the location to be sealed for search and exploration, with certain specific requirements; i.e. the sharing of gold and jewelry if found and the particular percentage of each share. It is worth mentioning that these privileges were given only by a decree of Muhammad Ali in person, the highest authority in the country. To Muhammad Ali it felt like a private matter, and he used his negotiations as a political means to achieve the greatest possible gains and protection from his new friends (England and France).

The British and the French consuls in Egypt during this time were the most important figures in Cairo, actively gathering artifacts from across the country, from Alexandria in the north to Abu Simbel and Nubia in the far south. Henry Salt, the British ambassador, and his enemy and rival, Drovetti, an Italian with French nationality, acted as ambassadors to Egypt—two men representing competing European diplomacies in the Middle East at the same time. No surprise, they did not mind making a profit for themselves by collecting extra artifacts from Egypt and selling them to major exhibitions in Europe and the big museums.

They were both controversial persons. They were the first men tied to politics involved in the exploration of Egyptian antiquities and the game of concessions, the game that overshadowed the rules of the conservation and preservation of Egyptian antiquities and the process of discovery for nearly two centuries.

As we shall see, these two men exploited their positions as consuls to win over Muhammad Ali and accordingly to obtain special privileges for extensive explorations and digging up of artifacts to ship north to Europe. We can only imagine the exciting competition between them to secure or prevent these privileges!

When Drovetti had the privilege of digging at the Temple of Karnak, Salt quickly complained and was compensated with the privilege of digging in western Luxor and the Valley of the Kings in the same week. Thus, the two big players, and with them Egypt, set in motion the era of big discoveries and international exhibitions of antiquities. Through them, trade in Egyptian antiquities spread throughout Europe, from statues to scarabs and even to mummies (having a big impact in creating a climate of paranoia with all things from Ancient Egypt). Antique collectors, treasure hunters and adventurers, and thieves focused their attention on Egypt. They all came to Egypt to try their luck. Here we pause to introduce the quintessential leader of all adventurers, the great Italian Belzoni, and his most important discovery in Egypt, the greatest of all the tombs in the Valley of the Kings.

Discovery Story

On November 5, 1778, Giacomo Belzoni, a poor barber from the Italian city of Padua, was blessed with his fourth child named Giovanni Battista Belzoni. This child lived in his hometown until he reached the age of 13. He studied theology and hydraulics at a time when Europe was plagued with battles, after the French Revolution, affecting the city of Rome in 1798. This unrest is what forced Belzoni and his family to flee to the north as far as the Netherlands to escape and search for a better place to live. Belzoni next moved to London in 1803 where he attracted attention with his great size and astounding physical strength. He worked in London theaters, mainly for the Sadder Wales Theatre, as an acrobat. A veritable behemoth, he carried a metal rod weighing 60 kg and 12 persons on his shoulders, an act that was presented as Samson of Patagonia. It was during this time Belzoni met an English woman named Sarah and married her, and they were to enjoy quite an out-of-the-ordinary marriage until his death.

With his wife Sarah and his Irish servant and assistant James Curtin, Belzoni moved again in 1813, this time to Spain, in search of better business and after that on to Sicily in 1814. Belzoni's goal was to reach Constantinople (Istanbul), the capital of the Turkish kingdom, which acted as a magnet to the best acrobats and magic circus acts. In preparation for this venture, Belzoni moved with his family to Malta where he encountered Captain Ismail Bey Al Jebeltar, a special agent of King Muhammad Ali Pasha. Ismail Bey was tasked with searching for engineers and experts who had the ability to develop systems of agriculture and irrigation for Egypt. In turn, Belzoni persuaded Ismail Bey that he had new ideas for modern irrigation as well as the knowledge and ability to make a waterwheel with the power and force equivalent to six traditional wheels together while being powered by only one bull.

Ismail Bey persuaded Belzoni to go to Egypt to implement this project and present it to Muhammad Ali Pasha. Belzoni and his family left Malta on May 19, 1815, arriving in Alexandria on June 9, 1815. He wasted no time and immediately sought to interview Muhammad Ali Pasha. Baghos Bey, one of Muhammad Ali's close advisers, set the interview for them, but due to the general conditions of the recent political turmoil in Egypt, the interview was delayed for several months. At last, Belzoni was able to convince Muhammad Ali to proceed with his project, and he built and tested the new water wheel in the middle of 1816.

However, a small human error occurred. The pasha decided to replace the one bull with one man. He then chose Belzoni's servant, the small Irishman, who could not manage to turn the waterwheel and eventually broke his leg. After that, Muhammad Ali decided the new waterwheel was a dangerous and deadly machine and dropped the entire idea of hiring Belzoni, who had come to Cairo without another job. That is, until he met the Swiss Orientalist, John Lewis Burckhardt, who was then living in Cairo, had converted to Islam and was working as a Shari'a law judge. He called himself Ibrahim Ibn Abdullah Burckhardt. Burckhardt had a good relationship with the English Consul in Cairo, Henry Salt, who, as mentioned before, was very interested in collecting Egyptian antiquities and selling them to the British Museum and to wealthy owners of special collections in Europe.

Burckhardt persuaded Consul Salt that Belzoni would be the right person for the mission, a simple one: to obtain a collection of exceptional Egyptian antiquities from Upper Egypt. Belzoni traveled to Upper Egypt on his first trip in 1816 with the support of Henry Salt, his new employer. He traveled as far as the temples of Abu Simbel and collected a large number of antiquities. He also explored in the Luxor area, under the control of Khalil Bey as district commissioner to Muhammad Ali Pasha.

As overseer of the Luxor area, Khalil Bey was in charge of both the east and west banks of the Nile, and his Deputy Governor, Mahmoud Agha, was in charge of the Armant area southwest of Luxor. Belzoni did not appreciate Mahmoud Agha, especially after learning that Agha was a close friend to Drovetti, the French Consul, who was competing with Henry Salt in collecting antiquities. Required permission had to be obtained from the Director of Luxor who had already given exclusive license to Drovetti to excavate the area around the Karnak temples. Belzoni was, however, able to explore in the West Bank across the Nile.

Belzoni returned to Cairo on November 21, 1816 from his first trip after having collected a great wealth of antiquities and having discovered the Tomb of Pharaoh Aye from the 18th Dynasty in the Valley of the Kings on the West Bank.

Despite Belzoni's great achievements on his first trip and all of the difficulties he faced because of Drovetti's strong connections with the directors and local officers in the Luxor area, he realized that fame and profit which he had dreamed about all his life had not yet been achieved, that all credit was reserved for the British Consul. Therefore, Belzoni prepared for a second expedition to excavate a new collection of artifacts and left Cairo on February 20, 1817. Two British embassy staff, Henry William Beechey and Yanie Athanasius, the Greek translator accompanied him.

Belzoni arrived at Luxor and after mending his relations with Mahmoud Agha, he began to search for a place to work. Unfortunately, he found that Drovetti still had exclusive rights to dig in the Karnak area and that he had hired all the available laborers in his digs. Belzoni was obliged again to transfer his work to the West Bank of the Nile to the great cemetery of Thebes and its mortuary temples.

During that period, Belzoni was able to establish good relationships with the local population in villages in western Thebes (the village of Qurna) and bought several relics of great value, enough to fill a large ship. He had already gained in-depth knowledge about the forms and various styles of tombs, even the methods the Ancient Egyptians had used to construct them.

On June 5, 1817, Sarah and their Irish servant joined Belzoni in Upper Egypt where they traveled together on a voyage to Nubia for the second time to further explore the temples of Abu Simbel. They fully excavated and revealed the temples on August 3rd. Afterwards, they returned to western Thebes where Belzoni read a history written by Strabo, a Roman historian who had visited Egypt in the 1st century AD. Strabo claimed there were 47 royal tombs in the Valley of the Kings, known at the time by the villagers as *"Beban El Meluok,"* meaning the Kings' Gates.

Belzoni decided to concentrate all his further efforts in the Valley of the Kings hoping to find the treasure he had been dreaming about since his landing in Egypt. He successfully managed to hire 20 workers from the nearby village of Qurna with the approval of the mayor, and he started the excavations on October 1st. The digging began near the Tomb of King Aye where, almost a year before, Belzoni had made another tomb discovery, that of a prince named *"Montuherkhebeshef"* from the New Kingdom. Belzoni stated that his experience with Egyptian tombs allowed him to locate this tomb easily, as tombs were normally cut into the cliffs under the edge of the mountain (escarpment). Due to erosion of rock and continuous falling pieces of stone from the hills, the tombs' entrances created small hills and piles of rock clearly visible to the eye. Close to many of these tombs, remnants of stone cutting tools and parts of the workers' gear could be found. Belzoni claimed it was possible to determine if there was a tomb in the location by comparing the different kinds of deposits and stones in the area. Using this method, in mid-October, Belzoni discovered yet another tomb in the valley, the Tomb of Ramses I from the 19th Dynasty. Searching further, not far from the entrance to the newly discovered Tomb of Ramses I, he found an old dry water channel that cut into the mother rock of the mountain but suddenly disappeared under a significant quantity of rubble. He ordered water poured into the channel to see where it went. He was surprised when the water disappeared somewhere under the rubble and immediately ordered his team to start removing the piles of rubble to see what was hidden beneath it. None of the workers understood him, even his own assistant Peachey and his servant Curtin laughed at his idea, but he insisted on digging.

On October 16, 1817, Belzoni had his team make a wooden machine of palm tree trunks hanging on a stand to be used as a battering ram to hit the piles of solid debris and to help disintegrate the rubble. (This machine was similar to war machines of the Middle Ages used to break down the doors of forts.) On the following day, toward the end of the work, Belzoni reached an artificial cut in the stone under the rubble, which confirmed his theory and all his expectations. On the morning of October 18th, he continued work until they opened a gap in the middle of the deposited rubble to a width of almost six meters. This made it possible for a single worker to enter. From the start, everyone believed that the tomb was large and of great beauty, but the workers found the entrance blocked with large quantities of deposited rubble. After removing the stones the following day, workers found a long corridor fully decorated with beautiful hieroglyphic writings.

Belzoni entered first followed by his wife Sarah, his servant Thomas Curtin, British embassy employee William Beechey and other workers, pushing inward until they arrived at a number of stone steps which led to a sloping passage that dead-ended with a deep well. Colorful scenes decorated its wall. Belzoni noticed that the corridor beyond the well was blocked by a stone wall, also decorated to deceive thieves and tomb raiders into thinking the wall represented the end of the tomb.

However, ancient tomb robbers had discovered the corridor beyond the well and its fake walls. Belzoni and his companions noticed the wall on the far side of the well had holes with a wide opening overhanging it, and there was an old rope made of palm fiber hanging from the slot to the depth of the well. Belzoni also noted that there were remnants of another rope on his own side of the well that also hung down into the well. Because of the extreme depth of the well, it was impossible to continue working that day, so Belzoni was forced to wait for the following morning. The next day, Belzoni brought in some of the palm tree trunks, rolled them over the well and reached the hole in the wall on the opposite side. He sent one of his workers in first to see what was behind the wall. Later, he crossed and his companions afterwards. When he entered through the small wall opening, he found a large square room with four pillars supporting the ceiling. He named it the "Entrance Hall." Running off this square room was a small side hall carried by two columns, embellished with religious scenes. Belzoni named this the "Drawings Hall."

The team continued descending into a large room before reaching the main hall at the center of the tomb. It was fully decorated with scenes dedicated to most of the major Ancient Egyptian gods and goddesses. The art in this room was finished to a high degree of splendor. Belzoni named it the "Hall of Magnificence" for its exceptional beauty. Next, he enthusiastically entered a large hall carried by six columns in two rows leading to the burial chamber. It contained theological texts and pictures for funeral gods. Belzoni named it the "Hall of Pillars." This hall had two accompanying small side chambers decorated with scenes from the *Book of the Celestial Cow*, which shows the Goddess Nut, Goddess of the Sky, in the form of a cow carrying the sun disk on her back.

Belzoni mistakenly thought the goddess was Isis, so he called it "Isis Hall." In the other side chamber were religious scenes, but Belzoni could not understand these so he called the chamber the "Wonder Room." The team continued further until they arrived at a large hall Belzoni named the "Salon." It contained a small chamber to the left that he called the "Side Hall" and explained its presence as a necessity for preserving magical texts and religious writings for the tomb owner. The other side chamber of the "Salon" was found empty. The team proceeded until they arrived at another hall decorated with scenes from the *Book of the Earth* and the *Book of the Gates*. The team found in this room some remains of mummified bulls, so Belzoni called it "Apis Hall" (Bull Hall).

In addition, he found in this hall a large number of small, hollow, blue, human and pharaoh-like figurines, called *"ushabti."* He misunderstood their function and oddly thought they were containers in which to keep papyrus. He also found a small wooden statue whose dedication was unclear, and the greatest surprise of all in this room, the royal coffin of the pharaoh owner of the tomb, which Belzoni called "The Hero!" The coffin was made of fine, translucent alabaster and decorated with many religious texts in elegant carvings, a masterpiece that exceeded every description. (This wonderful coffin is currently located at Sir John Sloane's Museum in Holborn Station in the heart of London.)

Beyond that, the room was empty, but Belzoni was extremely happy and greatly impressed with its splendor and beauty. Belzoni later found at the end of this hall a long deep tunnel dug from the ground floor of the burial chamber but never completed. He went inside to explore the tunnel but found it in bad condition and with no scenes, and he explained that it was the entrance to the tomb from another side or perhaps the work of tomb robbers.

Belzoni began working on a detailed description and took exact measurements of the inside of the tomb. With the help of Ricci, they made copies of all the drawings on the walls throughout the entire tomb.

People in and around Luxor began hearing about the great new discovery in the Valley of the Kings, and eventually the news of the great treasure inside the tomb reached the Director of Qena, Hamid Agha. Wasting no time, Hamid Agha and a small force of police headed down to Luxor to learn more about the treasure. They traveled on horses, covering the Qena to Luxor distance in only 36 hours, a distance that normally took two full days, straight into the Valley of the Kings. When they arrived, the workers told Belzoni that many horses had arrived from away. The director and his police force announced their arrival by firing gunshots in the air. Belzoni thought an army of Turks had come to loot the entire valley; this is how he read the situation at first.

In spite of Hamid Agha being Governor Director of Qena (a town 50 km. north of Luxor), he was well known for his might and greed. He came to Luxor to plunder this treasure for himself, without giving any account to the Governor of Luxor, believing this trophy might be claimed by whoever could grab it first. When he met Belzoni inside the tomb, Agha paid no attention to, nor did he care about, the tomb pictures or great scenes on the walls. He ordered his army to start searching like hungry wolves in every corner of the tomb, inch by inch, while Belzoni sat on the alabaster coffin. Hamid Agha stopped in front of him.

Hamid shouted, "Tell me where you put the treasure."

Belzoni replied, "What treasure?"

"The treasure that you found in this place," an angry Hamid answered.

Belzoni smiled at Hamid's words, raising doubts in Hamid Agha, and said, "We did not find any treasure here."

Then Hamid Agha laughed loudly, the echo of his voice filling the air of the burial chamber of the Tomb of Seti I. "I was told by people I thoroughly trust that you have found in this place a large cock made of gold and ornate with diamonds and pearls, and I must see it. Where is it?"

Belzoni tried to stop himself from laughing at this crazy notion and tried to assure him that he did not find anything like that in the tomb. Hamid Agha seemed very disappointed, but suddenly the alabaster coffin of Seti I, beneath Belzoni during the entire conversation, attracted Hamid Agha's eye. Belzoni was afraid that Hamid Agha might covet it and want to steal it. He sought to change the conversation and asked him about his opinion of the beauty and magnificence of the painted walls around him (clever misdirection).

Hamid Agha looked around carelessly then said, "This place is suitable for women where they find some pictures to look at." In a rage, Hamid Agha took his men, left the Valley of the Kings and returned to where he had come from, the city of Qena.

Belzoni started earnestly to make transcripts of the scenes found in the tomb, particularly the name of the tomb owner. He mistakenly thought the two royal seals (cartouches) indicated the tomb owner and the name of his son or his father because it identified two royal names of the king (*sa a* and *neso pete*, honorary titles every pharaoh must take, which means son of Ra and Lord of Upper and Lower Egypt).

In Belzoni's eyes, it was the greatest tomb discovered, and this major find changed his life and gave him the glory and the satisfaction that he had dreamed of, something no amount of money could buy.

For three full weeks, Belzoni continued copying wall scenes from the tomb. During these weeks, three large, river cruise ships arrived in Luxor with British tourists guided by Henry Salt, the British Consul. They entered the Valley of the Kings and visited the enormous Tomb of Seti I. Belzoni himself was their guide inside the tomb and to all the temples of Luxor (the first tour guide in the area of Luxor!). After completing his work in the tomb, Belzoni left Luxor carrying with him a wealth of antiquities collected over the six months and returned to Cairo arriving on December 21, 1817. In 1818, Belzoni worked to prepare an exhibition in Europe to display the artwork he had collected from the great tomb of Seti I, to reap the profit and glory that were the allure of his dreams.

With the exhibition in mind, he traveled once more to Egypt and the Luxor area with Italian painter Alessandro Ricci to make more wax copies of the most important images and scenes of the great tomb. The work continued for two months, and they lived inside the tomb for most of the summer of 1818. The weather was much nicer inside than it was outside in the Valley of the Kings (average 110 F during the day in the shade and a slightly cooler 90 F at night). Creating these wax copies was very difficult due to the extreme heat. However, Belzoni counted 800 reproductions of small-sized scenes, 182 normal-sized scenes and nearly 500 copies of hieroglyphic inscriptions made. To secure the tomb while working, he made a wooden door and locked himself in most of the time.

When Belzoni returned to London in 1820, his fame had been widely established, newspapers having reported on his discoveries in Egypt and his return to London after five adventurous years in Egypt. The largest British publisher, John Murry, had published stories of his trips in his famous book, *Narrative of the Operation and Recent Discoveries within the Pyramids, Temples and Tombs*. The book was a big success and was translated into Italian, French and German.

In Piccadilly, in May 1821, Belzoni celebrated the opening of his art gallery and showed his private collection from the Tomb of Pharaoh Seti I. (At this point, no one yet knew the pharaoh's name.) It was an unforgettable day and 1,900 people jammed into the opening on the first day alone.

Belzoni presented the cartouche of the pharaoh and tomb owner to Dr. Thomas Young, a known linguist. He tried to read it as a cartouche belonging to Pharaoh Nekao (from the 26th Dynasty) and his son Psmatik. Belzoni was particularly happy with this scientific breakthrough and declared that for the first time the name of the royal cartouche had been read with precision.

Dr. Young's way of reading the ancient names was correct to a certain extent and it was a revelation that gave hope to decoding the Ancient Egyptian symbols. The expectation was that it would reveal the secrets of the world's oldest civilization.

Even Belzoni made interpretations of the wax copy scenes from the tomb on this incorrect basis. The explanations of scenes from the *Book of the Dead* and the *Book of the Gates* depict only four nations of worlds worshipping the Egyptian Sun God Ra: the Persians, Jews, Ethiopians and Egyptians, who were all under the control of the great Pharaoh Psmatik. Up to his death in 1823, Belzoni still did not realize that the tomb he discovered in the Valley of the Kings actually belonged to the great King Seti I from the 19th Dynasty, the first son and successor to the founder of the 19th Dynasty, Ramses I.

Seti's is the greatest tomb in the Valley of the Kings. Sarah Belzoni must have understood this, too, having lived with her husband for 50 years, with his memory, fame and wealth.

Finally, this great discovery opened Europe's appetite to acquire even more Egyptian antiquities. After the deciphering of the symbols of Ancient Egyptian writing, it became imperative for the elite society in Europe to secure permission to be able to collect as many relics as possible with Ancient Egyptian texts to supply material needed for translation and research into the vague texts. If Ancient Egypt's secrets could be revealed, it would help to understand and explain history. It would also answer questions regarding the origin of Europe, religious history and the Holy Bible.

It became clear that the status of Egypt and its importance increased with the deciphering of the Rosetta Stone and the year 1820 saw the beginning of a series of great discoveries.

The story continues.

CHAPTER 3

Serapeum at Saqqara

WHEN CHAMPOLLION VISITED EGYPT, THE land of the pharaohs, for the first time in 1829, he was loaded with hopes of reading all the Ancient Egyptian texts he could find. A few years before, he had advertised his ability to decipher the symbols of the Rosetta Stone. He announced that all of the pharaohs' secrets and their mysterious civilization had finally opened their arms to him, to Europe and to humanity, by disclosing of all their secrets through the texts carved on the walls of temples and tombs and on papyrus rolls.

His visit to Egypt was shocking in every way as Champollion had trouble understanding the symbols and signs of the Ancient Egyptian texts! Slowly, he began to comprehend. He seemed to realize later that the Ancient Egyptians had written their ideas through images, the use of determinatives in the language and multi-purpose methods and shapes; here was a true challenge.

The historic visit ended with the shipment of a large collection of Ancient Egyptian artifacts to France for his further study. In addition, the young scientist broke off one of the two obelisks that stood in front of Luxor Temple and shipped it to France in 1836 through a special permit from Governor Muhammad Ali Pasha. This obelisk is now in Paris in the heart La Place de la Concorde, in front of the Louvre Museum's garden.

In Cairo during this time, there was an intrepid Italian doctor, Filiberto Mariucci Moncalieri, who hailed from Belmonte, Italy who was employed as a doctor to Ismail Pasha Al Daftardar, Head of the Government Secretariate. Mariucci soon became a well-known figure in the field of exploring the archeological sites surrounding Cairo, possessing a large collection of relics and subsequently selling artifacts to the consuls of European countries in Cairo and Alexandria. His love and passion for the pursuit of wealth changed his medical plans and caused him to work for the benefit of foreign consuls excavating and collecting Egyptian antiquities.

One lucky day, the young doctor accidentally detected many Sphinx statues in the desert north of the Step Pyramid, the Pyramid of King Djoser, at Saqqara, the great necropolis of Ancient Memphis. This discovery helped him by providing a clue to another discovery a few years later: the tombs of the sacred bull Apis in the impressive underground burial Serapeum at Saqqara. Mariucci started his field experience in 1817 when he participated with Belzoni in his excavations at Karnak Temple near the small Temple of Goddess Mut. Next, he moved one year later, to settle in the City of Assyut in Middle Egypt where he was a vigorous and active collector. Later, in 1832, Mariucci was hired to work for M. Minuet, the French Consul in Egypt. In the spring of that year, he began his excavations and search for treasures in the great cemetery of Saqqara.

Digging a small, narrow groove deep in the sand, he found himself, by chance and fortune, right above the ancient Avenue of the Sphinxes that led to the ancient Temple of Serapeum. On that day, Mariucci found two large stone statues in the forms of seated lions, but they were in very poor condition. Mariucci left them in the desert where visitors of Saqqara later were able to see them half buried in the sand where he had found them. He did not complete the excavation in that area because he assumed it was not a fruitful site and not worthy of spending more time or effort.

A few years later, a famous antique dealer gained permission to dig in the desert of Saqqara. He was likely the famous dealer called Fernandez, who had close contacts with most of the wealthy families, consuls and foreign diplomats in Cairo. Fernandez completed what Dr. Mariucci had started earlier, but it was his good fortune to find the complete, original Avenue of the Sphinxes with 30 previously unseen statues in good condition buried in the sand. The 30 pieces were divided and sold immediately. Twelve of them were sold to Cesena Pasha, Consul of Belgium in Egypt, who kept the statues in the garden of his palace in Alexandria.

Two other statues were sold to the famous Clute Bey, who was a well-known physician, a surgeon, the founder of the modern School of Medicine in Cairo and head of the Department of Health in Egypt at the time. Another two statues were sold to Varine Bey, Director of the Giza Horse Club, and two more statues to Linan de Belfond, Director of Irrigation in Egypt. Finally, the government of Great Britain bought the remaining 12 statues and shipped them to Calcutta, India, in 1844 where they remain to this day.

The hunt did not stop at this point. The wealthy British business citizen, A. C. Harris (1790–1869), credited with many archeological discoveries including famous papyrus rolls (which still bear his name in the British Museum), initiated excavations at Saqqara during the 1847–1848 season to rediscover the Avenue of the Sphinxes at the entrance of the Serapeum. On June 28, 1848, Harris announced his great find of the original Avenue of the Sphinxes leading to Scrapeum at the British Royal Society of Arts in London.

The full report was published in the annals of the association in the same year. However, after all of these efforts and finds, no one had revealed the actual entrance of Saqqara's lost Serapeum, the resting place of the sacred, mummified Apis bulls of Ancient Egypt.

The Cult of the Sacred Bulls

I would like to shed light on the importance of worshiping the sacred bull in the ancient city of Memphis, how the divine bull was selected, and after its death, embalmed and prepared for its final burial in the desert of Saqqara. While the royal cemetery is devoted to the tombs of kings and nobles throughout different ages of Ancient Egypt, the great Serapeum is dedicated solely to the sacred bulls, the divine animal manifestation of the God Ptah, God of Creation, and patron god of Memphis.

Memphis

During the archaic period, when Egypt took its first steps under the authority of a unified political regime toward stability and progress, King Narmer chose the city of *"Inb hedij"* (white walls) to be the capital of his kingdom. *"Inb hedij"* was located in the first state of the regions of Lower Egypt and retained its glory and its historical position for more than twelve centuries. Ancient Egyptians considered the god of this ancient city, God Ptah, the Creator God, one of the most important gods in ancient history and worshipped him as the patron god of crafts and artists, master of the flood and the growth of crops. Ptah, deified as God of Creation, was equivalent to the God Re in his importance and glory.

Egyptians adored this god as the living embodiment of his glory on earth, represented in the form of a small male calf selected by the Egyptian priests through certain conditions and rituals. Herodotus referred to the qualities of this bull: it had to be the firstborn of a cow that had never given birth before, and was conceived through lightning from the sky. The priest's description of the divine bull was that it was of certain color, white with a black spot on its back. The black spot must look like a winged hawk. The bull's tail had to contain an odd number of tufts of twisted hair, and his tongue had to have certain shapes that looked like scarab bodies. Additionally, the sun hung from a lock of hair between his horns.

The Ancient Egyptians called this bull "*hib*" and believed that it represented the animal manifestation of the God Ptah. Manito, the Egyptian historian, who lived in the 3rd century BC, indicated that the great Cult of the Bull "*hib*" was centered in Memphis, "*inb hedij.*" During his lifetime, the sacred bull was considered to be equivalent to the God Horus on earth and an incarnation of the pharaoh. Moreover, he was thought to be one of the images of the Sun God Re.

The sacred bull was different from all other sacred animals in Ancient Egypt. Its selection was thoroughly scrutinized, and it remained inside the Temple of the God Ptah at Memphis with a special priest assigned to serve the holy animal. The priest was fully dedicated to interpreting all its moves and voices because these were thought to be divine prophesies for the people.

Egyptians also linked the sacred bull *hib* to the netherworld as they considered him the master of entrances to the world of the afterlife. *Hib* was the only god who could leave for the realm of the dead and return.

The death of this bull brought about mourning throughout all of Egypt, and sadness prevailed in all towns. People believed that the dead bull would be united with the God Osiris in his netherworld kingdom and that Osiris would become *hib*. For this reason, Ancient Egyptians mummified the bull in his temple in Memphis and then transported the embalmed body for burial in solemn procession to his final resting place of Serapeum in the cemetery at Saqqara.

During the New Kingdom, the bull was buried in an individual tomb, a tomb in the form of a deep well containing a huge coffin that held the body of the deceased animal. In the meantime, the priests started searching for another new god/bull with the same qualities. But toward the middle of the 18th Dynasty (Amenhotep III and IV), the priests at Saqqara's Serapeum began connecting several burial wells together with a series of links, corridors and passageways, and this became the new burial ground reserved exclusively for the divine bulls of Memphis. The main task of the high priest of the God Ptah was managing and serving in the elaborate underground burial corridors within the ancient city of Memphis.

Therefore, it is undeniable that the largest and most important building in the entire cemetery was the Serapeum. The high priests of the God Ptah in a later period of Egyptian history were persuaded to build one of the largest temples in Egypt dedicated to the God Apis/Osiris atop the Serapeum at Saqqara. The new temple was connected with the large Temple of Ptah in Memphis with a long shaded avenue and decorated on both sides with seated statues of rams and sphinxes. This avenue ran for a distance of about 5 km, the longest avenue of rams and sphinxes in Ancient Egypt.

The temple above the Serapeum reached the zenith of its glory and fame in the late Dynastic period, was considered the main shrine for all pilgrims and a place for divination and prophesy. The temple was associated with a group of priests from many parts of Egypt who had devoted their lives to the Cult of the Apis bull. It is important to note that the death of Alexander the Great in 323 BC brought much glory to the burial of the bulls at Saqqara, as Alexander himself was thought to have been embalmed and buried in the Serapeum for two years before his body was taken to Alexandria! When the Ptolemys later ruled Egypt, King Ptolemy I chose God Osiris/*Hib* to be the main god of all of Egypt, but he used the Greek name *Serapes*.

At that time, the Temple of God Apis/Serapes at Saqqara was completely rebuilt to fit the god's unparalleled state and honor, and this temple retained its glory until the first century AD when Strabo, the Roman historian and geographer, described its ruins. Strabo said:

> "*The Serapeum temple was built in an area in the desert fully covered with sand to the extent that the impact of wind - formed real sand hills. When we visited the site, the statues of the Sphinx were already buried in the sand and some were even covered to the head and others only to the mid-body.*"

In spite of the glory granted to the Serapeum at Saqqara and its underground burials of the sacred bulls, the Declaration of Theodosius, the Roman Emperor in 384 AD, prohibiting all pagan beliefs throughout the Roman Empire, marked the end of this temple. The temple building was destroyed and turned into ruins, and the sphinx statues outside the temple leading the way toward the cemeteries of the sacred calves were all lost and remained only in the memory of historians and their old scattered writings for hundreds of years. Not until modern times was the location rediscovered. Based on Strabo's writings, the young French engineer E. Joumard, who had arrived in Egypt with Napoleon in 1798, postulated that the Serapeum and its special Avenue of Sphinxes leading to the sacred underground burials of the bulls might be located north of Saqqara.

Joumard said:

"The Serapeum, or the Temple of Serapes, was only to be close to the Libyan western hills and to find it, large excavations at Saqqara must be done and also near the step pyramid from the north and by removing all the sand, it shall help to find and detect its sphinx statues."

However, the political and military circumstances that surrounded the French campaign in Egypt did not enable researchers to carry out this excavation. There is nothing about the ancient Serapeum except what was mentioned by Strabo to refer to the fact of its existence.

Discovery Story

In 1850, the French Louvre Museum, decided to buy a collection of Coptic papyri from Egypt. To that end, the museum commissioned the young archeologist August Mariette to purchase these papyri. Mariette was young, well-built, with a light beard and the son of a middle-class family from the city of Borsomir in France. His passion for antiquities and the field of archeology appeared early in his life, perhaps because he was related to the artist Nestor

Lott, the companion and close friend of Champollion. Mariette was also well aware of the lesser historian's writings, especially on Ancient Egypt and its history. It was therefore a good opportunity for him to travel to Egypt to acquire these papyri.

He arrived at Alexandria on October 2, 1850 and was invited as a dinner guest to the palace of Cesena Pasha, the Consul of Belgium. While sitting in the garden, Mariette was taken by surprise by the presence of large sphinx statues decorating the palace garden. When he examined them, he surmised that those statues belonged to the ancient Temple of Serapeum at Saqqara, as was mentioned in Strabo's account. So, when Mariette failed in obtaining the Coptic papyri, he directed his attention to the site in Saqqara that Mariucci had excavated earlier. Mariette hired 30 laborers and started digging at the site on November 1, 1850. In less than a month, the digging revealed the Temple of Serapeum and its underground labyrinthine tombs. Despite the fact that Mariette has been credited with the discovery of the great Serapeum, he confirmed in his personal memoirs that he had simply completed the digging started earlier by Mariucci at the site and that Mariucci's work was his guide to the discovery. Unbelievably, to speed up the work and to excavate the desert sands, Mariette used explosives to remove the huge amount of sand that covered the Avenue of the Sphinxes that led toward the Serapeum entrance. Sadly, many sphinxes were destroyed and sent flying high into the air in small pieces. Mariette later shipped to France most of the intact, discovered artifacts from the Serapeum, the wall engravings of the original, lesser vaults that commemorated the celebrations of the mummified sacred bulls. The contents of these lesser vaults are now in the Louvre Museum in Paris.

Through this exciting story, we find that Mariette's dinner invitation to the garden of the Consul of Belgium in Alexandria was the spark for the beginning of excavations in Egypt for more than 30 years. It is important to say that the discovery of the temple and tombs of Serapeum in 1850 is the single most important such discovery during the mid-19th century and marked another new era of research and exploration.

Egypt and France: A Special Relationship

Young Mariette became the main player and explorer in Egypt resulting from his close relationship developed with Said Pasha, a son of Muhammad Ali Pasha. Special concessions and privileges were pouring onto Mariette allowing him to continue his research and exploration throughout Egypt. Eventually, he became one of the most important figures in the second half of the 19th century. Following the great founder of the family, Muhammad Ali, there was a series of weak governors. This was also the era of Egypt's great opening to western culture, in particular to the French, along with the entry of many investment groups and institutions that were interested in initiating long-term investment projects in partnership with the State and the Governor of Egypt, Said Pasha, and later, Ismail Pasha.

At that time, Khedive Said's most important achievement was the planning and starting of the Suez Canal project that would link the Red Sea to the Mediterranean, a project conceived by scientists of the French Revolution, many of whom had come with Napoleon to Egypt to study its possibilities. However, their surveys and studies at the time were not able to determine the difference in ground elevation between the two seas. Soon after the days when Napoleon appeared in France, a group of young investors, mostly civil and road engineers, calling themselves the Saint Simonians, established a group whose objective was to create a global investment climate by linking the seas and rivers together, thereby establishing new trade links and roads. Their most important projects were the Suez Canal in Egypt and later the Panama Canal in Central America.

It is noteworthy that the 1850s saw Egypt standing at the gates of European modernity. The railway entered Egypt, mail service was introduced, and maritime trade grew rapidly in seaports and along the River Nile. The King of Egypt, Said Pasha, was deeply influenced by every French idea to modernize Egypt, such as the Suez Canal project, presented to him by his childhood friend Ferdinand De Lesseps, an engineer and investment partner with the Simonians, and the son of a French diplomat who lived and served in Egypt in the years 1840 to 1850. No doubt, De Lesseps took advantage of his childhood friendship with Said Pasha. It seems fate put De Lesseps, the engineer, and his huge project, the Suez Canal, in front of his childhood friend, the only decision maker in Egypt.

These are the circumstances surrounding the rise of August Mariette in Egypt, who would later be granted the honorary title Pasha by Said's successor Khedive Ismail later in the 1870s. In 1863, the relentless efforts of Khedive Ismail and August Mariette led to the creation of Egypt's Department of Antiquities, the purpose of which was to regulate and control all methods of research and archaeological work in Egypt being conducted by foreign missions, which were mostly dominated by individual characters and adventurers.

Little by little, with its Chief Manager Mariette Pasha, the Department of Egyptian Antiquities became responsible for providing privileges and permission to dig in Egypt, but always with the required approval of Khedive Ismail, in person. We can only imagine the amount of coordination required between the "French ambition" Director of the Department of Antiquities and the enlightened Khedive who was passionate about everything French.

There is an interesting story that demonstrates the strength and influence of Mariette Pasha in the 1860s. South of El Fayoum, Mariette discovered the treasures of royal jewelry of Illahoun inside the burial tombs of the queens from the 12th Dynasty, located behind the mud brick Middle Kingdom Pyramid of Illahoun. This marvelous collection of royal pharaonic jewelry was the most important and largest treasure yet to be found from the times of the pharaohs, and the collection was sent on a promotional journey of exhibitions to Europe courtesy of Khedive Ismail and Mariette Pasha.

When she saw the collection of Illahoun royal treasure, Queen Eugenie of France was truly impressed (the queen was well known for her love of luxury clothing, drink, and expensive jewelry). She asked in a formal letter to Khedive Ismail that she be allowed, after the exhibition, to retain that collection in France and not return it to Egypt. The response of Khedive Ismail was quite surprising as he wrote back to the queen with regrets saying that if the matter was in his own hands and not under control of the Department of Antiquities, he would give her the collection, but it was all in the hands of the Director of Egypt's Department of Antiquities, Mariette Pasha. Mariette, in turn, strongly opposed the idea of offering the collection as a courtesy to the

French Queen and insisted on the return of the entire collection to Egypt. It is now in the Cairo Museum, its only rival in beauty and splendor: the jewelry collection of King Tutankhamen.

This story points to the beginning of change in the general climate surrounding Egyptian antiquities, the management of discovered artifacts and the need to retain them in Egypt. However, at the time, Egypt did not have any museums or permanent exhibitions. Consequently, Mariette Pasha was obliged to display and store the pieces in the royal palaces on the banks of the Nile, one of which he later claimed and converted into the Museum of Antiquities, south of central Cairo and several kilometers from the current museum.

Strong colonial powers had taken their fair share of these artifacts in the first half of the 19th century during the era of Muhammad Ali, but the second half of the 19th century were the awakening years with the birth of awareness of the importance of preserving the heritage of the archeological sites and their discoveries.

At that time, the completion of the digging of the Suez Canal was Khedive Ismail's main concern while building Egypt's first great museum was the overriding concern of the Director of the Department of Antiquities, August Mariette.

CHAPTER 4

Royal Mummies, Deir El Bahari Cache

THE LEGENDARY INAUGURATION OF THE Suez Canal in 1869 was heralded with imperial celebrations, extravagant parties and spectacular banquets along the canal and its new main cities, Port Said, Ismailia and Suez. All these cities flourished rapidly after the canal was opened and attracted ships of all types to use the canal rather than the usual naval routes around Africa's Horn of Good Hope. Due to the increased interest in supporting the canal by all necessary means to guarantee success and immediate growth, Khedive Ismail ordered the digging of a new fresh water canal from north Cairo stemming from the eastern branch of the Nile—Damietta—all the way to the desert area near the Suez Canal. It was there that he had built a new town to commemorate his name, Ismailia. This fresh water canal converted the barren desert into green fields and fruit orchards, known now for the best mango farms in Egypt. It was all a sweet dream.

In Cairo, the Khedive built several palaces along the Nile to host the European visitors who would attend the canal's great celebrations (e.g. Omar El Khayyam Palace on Zamalek Island, a Marriott Hotel now). He also built a palace in the desert of Giza just below the Great Pyramid of Khufu (Mena House Hotel now). Finally, Egypt's generous Khedive crowned his efforts by building the first opera house in Africa, and Egypt, right in the heart of the newly modernized city of Cairo.

In Opera Square near the famous Azbakia gardens, the opera house was designed to copy the one in Paris and was prepared to witness Verdi's Aida on its first opening night, as the principal show of Cairo's celebration of the canal. However, Aida was not ready in November 1869. Instead, they showed Opera Rigoletto and Aida was performed a year later.

Too much celebrating and too many new buildings along the canal and in Cairo in a short time period forced Khedive Ismail to borrow a significant amount of money from European banks and financial foundations to cover his enormous costs. He dreamed there would be money raining down on him, on Egypt and on all the stockholders and financial partners with opening of this grandest of canals. He thought there would be more than enough income to pay back all his loans and set Egypt's economy on the road to strength. But winds often do not blow as ships desire. The Suez Canal became a curse on Ismail and Egypt together, as the country started to sink into financial trouble with international loans, and the canal itself was not enough to save Egypt from looming economic catastrophe. Due to tremendous international pressure, Ismail found himself obliged to sell all his personal stock in the Suez Canal Corporation on the markets in Europe, unhappily allowing him to pay only a small fraction of his loans.

Eventually, the Khedive dwindled in financial crisis. Alternatively, the British government waited, hoping to purchase every possible Suez Canal Corporation stock to ensure control of the most important water corridor on the world map. Control of the canal was important not only for world trade but also for their own colonial purposes, as India, the jewel in the colonial crown, would in effect become closer to Britain. Acquiring Suez Canal stock was the first step in gaining full control of the canal, and the next step was evidently to send the British army physically into Egypt to operate and protect the canal, and this took place in 1882.

The British Prime Minister personally responsible for buying the Suez Canal stocks on European markets was Benjamin Disraeli, who did anything he could to make sure England acquired of all the Suez Canal stock on the market. Controlling the Suez Canal Corporation later became one of his major achievements. This hot and vigorous operation happened under the full supervision of Queen Victoria.

These days were full of events, and archeological discoveries increased rapidly with the rhythm of digging out the Suez Canal: first celebrations, then depredations, as August Mariette, Head of the Egypt's Department of Antiquities, directed most of the archeological sites and heavily regulated the black market in Egyptian artifacts. Farmers and villagers along the Nile plundered artifacts lying in the sand unattended, and the Department of Antiquities was aided greatly by police forces who confiscated those relics directly from the villagers and farmers. Mariette led a campaign to try to ban the trade in Egyptian artifacts and the constant looting by poor farmers, antique dealers and rich collectors from Europe.

At the time, Egyptian laws did not allow Mariette to practically control all archeological sites along the Nile for the thousand miles between Alexandria in the north and the far Nubian Desert in the south. Nor did laws allow him to provide the necessary guardianship to all temples and tombs scattered at the edge of Egypt's deserts.

This period witnessed the appearance of the first generation of real archeologists who put effort into scientifically recording the digging sites and excavated areas. We have received copious materials from this pioneering generation that shed light on the rise of Egyptology as a new science. Their journals and handwritten records still function as respectable sources and references to research the history of excavations in Egypt.

These days saw the discovery of many tombs and revealed many pyramids that had been veiled under the sands. But the greatest and most fantastic discovery was reserved for an accidental moment, finding the secret cave in the mountains of western Luxor where a number of royal mummies were coffined and cached. These were pharaohs' mummies in their light wooden coffins from the New Kingdom (18th, 19th and 20th dynasties) and later pharaohs of the 21st Dynasty. These mummies had been transported into a well-hidden cave around 1050 BC from their original tombs in the Valley of the Kings after having been systematically violated and looted by grave robbers.

Before I narrate the story of this fascinating discovery, I would like to give a brief history of the later days of the New Kingdom and the general circumstances that led to moving all the pharaohs' mummies to the cave.

Historic Background

The coronation of Pharaoh Ramses XI, the last king of the famous 20th Dynasty, was the signal of Egypt's political twilight and the sunset of its glory. Domestically, the country was in civil strife with chaos and corruption overwhelming its every corner. Its regional power beyond the border was lost forever. It is important to mention that the pharaoh was weak and unable to face the domestic troubles coming from the local governors and strong families in Egypt. There was obvious deterioration in security throughout the country leading to a decline such that plundering of the royal tombs in various royal cemeteries became an infuriating matter, but the king was simply unable to stop the violation and looting of his own ancestors.

In the meantime, the power of temple priests was increasing alarmingly and challenging the king's authority in their regional states and temples; and with the death of Ramses XI, not surprisingly, Egypt fell into domestic disunity. The north had become separated from the south under the rule of powerful local governors. Each proclaimed the throne of Egypt and called for themselves to be legal rulers of the country. In the north, *"nesbanebjed"* claimed to be the King of the North of Egypt and the Delta, establishing for himself a new ruling dynasty. At the same time, the High Priest of Amun at Karnak Temple in Thebes claimed himself to be sole King of Egypt from the old southern capital, established a new dynasty and toward the final years of his life, even secured his own son to co-rule with him. Thus, *"Piankh"* became pharaoh, but the sudden death of *"Piankh"* led the way for his son *"Pinedjem,"* also an Amun priest at Karnak Temple, to become the Pharaoh of Egypt in the South.

Pinedjem was an active pharaoh/priest. He continued building in the Karnak Temple complex and finished the side Temple of Khunsu, the son of God Amun and Goddess Mut. He repaired much of what had been damaged in Thebes and its surroundings, but his greatest achievement, forever remembered in history, was the collection of a great number of the royal mummies from the Valley of the Kings and re-embalming and reburying them together in two different caches. One cache was in the Valley of the Kings, in the Tomb of Amunhotep II, discovered by V. Loret in 1899; and the other cache was placed outside the valley on the other side of the mountain from the Temple of Queen Hatshepsut, inside the Tomb of Queen *Inhape* from the 18th Dynasty. We accidentally found this large collection of pharaoh mummies in extremely well-preserved condition, and the story of this great discovery is one of the best stories we have from the second half of the 19th century.

Discovery Story

One gusty, winter day in 1871, on the West Bank of the Nile, Ahmed Mohamed Abdel Rasoul, a son of the powerful tribe Al Harabat, was herding his sheep in the area north of the village of Abdel Qurna near the ruins of the ancient Christian Monastery of St. Phoepean. This area, just south of the El Deir El Bahari Temple, was well known among the local villagers by the name of "the northern monastery." The villagers also knew of another monastery in the area, just south of the village, the Monastery of St. Apanopher, "the southern monastery."

In the area of Luxor's West Bank, the Abdel Rasoul family was known for working in various fields such as agriculture, animal herding and most interestingly, trading in the Ancient Egyptian artifacts they collected from the surrounding monuments. Their clients were mainly foreign visitors and wealthy collectors who came to the area, attracted by the large number of tombs cut into the mountains and temples built on the edge of the desert.

One of Ahmed's sheep went astray while he was herding in the mountain area above his village. The missing sheep had climbed the mountain and disappeared into a rocky alcove where Ahmed was unable to see it. This place was not far from the ruins of the ancient monastery where he often came, but he couldn't remember having seen this alcove before. Trying to retrieve his missing sheep, he found the alcove to have been carved remarkably deeply into the white limestone mountains, leading him toward a steep gorge. His experience with looting tombs in the mountains had taught him this must be some kind of a tomb yet undiscovered. However, it was sealed with sand, rubble and a great deal of rock. At that moment, his dreams of finding a large tomb full of treasures passed before him, and he began planning to dig his way down to the tomb that he guessed lay beneath the sand.

He returned home to the village to tell his brothers about his new find at the edge of the escarpment. At night, he and his two brothers, Mohamed and Hussein, returned to the place and scouted the location and its surroundings carefully to make sure no one was around to see them before they dug in the deep gorge toward the vertical shaft. A few meters down, they reached a small square room with a small door that connected to a long horizontal corridor with a small side room cut into the rocks. The side room contained a number of wooden coffins, many papyrus scrolls, stone vessels, jars, reed baskets and small statues. Next, they walked to the end of the small narrow corridor and found themselves in a much larger room. They held their collective breath when they saw the room in front of them. It was packed with over 40 wooden coffins and their mummies.

The three brothers harvested a superb collection of artifacts grabbed from the coffins and mummies; small, easy-to-carry objects and at the same time, ones they could sell for a high price. They closed the tomb entrance and hid it perfectly, exactly as it was before, and took a family oath never to return to the tomb unless they were all together and only after having sold what they had plundered. They all agreed to keep the secret, knowing this private family treasure could keep them rich and happy until the sunset of their lives. They returned home with only one great fear: the powerful hands of the Antiquities Department officers and employees who had eyes everywhere in Luxor and were always sniffing around for new finds and artifacts for sale. Therefore, the Abdel Rasoul brothers were extremely cautious about showing their royal artifacts to strangers. They would never sell to just anyone who visited their village. They selected their clients carefully and only visited the tomb/cave three times in the ten years that they kept their secret. It was all working well for of the family, but village eyes were suspiciously watching even these careful moves.

During these ten years, Mariette in Cairo was hunting for every possible artifact from all over Egypt. He was negotiating with villagers and antique traders to buy unique pieces to build his first collection of Egyptian artifacts for his Boulaque Museum, which he planned to open in one of the palaces in Cairo. Therefore, he studiously watched the antiquities trading markets in Egypt, especially in the Luxor area, as it was the principal source of artifacts in the country.

Gaston Maspero, Mariette's assistant, was occupied with searching for a royal tomb in the Luxor area where most of the finest artifacts sold in antique markets came from. He was searching for the source of all the pieces rather than hunting for the pieces themselves. To do so, Maspero used a number of friends, students and assistants who had experience with Egypt, its people and its illegal antique business. Among them were Marquez de Rochemonteix, Emile Brugsch and Charles Wilbour.

Early in his life, Charles Wilbour was a man from a wealthy American family with the obvious classic look reflecting riches and honor. He had studied international politics in the United States before traveling to Paris where he began studying Egyptology under his mentor Gaston Maspero who persuaded him to travel on to Egypt. When he arrived in Egypt, he was 48 years old, a heavy man with long beard looking older than he actually was.

Wilbour was sent by his teacher up the Nile to Luxor on a special secret mission. Acting like a wealthy tourist looking to purchase Egyptian artifacts from the local antique dealers and traders, he arrived on January 21, 1881 and stayed at the Luxor Hotel on the east side of the Nile, near Luxor Temple. There, he met with Mustafa Agha Ayat, a wealthy Turk, who lived in a spacious house just inside Luxor Temple, close to its hypostyle pillars. Ayat was the consul for several countries in Luxor, representing Britain, Belgium and Russia as well as several well-known antique dealers in town. Protected by his political titles, connections and his bright name among tourist groups arriving in winter to visit the monuments of Luxor, Mustafa Agha Ayat and his son had a long and strong relationship with the famous family of Abdel Rasoul from the village of Qurna on the West Bank. The Abdel Rasoul family was the main supplier of antiquities and artifacts found during their looting in the mountains behind their village. Within a week of his arrival, Wilbour heard from one of his sources that Abdel Rasoul's family was in possession of a large number of very unique and important artifacts and that they were willing to sell them for the right price. Wilbour accordingly planned to visit the village of Qurna and met with the family to examine their treasure. He visited the family in their house located behind Ramesseum Temple and after a suspicious welcome, they showed him a magnificent papyrus including a long hieroglyphic text but without any images or pictures recorded. Ahmed Abdel Rasoul asked 350 pounds for the papyrus but Wilbour refused it saying it was too expensive. Cleverly, he realized that the papyrus was not complete, that they had cut it into three parts and had showed him only one part in an attempt to make more money out of the papyrus. Wilbour sensed they hid something bigger, so he asked them if later they would show him some real things and artifacts that would more interest him. They did not make any promises.

A short time before this, at the death of August Mariette, Gaston Maspero had taken his place as Chairman of the Department of Antiquities. His hope to find the source of all royal artifacts sold in the markets continued, and he supported his student and assistant Wilbour's search in Luxor to uncover the source. Days later, while exploring the tombs near the village of Qurna, Wilbour was approached and offered a number of leather and linen scrolls originally coming from a royal mummy. Wilbour examined the scrolls and noticed the colored royal cartouche of a king, later identified by Maspero as Pharaoh "*Pinedjem.*" He also noticed that the royal scrolls must have been collected recently from their tomb, and he felt that this could direct him to the source he was looking for. He immediately sent a message by telegraph to Maspero in Cairo with an update and asked for permission and funding to start his excavations near the village of Qurna where he thought he might find that same royal tomb, but Maspero asked him to wait until he could join Wilbour in Luxor. In the meantime, Wilbour was still trying his best with the Abdel Rasoul family to convince them to show him more royal artifacts from their secret tomb, or to show him the way to the tomb itself. Naturally, they strongly refused all of his requests and realized their fatal mistake. Showing this man their unique artifacts had been a gamble, and now, in order to sidetrack Wilbour, they took one of the mummies they had and placed it inside an empty tomb near the village. They took Wilbour there and told him this was where they had found the leather and linen scrolls, but it was obvious to Wilbour that it was not the source and that they were only trying to fool him. He confirmed with Mustafa Agha Ayat that the Abdel Rasoul family was still keeping the secret of a large tomb in the mountain that was full of great artifacts. Mustafa Agha Ayat tried using Wilbour's power to induce the locals and the Abdel Rasoul family to sell only to Ayat, or face the authorities. At the same time, Ayat was trying to befriend Maspero in Cairo and acquire permission to dig for himself in the area of Luxor and split the finds with the Boulaque Museum.

On April 3, 1881, the Department of Antiquities Boat 11 arrived at Luxor with Gaston Maspero and his wife onboard along with two of his assistants, Victor Loreh and Bouriant. The journey had originally been scheduled to inspect all monuments and archeological sites in Upper Egypt between Luxor and Aswan. At night, they all met with Wilbour, who had come to meet them and have dinner onboard. During the meal, Wilbour explained in detail about his finds, recounted stories from the village in the west and told of his deep suspicions of the Abdel Rasoul family's knowledge of a secret royal tomb in the mountain.

The following morning, Maspero paid a visit to Wilbour at Luxor Hotel and told him that he had sent a request to Luxor's Chief of Police asking for the arrest of Ahmed Abdel Rasoul. Maspero also demanded that Police Headquarters in Qena arrange to interrogate the Abdel Rasoul family members. A few hours later, Ahmed was arrested and brought to Boat 11 where he was interrogated first by Emile Brugsch and Marquees De Roshmenteou in front of Gaston Maspero. He denied all accusations, denied any connection to stealing or trading in Egyptian artifacts and eventually denied any knowledge about the alleged royal tomb they kept asking about.

Even with threats of torture and imprisonment, Ahmed did not speak; rather, he offered his house to be searched. The following day, the Abdel Rasoul residence was carefully searched by police forces. Rumors in the village suggested the secret tomb lay underneath the house itself. It was a large house, painted white, with a huge open courtyard inside that might have allowed for easy digging toward the mountain if the family had wished. The house reflected an obvious economic status far above the average family, in the area in a society cursed by severe poverty. The search group found nothing in the house, and Ahmed was released the next night. The next day, Mustafa Agha Ayat informed Wilbour that another warrant had arrived from Police Headquarters in Qena for the arrest of all the Abdel Rasoul brothers to be investigated at headquarters in the city of Qena.

The following morning on April 7th, Ahmed and his brothers were arrested and sent to the city of Qena. Dawoud Pasha, the Chief of Police in Qena, well known as a cruel, heartless and brutal policeman, interrogated them personally for several days. The brothers were physically tortured: Toenails were ripped from Ahmed's foot, and he became disabled and limped for the rest of his life. For two more months in detention, the brothers did not speak, no mention of their secret tomb in the mountain, until several old sheikhs from the village of Qurna came to Qena, met with Dawoud Pasha, and pleaded for mercy to let the brothers go home. Under pressure, Dawoud allowed them to return to the village where they found their house had been aggressively searched by Dawoud's policemen who had found and immediately confiscated three papyrus scrolls. When the brothers arrived home and heard what police officers had done in their absence, they knew they were going to face some difficult times.

The entire Abdel Rasoul family assembled at home and after a long night of discussion and weighing all their options, they recognized clearly how tough the situation ahead would be for them. Just having the papyrus papers was a crime on its own, and Dawoud Pasha could easily issue another arrest warrant and the brothers would have to face yet another round of interrogation and torture in the city of Qena. They well knew that in October, when the antiquities managers returned to Upper Egypt after spending the summer in France, the family could not count on the usual cover from the Turkish dealer Mustafa Agha Ayat working any longer. With important police officers from Cairo and Qena getting involved in their business, the family could not fight the pressure. So, the family made a strategic decision as they saw only one way out of this looming family catastrophe. It was to disclose the family secret to the authorities in exchange for a solemn guarantee that they would not be legally punished.

The head of the family, Mohammed Abdel Rasoul, was obliged to travel north to Qena to meet with Chief of Police to confess and make a deal as a witness to lead the authorities to the location in the mountains. The family members requested to work as local guides for Egypt's Department of Antiquities officers in all future digs taking place in the area of the great cemetery of Luxor. Dawoud Pasha accepted the deal and telegraphed all details to Cairo's Chief of Police, who at once informed the Khedive Tawfik, King of Egypt and son of Ismail. The Khedive was very excited and commissioned Emile Brugsch to lead a team immediately to go to Luxor to open the tomb. The team was made of three members, Emile Brugsch, Ahmed Efindi, and probably Victor Loreh. They stopped in Qena to meet Dawoud Pasha who welcomed them, giving Brugsch the three confiscated papyri from the Abdel Rasoul family house, and provided them a small police force to go down to Luxor.

On July 4, 1881, the inspectors and the police force arrived at the village of Qurna and met with the family members. It was a friendly gathering and the following morning the Abdel Rasoul brothers guided the inspectors toward the mountain escarpment close to the Temple of Hatshepsut at El Deir El Bahari. They climbed above it toward the peak, and there Mohammed led them to the sealed entrance of the tomb where they removed all sand and dirt to enter the tomb. Mohammed entered first, followed by Emile Brugsch and his colleagues. To their astonishment, the tomb was much larger than expected, and the number of wooden coffins with mummies inside far exceeded anyone's imagination. Brugsch knew at once that the tomb was now no longer safe. The police officers, the villagers and everyone around knew its location and contents. The tomb had to be emptied at once, before the people from Qurna could come and loot the treasures in the tomb. It was a critical moment, and he knew he had to act very quickly.

With help from Dawoud Pasha, Brugsch hired 300 men from the surrounding villages to work in the tomb for two continuous days. He telegraphed to Cairo urging the dispatch of Boat 11 to carry all their finds to Cairo. By late afternoon on July 11th, every item in the large tomb had been carried from the mountain to the banks of the Nile. It must have been quite a scene to see hundreds of men carrying royal accessories, coffins with mummies and boxes of all kinds. It looked like a giant snake starting high above on the mountain all the way to the river accompanied by hundreds of policemen on horses, watching the workers carefully, guarding the treasures and diligently making sure villagers didn't interfere with the operation. It was a sad time for the village and a very happy time for the antiquities officials.

On July 14th, the boat arrived at Luxor and workers began loading the ship with all the treasures they had collected from the mysterious tomb. Early in the morning the following day, Boat 11 headed back to Cairo heavily guarded all the way, a trip that took several days. When the ship arrived at Cairo's river port at Boulaque, fees and customs were paid on all cargo. Not surprising, port clerks had no idea what to charge for a cargo of ancient mummies, items not normally shown on the tariff charts. The port clerks finally decided to charge the same taxes as for salted fish cargo from Upper Egypt.

The Antiquities Department kept their word with the Abdel Rasoul family. They paid them 500 pounds as a reward for cooperation with the authorities and all the brothers were hired by the Department of Antiquities in the Luxor area (one of the sons of the Abdel Rasoul family later helped find the famous Tomb of Tutankhamen and worked with archaeologist Howard Carter for decades). Many of the family members still work for Department of Antiquities.

Now, let's take a look at the contents and the great finds from the mysterious tomb. Brugsch was able to recognize right away the mummies of the great pharaohs Seqenre, Ahmose I, Amunhotep I and Thotmosis I, II, and III. Seamun and ten royal princesses were buried together in caches, among them Queen *Ahmose Nefertari*. They also found the mummies of pharaohs Seti I and Ramses I, II, III and IX and pharaohs *Pinedjem* I and II, *Jedptahiufankh* and several royal priestesses, among them *Hinutawi*, other unknown mummies and a large number of funeral accessories such as stone jars, papyrus rolls, jewelry boxes, wigs and others that later filled many rooms in the Cairo Museum.

The story of this great discovery inspired the famous movie director Shadi Abdel Salam in 1969 to make his wonderful documentary about the discovery and the people of the Qurna. The movie was called *The Mummy*, and it was the best artistic approach to this great discovery ever made. Another point, the discovery of the caches of the great royal mummies resulted in new changes in the field of exploring Ancient Egypt. It demonstrated the growing power being displayed by the government and the Antiquities Department to protect monuments and to chase down locals trading in artifacts. It was also an alarming sign for villagers about the consequences of raiding ancient tombs and temples. What the Abdel Rasoul family did by leading the authorities to the location of the tomb was a game-changing factor. The family realized the futility in fighting the police and the constant harassment of Egyptian authorities. The Department of Antiquities declared itself profoundly as the protector of all monuments and stepped up to take responsibility for guarding all sites against illegal looting by villagers, greedy collectors and antiquities traders.

Toward the end of 1881 and the beginning of 1882, Egypt was at the gate of political turmoil and heading to significant social changes because of uprisings against the weak Khedive. Drums of war could be heard throughout Egypt as the crushing pressure of Great Britain mounted because of the Suez Canal and the related unresolved loans. A British military occupation of the country was inevitable. This hot political situation was tied to the development of exploring Ancient Egypt as we learn in the next story.

CHAPTER 5

Naucratis, the Greek town in the Delta

AFTER KHEDIVE ISMAIL WAS FORCED to resign, pressure from Britain set the path to make his son Tawfik, a person sadly imbued with a weak personality and lacking political vision or insight, the next Khedive. Hard times were here for him and for all of Egypt as Britain, the largest stockholder in the International Suez Canal Corporation, decided to occupy Egypt by landing its armies near the canal to protect its rights. There were also a number of other reasons for the British army to enter Egypt in 1882. One was to provide protection to ethnic and religious minority communities, such as Christians, Jews, Armenians and Maltese, from the increasing harassment by both the government and the people of Egypt, especially in the environs of Cairo and Alexandria where most of these minority communities were living.

A fight in a local market in Alexandria between some Egyptians and a Maltese trader, who was murdered, was the signal to start a series of political debates between the two countries. Malta was under British protection, so Maltese people in Egypt presumably enjoyed the protection of the British Consul in Alexandria. The murder prompted Britain toward escalation, and suspicious persistence, in sending their army to Egypt solely to protect minorities.

This provided the excuse to initiate the invasion plan, and the moral and ethical justification was enough cover to sell the idea to the British public with a media campaign in Britain. But the truth was, since the opening of the Suez Canal, Britain recognized the paramount importance of this corridor, and the imperative for Britain to fully control this strategic connection, not only for the purposes of dictating world trade but also for communications and travel to its vast empire in the Far East. Buying all the canal stocks available on the market a few years earlier was only the first step in this critical control operation, while the murder of the Maltese trader in Alexandria was the excuse for launching the military campaign first on Alexandria and afterwards on the Suez Canal, the ultimate intention being war.

The reason and the excuse is an old game that powerful colonial countries play with poor, weak and targeted countries in order to invade and colonize or just access rich resources or strategic locations, and this was most certainly the case with the Suez Canal.

The British army faced the small, untrained Egyptian army near Ismailia (Tel el-Kebir). After defeating it, they marched toward Cairo where Ahmed Orabi, the young army officer in charge of reorganizing the defeated troops, made his last stand. The Egyptians were crushed easily, and the British army faced no serious resistance upon entering Cairo. Having ignited nationalist feelings and pride against the palace, the Turks and all foreign involvement in Egypt's local affairs, only the solid Officer Orabi displayed anger toward the weak Khedive Tawfik, who ironically had welcomed the attacking British troops, believing they represented protection from his own angry, nationalistic army officers. Tawfik desperately needed the British army to crush his rising opposition in Egypt.

Paradoxically, soon after entering Cairo, Britain claimed they were in Egypt for a specific mission, not to stay more than three to four years, and remaining indefinitely was certainly not their plan. However, the fact is the British army remained in Egypt for 74 years and did not leave Egypt voluntarily. Instead, they were forced to leave after a war with not only the army of Egypt but also the entire country of Egypt, aided by international pressure in the 1956 Suez War.

As an introduction, I want to clarify the general social and political situation of Egypt at the time of the British troops' arrival, the period that witnessed the birth of Egypt's national awareness through the young Egyptian military officers who represented the wide circle of Egyptian farmers and village people. This new wave would lead Egypt politically for several decades through liberation from British occupation. The Battle of Tel el-Kebir would remain in Egypt's modern history as an indicator of the birth of a new nationalistic movement to promote the slogan of "Egypt only for Egyptians, not for the Turkish royal family, not for French and certainly not for the Britons."

Obvious growing patriotic feelings began surfacing after overwhelming public support and sympathy for Ahmed Orabi arose throughout Egypt, especially among farmers and poor people who saw the young officer as a hero and a voice of righteousness trying to reach the Khedive. He fought his battle with pride and honor, even though he knew that there was no chance to beat the invading British army. His deep sense of national responsibility to defend his country and its land had clearly reached every house in Egypt. Citizens reserved a special place in their hearts for their army, its officers and soldiers, something that continues with Egyptians to this day.

This turmoil and these changes have strong ties to this book. As the British army entered Egypt in 1882, significant changes in the archeological field arose. On realistic grounds, the discovery of Ancient Egypt and the exploration of its fascinating monuments and relics was and is the mission of Egypt's Department of Antiquities. This particular government body became the new battlefield of the struggle between the first generation of French managers, Mariette and Maspero, on one hand, and the military British ruler of Egypt on the other hand. The weak and helpless Khedive who lived in Abdeen Palace no longer had the upper hand like his great-grandfather Muhammad Ali had.

At this point, politics became deeply involved in the field of Egyptology, contrasting the mere political card it was when Muhammad Ali maneuvered with the French or British consuls in Cairo. By 1882, the cards were shuffled, and the situation had become more complicated. With Egyptian monuments scattered across the country in the hands of Egypt's Antiquities Department and its French managers; with a weak and careless Khedive in the palace under the thumb of shrewd British military rulers on another side; and the entire nation of Egypt's poor, uneducated farmers and villagers, ignorant of the true value of their history and its treasures, willing to sell anything for a few pounds, on the final side; this was definitely a troubled triangle. Like a faint light at the end of a long dark tunnel, we saw the small community of educated Egyptians, mostly in Europe, and young army officers trying to build a nationalistic movement to lead the nation to a better future. This was Egypt in 1882.

Within a few months of the British army taking the Suez Canal, we started to see the first generation of British researchers and archeologists who traveled to the land of the pharaohs to explore the ancient wonders. We also began to see organized tourist groups from Britain who visited Egypt in wintertime and enjoyed the Nile steamer cruises under the warm sun of Upper Egypt. With such changes, trade of Egyptian artifacts increased, and villagers supplied more and more relics to the winter visitors and collectors. These times also witnessed the rise, in 1883, of a young English surveyor named Flinders Petrie whose work in the Giza pyramid area utilized the first true scientific measurements at the only monument still in existence from the Seven Wonders of the Ancient World.

Flinders Petrie

On June 17, 1853 in the Charlton area of London, England, one of the giants of Egyptology was born, a true pioneer in the field of archeology. The child was William Matthew Flinders Petrie, son of a famous civil engineer and surveyor. His mother was the daughter of the famous geographer and explorer Matthew Flinders. The parents were keen to educate their child with a foundation in mathematics, geography, measurements and surveys. His father even took his son to help him survey the famous Stonehenge monument in Wiltshire, England. Naturally, the child grew up in love with archeology, surveying monuments and ancient places.

In 1883, Petrie traveled to Egypt with the objective of studying and surveying all measurements of the Great Pyramid of Giza. His research concerning the Great Pyramid was the first true scientific survey of this ancient monument. At that time, theories abounded that attributed the building of the Great Pyramid to some technologically advanced, but vanished, humans, perhaps inhabitants of Atlantis. If not humans, perhaps some other interplanetary beings such as Martians? However, through his meticulous surveys and measurements of the Pyramid and its inner chambers, Petrie discovered what he called the Egyptian measurement system, which included ratios, triangulation and symbolic use of numbering values. During this process, he realized the human elements and fingerprints of real people with solid thinking patterns and dominant religious values. Petrie's precise measurements tied everything to local Ancient Egyptian society and culture. His sound research and results boosted Petrie into the limelight of Egyptology and made his name well respected.

Flinders Petrie was the founder of an entirely new school of Egyptology, the school that began amidst the confusion and political turmoil in Egypt that occurred with the British military occupation of the country. He was the first benefactor of those changes and worked in Egypt peacefully, protected by the British Military Commissioner and ruler of Egypt who, little by little, pulled the rug from beneath the generation of French managers of the Department of Antiquities. The British shifted the powerful government department to new leadership, a leadership that complied with their self-interested changes in Egypt. Consequently, many British, and later American, researchers and explorers took advantage of this change in leadership and began to travel more freely in Egypt, acquiring special authorizations to excavate in Egypt, searching for treasures and glory.

For more than three decades, Petrie excavated thoroughly all over Egypt, and his name became associated with many great discoveries. He established a new era of excavation of Ancient Egypt. One of his greatest discoveries in Egypt happened by mere accident: An event took place in 1884 and led him to unveil the lost Greek city of Naucratis in the Nile Delta, at one time a very famous Greek colony in the land of the pharaohs dating back to the later days of Ancient Egyptian history.

Before I tell the story of this interesting discovery, I would like to present a quick review of the historic background of this Greek settlement in Egypt's Delta.

Historic Background

As Egypt entered the epoch of the later days of its long history, with the turn of the 10th century BC, the ancient glory of Egypt after centuries of victories and richness was lost. Its military and royal glamour had waned after several successive waves of attacks from outside enemies and the continued rising struggles of its local lords and emirs to control their own regions and proclaim themselves pharaohs on Egypt's throne. Each alleged the honor of being a true royal-blooded leader, worthy of the throne, and these domestic disturbances led to the downfall of the country.

At the same time, several small regional powers were rising and seeking to build their territorial kingdoms on Egypt's weakness. Changes transpired that prophesied the sunset of Egypt as an old power and the sunrise of several individual regional kingdoms under the auspices of the Hittites, Syrians, Hebrews, Assyrians, Babylonians, and later Persians and Greeks, in the area known as the ancient Near East.

Despite Egypt's gradual weakness in its later days, its central geographical location nevertheless gave the country certain economic advantages and strength. Even though the dynastic rulers were not as powerful, the traditional trade routes in both the Mediterranean and the Red Seas remained safe and active destinations for the old world traders and caravans. This is one reason why, around 600 BC, Egyptian markets enjoyed the arrival of Greek and Aegean Sea islands' traders who built strong mutual trade connections between their countries and Egypt. Egypt was an important market for their goods. Many of the Greeks and Aegean Sea islanders chose to join the Egyptian army as hired mercenaries serving the pharaoh. Their numbers increased steadily in such a way that Pharaoh Psmatik I allowed the Aegean and Greek mercenaries in his army to build colonies of their own in the Nile Delta, where they could start their own families and enjoy their local culture, traditions and language. Thus, several Greek towns/colonies were comprised of large populations who had come to Egypt to work in trade or serve as soldiers in the army. We know of several Greek towns from this period, such as Defneh, Maria, Sais, Canup and others, in the Nile Delta near the Mediterranean coast.

The Roman historian Strabo once mentioned that Greek and Aegean communities appeared in Egypt around the 26th Dynasty. He suggested the earliest wave of Greek settlers in the Delta had come from an area called Miletus. A group of merchants from this island established a small town and trade colony near the eastern Delta town of Sais and they called it the Citadel of Miletus. The Citadel grew bigger in the 26th Dynasty during the reign of Psmatik I, the pharaoh who welcomed members of all Mediterranean nations to come to Egypt, live and, in some cases, serve his armies as mercenaries. Strabo indicated that old Miletus later became the largest Greek city the Nile Delta, changing its name to Naucratis, which soon became a shrine to immigrants, traders, artists and others who joined the armies in Egypt. All brought with them their native costumes and traditions from the Aegean islands and beyond.

When Pharaoh Psmatik II ordered the fort of Defneh closed down, its garrisons relocated to the ancient city of Memphis, and all Greek populations to be settled in Naucratis, the living conditions in Naucratis changed definitively. The new city grew rapidly to become the largest Greek and Aegean community in all of Egypt. Its citizens were able to choose their ruler and enjoy full religious freedom of practice and celebration of all their feasts; it in effect ruled itself independently as a city-state in Egypt's Delta.

Naucratis was situated on the western branch, the Canopus branch, of the Nile, and its proximity to the Mediterranean (only 80 km. away) gave the city a prominent economic position, enjoying both trade on the Nile and in the Mediterranean world. As a port, Naucratis became the busiest and largest in all of Egypt.

The town had been known in Ancient Egyptian records as *"n3yw krd,"* which means the settlement of *"krd,"* now located only three km. west of the modern city of Damanhour in the northwestern part of the Delta. The area is locally known as Kom Geaf. The town hosted many communities from various parts of the Mediterranean world, such as Carinthia and Miletus. Its Ancient Egyptian name was corrupted to become later Naucratis during the Graeco-Roman times and may well be the origin of the modern village near the archeological site now called Nuqrashi.

The city presented itself to Alexander the Great and his armies before they entered greater Egypt, and the people of Naucratis tried to form a bridge between the invading armies of Alexander and the people of Egypt. The town remained glorious for several centuries but the building of Alexandria under the Ptolemys stole the light and glory from Naucratis as it became neglected and finally totally abandoned during the later days of the Ptolemys. The memory of Naucratis remains now only in history records.

Discovery Story

At the birth of Egyptology, the name of the town Naucratis was well known through the records of famous historians such as Strabo and Herodotus, who often mentioned the lost town as a major Greek settlement in the Egyptian Delta. However, its exact location had been lost. Many archeologists were searching for the lost city in different areas of the Delta; for example, George Eberth excavated the area near the town Desouq in the town of Kafr El Sheikh, and August Mariette searched in Sais near Sa El Hagar, Tanis, in the northeastern Delta. Unfortunately, their efforts were fruitless, and they found no clues to indicate the location of the lost city of Naucratis or its harbor.

One day in 1883, while Flinders Petrie was visiting the Giza pyramids area, he met a Bedouin antique dealer who was attempting to sell his collection to Petrie. Amongst the collection, Petrie noticed a small, broken, marble statue missing its lower half. The obvious Greek look of the statue with its helmet and shield enticed Petrie to buy it from the trader and pay him very well for it. Next, Petrie asked the man to tell him where in Egypt he had found the statue. The man said it was from a village in the Delta called "*Nbiera*" not far from the city of Damanhour.

Two months later, Petrie decided to travel to this little known village Nbiera and find the site from which the statue allegedly was to have originated. He walked for more than 20 km. on foot since the village did not exist on any maps at the time. Petrie had difficulty finding it but when he finally arrived, he found himself standing by a huge mound of sand that the locals had thoroughly excavated, and he found many deep tunnels and holes at the site. As Petrie quickly examined the mound and the pottery shards scattered around the sand surface, he noticed that not all the pottery was Egyptian. Some appeared to be Greek in style and decoration. Petrie sensed the importance of this site and decided to launch further excavations.

He was unable to determine the origin of the site, but the type of archaic Greek pottery he found served to indicate the importance of the place and the wealth of its community. For these reasons, Petrie decided to work on the large, mysterious sand mound that, to date, no other foreign visitor had inspected. Not knowing the village of Nbiera or its exact location on the map made it difficult for him to obtain the permission from the Antiquities Department to excavate the area.

The following season, in 1884, Petrie started his excavation on the site of the village of Nbiera. He began his work by collecting all pottery shards and broken artifacts in order to collect any data that might refer to the name of the ancient town or its origin. On the fourth day of work, just before he had nearly lost hope of finding anything useful, one of his hired local laborers found a square, flat piece of limestone with an inscription on it. When Petrie examined the stone, he saw it was written in old Greek text. Perhaps the slab had been used in ancient times as a doorjamb in one of the city's houses. Another story recounts Petrie discovering the stone with the Greek text at the entrance of one of the farmer's houses nearby the sand mound while he was drinking sunset tea at the man's house. Regardless, when Petrie examined the text and translated it, he found answers to his questions as the text says:

"The city of Naucratis honoring Heliodor's son of Dorian Philo, the High Priest of Athens, and the forever guardian of its records, its righteousness and good will."

After reading the text, Petrie felt a shiver of excitement run through his body. He had finally solved the puzzle of the mysterious lost Greek town of Naucratis in Egypt.

He continued working on the site for two more seasons (1884–1885) with the help of Ernst A. Gardener, who later became the Manager of the British School of Greek Archeology in Athens. Over two promising seasons of excavation at the site of Naucratis, Petrie discovered many relics that confirmed the origin of the town, for example, the two temples of Apollo built of white marble stone dating back to 700 BC to 600 BC. Beneath the temple ruins, Petrie found a large foundation deposit that included a number of artifacts, tools and accessories that had been donated to the temple by the rich merchants of Miletus to honor their own local gods and goddesses, Pan, Zeus and Hera.

He found an entire area dedicated to the manufacturing of pottery with thousands of shards discovered nearby, and a factory to manufacture scarabs and small funeral statues, and many jars with their owners' names inscribed on them meant to have been offered at the local temples. In addition, Petrie and his team discovered an area where gold and silver jewelry had been made, and remains of silverware were found nearby the factory.

They found a large wall that included a number of niche temples and storehouses used for trade purposes. Two famous headless lion statues were found at the site, and a small temple for Goddess Aphrodite, and more than

20,000 broken shards of decorated Greek pottery. Petrie was able to reconstruct 25 jars that are considered some of the best in Egypt. Petrie found parts of broken wine cups made of glass inscribed with the name of the famous Greek historian Herodotus, which confirmed his visit to the ancient town.

The discovery of the ancient city of Naucratis was truly a wonderful achievement and a marvelous start for Petrie's experience in Egypt and for all Egyptology, especially for the British School of Egyptology established by Petrie. As one who made sound discoveries in many of Egypt's cemeteries and ancient tombs, Petrie established a new technique of excavation and introduced meticulous recording techniques to both the finds and the excavated sites. One visit to the Petrie Museum in London, part of University College of London, ratifies Petrie's importance in the field of archeology in general and Egyptology in particular.

Here, at the end of this chapter, we can see the tangible bond between the development of Egyptology and evolving politics in Egypt toward the end of the 19th century. Colonialism in Egypt had produced waves of new spirit within the Egyptian nationalistic movement, and the ensuing new breed of intellectual Egyptian leadership that sought liberation from British occupation and the Turkish rule of the Khedive set Egypt on the path of modernity. As a result, we witnessed the rise of Egypt's first generation of archeologists and Egyptologists and set the stage for the researcher and scientist Ahmed Pasha Kamal.

CHAPTER 6

Amarna Letters

AFTER THE BRITISH INVASION OF Egypt and full control of domestic matters had subsequently come into the British army's hands, a number of special archeology-, excavation- and research-related committees and organizations from England began to focus generally on Egypt and specifically on Egyptology. They clearly saw Egypt as a principle source of ancient relics and an endless source of unique art pieces dating to the times of the great pharaohs, 3,000 years ago and earlier. A few years later, the notorious journeys of the famous British explorer Emelia Edwards to Egypt and Nubia received a widespread public attention in Britain through newspapers and the geographical community. In groundbreaking new fashion, she recorded her observations and travels to the lands of the Nile and its monuments. Her journal became the bestselling book of the time, *A Thousand Miles up the Nile*, which she published in 1878. During this period, the relationship between Britain and Egypt became even stronger and political ties became even deeper, but more complicated, with the leadership of the British Military Commissioner Lord Cromer, and the military invasion and control of Egypt.

The early explorations to demystify Ancient Egypt were essentially the basis upon which the establishment of the Egypt Exploration Society hinged in the 1880s. This great foundation was built by the robust efforts of many great scholars who had genuine interests in history, archeology and ancient relics in general, people like Emelia Edwards. It is important to remember that one of the principal goals of creating this well respected foundation was to support both technically and financially all exploration and excavation teams working on the ground in Egypt. The goal was to unveil more of Ancient Egypt's secrets and to discover more of Ancient Egypt's monuments, and to read and translate more of Ancient Egypt's texts into modern languages. The British linguist Alan Gardiner spent years working toward the compilation of the first complete dictionary of the language of Ancient Egyptians. The Egypt Exploration Society worked to coordinate all efforts being made on various fronts at this time.

It is interesting to note that another principal goal of the Egypt Exploration Society was to support special excavation operations in various parts of Egypt with an eye to finding clues to explain or at least shed light on the major biblical stories, including events and crises related to the entry of the Israelites into Egypt. The Hebrews' story of settlement along the Nile in the Delta area and how they lived and multiplied intrigues us still today. For several generations leading up to the birth of Moses, the epic story of his birth and childhood, his life in the pharaoh's palace as an Egyptian prince and finally, his great escape from pharaoh's imminent oppression, as the story told in the Book of Exodus, all captured the imagination of the members of the Egypt Exploration Society. In fact, many efforts were put into excavations that were only looking for evidence to prove the stories of the Old Testament's Book of Exodus. In the beginning, exploring the legacy of the Ancient Egyptians was not at the top of the priority list for the first generation of explorers. Scientists of the early committees gradually realized the difficulty of explaining or proving religious stories that were obviously folkloric in narrative style and shape. It was due to such realization that explorers decided to turn their focus toward solid discovery of Ancient Egypt's history in order to rewrite it with clear detail to reach a much sounder image of Egypt during the times of the pharaohs. Basing their research on true scientific foundations such as original texts that had been carefully dated and translated was to become the established standard measure of every work. The policy requiring hard, scientific references became a cornerstone for the Egypt Exploration Society, which is still an active organization in London with a branch in Cairo affiliated with the British Cultural Council.

The previous arguments amplify my theory that the birth of Egyptology as a western science was strongly linked with 19th century politics. Egypt's relationship with the outside world, mainly Europe, influenced the new science of Egyptology and those institutions with the technical and financial means to send archeological teams to work and excavate in Egypt. Consequently, the umbilical cord for exploring Ancient Egyptian monuments was certainly tied to western European countries with scientists, research institutes, and great museums and most important, to wealthy, generous sponsors who provided financial support for archeological digs. Various benefactors had various goals. Some sponsored excavations only to collect monuments and relics, ship what they found to Europe and sell the precious artifacts in grand auctions and exhibits. This intent was plainly commercial in nature, while other types of excavation sponsorship existed for purely religious reasons, to prove the narrative of the Old Testament by discovery of texts and relics, with the occasional bending of facts, from Egyptian monuments. Among Egyptologists and archeologists around the world, a continuous dispute exists: How can we know what lies inside the consciousness of patrons and scientists, and how can we see into their hearts? Many of these scientists feel they must hide their true agendas to avoid accusations of racism or religious fanaticism, accusations enough to dishonor a scientist, eliminating him from the archeological trophy stage and forever preventing him from pursuing the glamor of archeological discovery.

At this point, I think we need to keep an open mind and flexibility in dealing with such complicated matters of science vs. faith, and we must give reason and logic greater weight to reach a better understanding of the intrinsic value of our religious heritage. Differing religious backgrounds lead us toward disagreements about the meaning found in texts and at archaeological sites from Ancient Egypt. We do not need to accept as proof that a review of religious books serves as a thorough examination of early religions and practices in Ancient Egypt. Signs of perpetual damage on the walls of Ancient Egyptian temples also stand as testimony to the continuing change in religious viewpoints that occurred throughout history.

Ancient Egypt was never exempt from severe disfigurement in the texts of the Old Testament, nor was it saved from the desecrating hands of early Egyptian Christian zealots. The early Christians made great efforts to damage and disfigure what they found inside the ancient temples, including the carved images on the temple walls. The celebration of the new Christian faith took place at the expense of Ancient Egyptian temples' desecration. Nor could these same temples withstand continued ruin at the hands of careless, early Arabian tribes who immigrated to Egypt with the rise and spread of Islam in the beginning of the 7th century AD. Muslim Arabs settled along the Nile sometimes near or inside the ancient temples of Egypt, and they deconstructed the temples and the obelisk stones to build their homes and mosques. So the question begs asking: Why do we, in the next story, find ourselves in the final years of the 19th century with the motive for financing digging operations still being to prove the legitimacy of religious books? These hard-nosed efforts continue even to this day.

Now, we return to the Egypt Exploration Society as the most influential organization at the time in obtaining special authorizations for excavations in various archeological locations in Egypt, wielding its power despite historic French control over the Antiquities Department. After the decline of the influence of August Mariette, the founder of Egypt's Antiquities Department, the government institution's power waned, and real clout transferred to the new strong man in Egypt, the British Military Commissioner Lord Cromer. As the field of Egyptology and permission for digs and authorizations of excavations became more sought-after, competition arose among other nationalities to fight the French over Egypt's cake. (History repeats itself. As in the times of Muhammad Ali Pasha, all authorizations and concessions for digging in Egypt were provided equally by the British Council and the French Council General of Egypt.)

The star of this exciting period without a doubt is Flinders Petrie who excavated all across Egypt without exception, and I have presented in the previous chapter one of his greatest discoveries in Egypt. However, now it is time to shed the light on another renowned English scholar who reserved a very special place for himself in Egyptology: Sir Wallis Budge, the manager of the Oriental Department at the British Museum. His role in the history of Egyptology made him a leading figure in the field but his greatest contribution was his ability to decipher the symbols and characters of the ancients written on clay, letters from the times of Pharaoh Akhenaton (1370–1360 BC). Budge made exceptional efforts to collect a large number of these unique cuneiform tablets for the benefit of the British Museum in London. However, before we indulge in the exciting details of Wallis Budge's discovery of these exceptionally important ancient letters, I would like to present a brief historical background of the letters of Amarna and the period when they were written, in the 14th century BC.

Historic Background

When Egypt started the golden era of the New Kingdom, it regained much of its ancient glory, power and regional influence, especially with its independence from Hyksos tyranny that had lasted more than a century. This was a period remembered in Ancient Egyptian history for its difficult, domestic and political complications and major shifts in the balance of territorial and regional powers. The expulsion of the Hyksos from Egypt created changes in the political map of the ancient Near East and resulted in rebirth of Egypt as the most important and powerful military force among all the kingdoms of the ancient Near East. That said, many regional monarchs retained local dominance over their own politics and economies while working continuously to keep mutually positive relationships with Egypt, as the greatest central power in the ancient Near East.

Consequently, pharaohs of Egypt during the 18th Dynasty strengthened their channels of political communications and maintained stable, friendly correspondence with their counterparts, the local kings of other ancient Near East kingdoms, such as the rulers of Akkad, Phoenicia, Ammoro and others in the Levant area. Even during the internal social strife that stormed Egypt during the time of Pharaoh Akhenaton with the building of his new capital at the village of Amarna in the middle of the land between Upper and Lower Egypt, political communication with the outside world was never affected. Good relationships with neighbors remained strong as letters and other communications continued between the royal palace at Amarna and regional kingdoms outside Egypt. This correspondence covered a wide range of subjects, but communications that were political in nature were the most important.

The Department of Royal Correspondence, one of various royal palace administrations in Amarna, classified all royal correspondence sent and received in ancient, mesmeric Akkad script, which was considered the official linguae franca of international relations at the time, circa 14th century BC. Because this language was commonly used throughout all small kingdoms in the ancient Near East, letters arrived in Egypt written in these scripts. They were translated and recorded on clay cuneiforms in the mesmeric script of the ancient Akkad language before sending them to the oven to be dried. This operation indicates that the royal palaces in Ancient Egypt had different professional departments in all fields, including experts in translation and preparation of letters and other correspondence with the various surrounding nations. Presumably, the employees of departments like these must have had a good command of foreign languages and dictionaries to help precisely translate all words and terms from and into the Ancient Egyptian language. We are about to tell the story of the Amarna letters, a living witness to this ancient correspondence from the times of the pharaohs.

We have been fortunate enough to have discovered well-preserved letters from the times of Pharaoh Akhenaton. His capital city Akhetaten experienced a rapid rise and fall. After the mysterious disappearance and death of its founder and the associated decay and vandalism of the city, its palaces and homes, the city was completely abandoned, and many of its relics and artifacts were buried underneath the vandalized palaces. Many of the buildings were destroyed, and the desert sands swept in to cover the foundations. Akhetaten was entirely forgotten and neglected for more than 34 centuries until a mere accident was responsible for revealing the ancient royal letters and bringing the state correspondence of the pharaoh back to light once again.

The Amarna letters are a collection of personal and state correspondence discovered accidentally inside one of the small, ruined side buildings that had once been part of the great royal complex of palaces that had served Egypt's Pharaoh Akhenaton. The letters had been deposited in a building classified by modern archeologists as the Department of Royal Correspondence, and their translations were found inside what was the House of Royal Documents, all very close to the palace where the pharaoh had lived. The discovered letters numbered 382 in total, and soon after they were found in Amarna they were sold and dispersed among the British Museum, the Louvre, the Vorderasiatisches Museum in Berlin and finally, a handful of letters remained in the Egyptian Museum in Cairo.

Scholars are still debating the true dates of most of these letters but the oldest letters we have in the collection date back to year 30 of the reign of Pharaoh Amenhotep III; the most recent letters in the collection date back to the first year of Tutankhamun's reign. The vast majority of the discovered letters were recorded in Akkad script, as the state language for all international correspondence at the time, but there are a few letters in that same collection recorded in other scripts, such as the language of the ancient kingdom of Mitanni, comprised of the Hittites, Assyrians, and Hurrians.

The nature of Egypt's political relations with its surrounding neighbors was clearly reflected in the Amarna letters, particularly during the troubled days of the late 18th Dynasty. It is quite certain the letters that were smuggled out of Egypt shortly after they were discovered included a large number of stories that were full of adventures and other personal accounts of ancient world rulers, but sadly, only a few have been well-preserved such as the letters Wallis Budge deposited in the British Museum in London.

The scientific truth about these letters and clay tablet cuneiforms is that they are really the oldest and most important state archives of unique political correspondence ever discovered from ancient times, and they clearly explain the nature of Egypt's complicated relationships with the surrounding kingdoms during the times of Pharaoh Amenhotep III and his son and successor Pharaoh Akhenaton. Local sovereigns in Asia Minor and the area of the Levant enjoyed a friendly channel of communication with Egypt for reasons we have discussed. They sometimes signed the letters they sent with a certain phrase "Your brother," and a number of other kings and leaders signed their letters with "Your servant and your sincere slave" from which we can understand the complicated range of political ties that Egypt had with small kingdoms and city-states in the ancient Near East region. This was a time when frequent wars, battles and struggles among the little kingdoms and city-states erupted for all sorts of reasons, for land, water, forts and even hills. In the 14th century BC, the Egypt of the pharaohs was the greatest kingdom in the region and on many occasions, Egyptian authorities were obliged to intervene in domestic matters of surrounding kingdoms, either with military force or by political means. Egypt's policy toward surrounding kingdoms and city-states was mainly to achieve balance in political and commercial relations with them, especially in the Levant lands. To achieve its goals, Egypt was known to instigate quarrels between certain kingdoms against others, while at the same time promoting different kingdoms, building and implementing allegiances of all kinds. Egypt sometimes created coalitions of several kingdoms and city-states to wage war against one common enemy, war by proxy, for control of topography.

To help secure Egyptian political and commercial interests in the region, there were small Egyptian military outposts stationed en route from the Sinai

Desert at Egypt's eastern gates, along the Mediterranean coast as far north as Lattakia in Syria, among famous valleys and atop strategic hills within the Levant and around the Canaanite city of Jerusalem. We have learned many stories of the entire region through the translations of the Amarna letters. These translations are truly one of Britain's greatest contributions to the field of Egyptology. Discovery of the letters occurred soon after the British army came to rule Egypt with the subsequent arrival British artists and archeologists.

Discovery Story

Early one winter morning sometime in 1887, a young Egyptian farm woman from the poor village of Hag Qandil in the area of Tell El Amarna was working near the ruins of Akhenaton's ancient capital city, once standing powerful and glorious. The young villager was looking for dry animal dung, which she collected from the ruins daily. She would use the dry wastes to fuel her oven to bake bread, as an organic fuel heated up a mud oven quickly. As she searched the sands for the dried, rock-like animal dung that mixed with sands of the ruins of ancient monuments, she turned rocks upside down with her hands and was surprised to touch a broken wooden box buried in the ground, looking very dirty. When she opened the box, she found inside a large number of what appeared to be small, different-sized clay tablets. She examined the tablets carefully hoping to find dried animal waste, but she found only clay tablets of a strange texture and with enigmatic inscriptions. (I searched many historic documents and resources, even the testimonials of experts, to identify the woman who made the discovery but unfortunately, no references could precisely identify, or even hint at, the name of the woman of discovery.)

It is important to note that this unnamed woman found the clay tablets arranged in perfect order and condition, and their total number was nearly 400. (The number of tablets preserved now in world museums is only 382 but perhaps she found more with only 382 surviving.) Initially, the woman thought these tablets were useless, valueless clay bricks, but she decided to collect them all in a sack with the hopes of selling them to one of the antique dealers in her village for whatever price they would go for. A few days later, someone in the village bought the whole bagful of clay tablets for only 20 piasters, but it seems now that the man who purchased the tablets suspected their originality and true age. The tablets' surfaces were covered with perplexing inscriptions and these were what caused him to buy them and send some of them to a number of antique dealers beyond the village, to Luxor and Cairo, to verify their age and originality, and even to try to authenticate them to later sell them at a much higher price.

In the later years of the 1880s, Gaston Maspero, the Manager of Egypt's Antiquities Department and undeniable expert as a leading international figure in Egyptology, was aging and wanted to retire from his government job. He offered his resignation to the government of Egypt and started preparing himself to return to Paris forever. Maspero was both loved and respected by Egyptians and surprisingly, by the antique dealers, too, because of his friendly attitude and generous compensation paid to people to help find monuments and deliver artifacts. Maspero had wanted the Swiss scientist Edward Neville to replace him as Manager of Egypt's Antiquities Department but Neville's Swiss nationality made it difficult for him to take the government post as the Egyptian government preferred a French person to replace Gaston Maspero. For this reason, the government settled on Grebaut, the student and assistant of Maspero, who took his place. Unfortunately, Grebaut was weak in personality and his lack of imagination and vision made him a poor manager for this powerful government institution. To improve his image to suit the esteemed position as a successor to the first two great managers, Mariette and Maspero, Grebaut wielded power with brutality, sometimes landing on both villagers and antique dealers. He attempted to fully control illegal trade and digs by Egyptians and used a large police force to arrest farmers and villagers who were convicted of illegal digs and/or trade in ancient relics. Occasionally, he became extreme and issued a government declaration or warrant to confiscate people's lands and houses as a punishment for conviction. This charged atmosphere of his own making became a barrier between Egyptians and the new manager Grebaut. They simply refused to cooperate with him or his people. This situation slowed the development of the Egyptian Antiquities Department's continuous efforts in controlling the widespread monuments across the country.

At that time in London, the British Museum received a telegram from Iraq informing them of looting having taken place at British Museum teams' excavated sites in Iraq from the previous season, in the two areas of Abo Haba and El Nabi Younis. This meant the museum might have lost a large number of the discovered artifacts, much of which included mesmeric script. Therefore, the British Museum authorities sent one of its curators to the excavated areas in Iraq to evaluate the looting and the scope of losses. The British Museum envoy was Wallis Budge, the Curator of the Egyptian and Mesopotamian departments at the Museum. As his exceptional knowledge of mesmeric languages was well respected, he was clearly the right choice for the mission.

When Budge was making his arrangements to travel to Iraq, the museum received a message from Egypt that mentioned the discovery of a very important new find and, that some of its pieces had surfaced in Luxor in the hands of antique dealers and that many of the pieces were for sale. The message from Upper Egypt indicated there were enigmatic scripts on clay cuneiform tablets that no one from the Luxor area was able to read and that while many of these clay tablets were floating around the antiquities markets in Egypt, until then, no one had been able to identify the true date or originality of the objects. When Budge received this message from Egypt, he changed his plans and went to Egypt first to check on the new finds and try to purchase all the clay tablets available in the markets before he continued on his original mission in Iraq.

To reach Egypt quickly, he headed to France's port of Marseilles where he boarded a ship bound for Egypt on December 8, 1887 and arrived at the port of Alexandria on the 16th of December. As soon as he landed, he went straight to meet the British Consul in Alexandria who briefed Budge about the latest news in Egypt regarding the new finds and that Grebaut, the Head of the Antiquities Department, was taking strict measures to disallow the selling of any of the new artifacts. He also told Budge that the Antiquities Department of Egypt somehow knew about his visit and was taking legal actions to prevent him from reaching the artifacts. The British Consul in Alexandria advised

Budge to avoid confrontation with local authorities, that he must abandon his goal of buying these new pieces that he had come to Egypt for and made him promise to visit only archeological sites if he wanted to enjoy his stay in Egypt. But the truth is, Wallis Budge had made up his mind before coming to Alexandria that he intended to purchase the new pieces at any cost, and he would do whatever was necessary to achieve his mission.

Budge decided to travel to Cairo where he spent a few days collecting information to prepare for his trip to Luxor. On the train to Upper Egypt, heading to Luxor, he realized Egypt's secret police and special surveillance agents who had been appointed by and were reporting directly to Grebaut, the lead of this operation, were following him. Budge clearly realized how difficult his mission would be and how seriously the local authorities in Egypt were taking Grebaut's orders and personal desire: "Wallis Budge and the British Museum should never ever reach the new finds, and the tablets and all pieces must stay in Egypt." Actually, this would be a very difficult task since the new finds and artifacts had already left their home in Amarna and had made their way into smaller collections in the hands of several antique dealers, some in Cairo. However, the large collections remained in Luxor and this was where Budge decided to go, following his instinct and trusted resources in Egypt.

As soon as Budge arrived in the city of Luxor and settled into the Luxor Hotel, he met with Mohammed Mehaseb, the well-known antique dealer from the villages of the West Bank of the Nile, who offered Budge a number of artifacts for purchase. One of these artifacts was the unique Papyrus of Ani, which included parts of the *Book of the Dead*, and the final judgment scene of Prince Ani, a unique piece now on display in the British Museum, purchased that day by Budge.

At the same time, Grebaut had decided to travel by boat from Cairo to Luxor but the ship grounded on a sandbar on one of the little river islands between Cairo and Upper Egypt in the area of Naqada, about 35 miles north of Luxor. When Grebaut realized he was late, he issued a letter to the Police Department of Luxor asking them to arrest Wallis Budge and the local antique dealer Mohammed Mehaseb. In his hotel, Budge received the news of Grebaut's approach and the police warrant so he had enough time to hide all the artifacts he had purchased from Mohamed Mehaseb. Budge was a smart man and managed to hide all the relics he had bought in large metal boxes and deposited them in a house behind the hotel where he was staying. When the police searched his hotel room, they found nothing at all. Luxor police released Budge after a few hours of unfriendly interrogation, and he returned to his hotel.

Days later, a man came to meet Budge in his hotel and told him he had traveled all the way from the village of Hag Qandil in the area of Amarna, south of the city of El Mynia (where the Amarna letters had been found). The stranger told Budge that he heard from his friends in Luxor that Budge was an expert in reading ancient, enigmatic mesmeric scripts and that he had a few clay tablets. He needed authentication and verification of them. He gave Budge 12 clay tablets, each the size of his hand, and asked Budge straightforwardly whether the inscription written on them was old or new. Budge knew right away that the man did not want to sell the tablets; he only wanted to verify their originality and value, which also meant there must be more of the clay tablets kept elsewhere.

Budge carefully examined the 12 tablets over the course of an entire day and was finally able to decipher some of their words well enough to understand that it was some kind of a letter mentioning the pharaohs of Egypt in the middle of the 18th Dynasty. In addition, the letters indicated a state political correspondence style of language rather than literature texts. Oddly, on the same night when Wallis Budge had nearly finished his work with the 12 tablets, another man came to the hotel carrying with him 76 clay tablets from the same collection and asked Budge the same favor. This man too only wanted to verify their originality and value.

Another gift in Wallis Budge's multi-talented make-up was that aside from being a scholar, he was also a great negotiator. He sat down with the two men and invited them to dinner and during the meal, he made an agreement with both of them regarding the tablets they had brought him. The deal was that he would authenticate all the pieces for free. He convinced the two uneducated villagers that his job was very specific, and it would cost them a fortune to obtain his services. Needless to say, they didn't have the money to pay. In return, they would sell all their clay tablets for a good price to him. The two naïve villagers accepted Budge's offer at once and agreed to sell all their pieces for free authentication, which eventually would help them to sell the rest of the clay tablets for a higher price later on. Budge purchased the 88 letters from the Amarna collection (no specific price has ever been mentioned). That night, he was quite certain of their importance.

A few days later, he received news from his resources in Egypt that some antique dealers in Cairo had sold a number of similar clay tablets from the Amarna area to someone who managed successfully to smuggle them to Germany. These are now on display in the Vorderasiatisches Museum of Berlin.

In the meantime, Budge put all the new clay tablets into more boxes, again hiding them in the house behind the hotel, but the Luxor police suspected that Budge was hiding something in the house. Suspicions arose because the house belonged to a Luxor resident close to the illegal antiquities trade in the city. Therefore, Grebaut issued another warrant, this time to search the house and confiscate everything they found in it. The details of how Budge was able to escape the city of Luxor with all the boxes full of artifacts make quite an interesting detective story. Budge used the help of the Luxor hotel manager, an Englishman, to dig a small tunnel between the house and the hotel garden. And all the boxes of artifacts were moved from the house through the tunnel under wonderful cover: A camouflage dinner was planned on the roof of the house for all the guards and policemen involved in the house search. While the policemen were eating and drinking on the roof, the hotel staff were moving all of Budge's boxes through the tunnel to the hotel garden and from the hotel garden to a commercial ship waiting on the Nile near Luxor Temple. Budge had hired the ship to take him and all the purchased artifacts to Cairo at once that same night.

It was a great escape from the city of Luxor on a little commercial cargo ship to Cairo. When Budge arrived in Cairo, he delivered all his boxes to the British army camp by the Nile where army officers secured them, transferred all the boxes to Alexandria and from there to London, which now houses all the tablets in the British Museum. After he had accomplished his mission in Cairo, Budge turned to his original mission in Iraq.

This is the true story of how the Amarna letters left Egypt. What an adventure!

The story continues.

CHAPTER 7

Tomb of the Horse

WHEN THE BRITISH SCHOLAR FLINDERS Petrie came to explore in Egypt, he recruited a number of assistants, young artists and surveyors from Britain, to assist him in excavation and systematic recording of all the working sites he was planning to explore. Howard Carter was one of those artists/surveyors hired by Petrie, and he first arrived in Egypt in the 1890s to make measurements and surveys of the sites discovered by Petrie. It was a period of ultimate

British influence over Egypt and Egyptology, particularly with respect to archeology. Authorization to dig in Egypt was exclusively reserved for certain circles of people from England and for wealthy collectors from the United States who exhibited obvious financial bonds with Britain, such as Harry Burton and Theodore Davis.

Lord Cromer, the British Military Commissioner of Egypt at the time, was in fact the most influential character on the stage, known for his love of ancient monuments and archeological places and his obsession with collecting Ancient Egyptian artifacts. He built a number of personal retreat houses close to the monuments, sometimes actually within the ruins, making it easy for him to enjoy conducting his own private digs for artifacts that he could then carry along to Cairo and smuggle abroad.

Toward the end of the 19th century, these were the cultural and political circumstances in Egypt that cast dark shadows onto Egyptology. In another way, Egyptian society was experiencing big changes, becoming closer to modern European life and adapting to new, scientific breakthroughs in Europe. In those days, Egypt felt successive waves of enlightenment that came from the other side of the Mediterranean, which were well received in the big cities such as Cairo and Alexandria. With such waves of modernity, a number of other values and elements surfaced in educated, liberal, intellectual Egyptian society, ideas such as liberation from colonialism, the spread of nationalistic spirit and the necessity for economic independence and self-reliance. These new ideas brought about a cultural, political and intellectual renaissance in Egypt that reaffirmed the solid foundation of the Egyptian identity and would allow Egypt to weather the European/British occupation. Many of these innovative ideas and feelings floated on the surface of educated Egyptian society and led to a great era that introduced impressive Egyptian leaders in all fields, men who took initiative and accepted responsibility for confronting challenges and expressing legal hopes for the nation. These were the days of Mustafa Kamil, a nationalist activist, lawyer and journalist, who called for independence from the British army and the corrupt Turkey-backed king. He became the voice of the nation, the tongue for all uneducated Egyptians and the spark for the birth of Egypt's new spirit affecting many people in many fields. Those days witnessed the rise of the first Egyptian archeologist and pioneer in his field, Ahmed Pasha Kamal, who led the first generation of Egyptian explorers, and Tallaat Pasha Harb, the leader of the modern Egyptian economy and founder of Egypt's first bank, Bank Misr. Finally yet importantly, among these great names from the civil society, we recognize Qasem Amin, the famous writer, journalist and supporter of women's rights, who published the famous book *Emancipation of Women* in 1900.

All the great names above are the fruits of the great cultural bridges that were built in the late 19th century between Egyptian and European societies. There were a number of other elements that impelled Egypt to reach for modernization and independence. There had been a tangible spread of schools and education among people living in big cities. Two objectionable foreign forces ruled the country at the time: on one hand, the occupying British army and on the other hand, the king in his palace supported by the Ottoman sultan residing in Istanbul. Against all odds, Egyptian society was motivated, confidently and steadily, toward liberation from all forms of repression and servitude.

In the field of exploring Ancient Egypt, the excavation and exploration process with its required legal authorizations and problematic restrictions was but one of many aspects of western dominion over Egyptian society. The appearance of Ahmed Pasha Kamal's generation was an historic sign that established the benchmark of the Egyptians' own school to research Ancient Egyptian monuments. Efforts begun at that time were followed by successive waves of hard work that continues today. Current leaders still carry flags of modernizing and "Egyptianizing" the field of Egyptology, men such as Ahmed Fakhry, Selim Hassan, Labib Habashy and Zahi Hawass.

The colonial period in Egypt devalued the country in many ways. It widened the gap between the cities and the villages, and by the end of the 19th century, there were fundamentally two Egypts. One was the Egypt of urban wealth and lifestyle where one could find education, health care, theaters and opera houses, and the other, the Egypt of the rest of the country, in the Delta as well as in Middle and Upper Egypt, the rural areas where the poor farmers living in their mud huts toiled endlessly. There were others as well far off in the country who lived in the isolated desert oases who were basically living outside the frame of time and modernity. They were virtually living in the Middle Ages.

In those days, the British Commissioner of Egypt, Lord Cromer, employed Howard Carter to be the General Manager of the Upper Egypt District in Egypt's Department of Antiquities. Howard Carter lived on the West Bank of the city of Luxor, close to the great temples and tombs of the Theban Necropolis. Carter built a small house near the Temple of Ramses III/Habu Temple where he lived the best years of his life, his career glowing.

Every day, Carter rode his horse into the western hills of the Theban Necropolis, supervising all the different groups working for various archeological missions on excavations, preservation, restoration and renovation. His ride sometimes took him as far as the Valley of the Kings and sometimes to the nearby workers' villages. One day he went to the area of the Temple of Queen Hatshepsut, El Deir El Bahari, where a wonderful moment, a small accident, came upon him leading to a wonderful discovery.

Howard Carter

Sometime in 1874, in the city of London, Samuel John Carter and his wife Mrs. Martha Joyce welcomed their sixth child and they called the child Howard. The father, Samuel Carter, was a well-known painter of landscapes and nature who raised his children in an atmosphere full of art and unique skills in drawing and painting. Young Howard absorbed instruction and developed his gifts in painting with watercolors. In his teenage years, he became a well-known artist attracting the attention of a few famous, wealthy, English families who encouraged and provided special care to young artists; notable among them was the Amherst family of Darlington Hole in Norfolk.

With Howard Carter's exceptional artistic abilities in drawing, painting and restoration and with great help and support from the Amherst family, in 1891, he was able to obtain employment with the Egypt Exploration Fund. He was hired as an artist, painter and surveyor to work closely with the famous scholar Nubry on his new project in Egypt in the area of the Beni Hassan tombs in Middle Egypt, in El Minya province. After only one year, Howard Carter received an offer to join Flinders Petrie's expedition in the area of Tell el Amarna just south of Beni Hassan, about 50 km. away in the same Middle Egypt province.

Carter was hired again as a painter and surveyor, but this time he was lucky enough to work under Petrie, the most important archeologist of the time and the originator of the first scientific, systematic digs in Egypt. Carter worked with Petrie for several seasons in the Amarna area, and he learned firsthand his scientific methods of excavation and preservation. He also learned Petrie's unique methods for organizing and classifying the sites and the exact, meticulous recordings of all excavated materials.

In 1894, Carter moved to work as an assistant to Edward Neville at his excavation in the area of El Deir El Bahari near the mortuary Temple of Queen Hatshepsut. His experience as an assistant to Neville gave Carter deep, practical knowledge that enhanced his archeological skills, over the five seasons of digging near Queen Hatshepsut's Temple between 1894 and 1899. Much of the astonishing temple of the queen was discovered in that period, and Carter's main mission was to help with the recording of finds, redrawing all temple scenes and helping with restoration of the severely desecrated temple scenes. The work of both Edward Neville and Howard Carter was published in a large six-volume book, *The Temple of El Deir El Bahari,* written by Neville. The book celebrated the marvelous artistic skills of Carter and stands today as testimonial to Carter's early years as a rising star in Egyptology, and to the Egypt Exploration Fund, the organization to which he belonged.

It is important to mention again the weakening elements that Egypt's Department of Antiquities faced soon after the British invasion of Egypt, as Lord Cromer focused his energies on eradicating the power of Antiquities Department and its French manager, Victor Loret. The British Commissioner systematically cut financial support, causing the department to devolve into a helpless government body with no real control over the scattered monuments along the Nile.

In 1899, when he was unable to work because of pressure from Cromer, Victor Loret decided to leave. Cromer tried once again to rehire Gaston

Maspero who was by then 53 years old, but before he appointed Maspero, Cromer insisted on employing two British managers to assist Maspero in running the Antiquities Department. James Quibble and Howard Carter were to be the assistant managers, Carter becoming the manager and chief inspector for all of Upper Egypt. Therefore, Carter moved to the new manager's house near the Temple of Habu and left the smaller house where he had lived for five years near the Temple of Hatshepsut.

Ironically, Howard Carter had lived near the El Deir El Bahari area for five seasons working with Edward Neville but had never discovered anything special himself. It was not until he moved to the new manager's house near Habu Temple and started managing the entire area of western Thebes and Upper Egypt that he made his first great personal discovery. He made it near the Temple of Montohotep from the 11th Dynasty and next to the Mortuary Temple of Queen Hatshepsut.

Historic Background

"Montohotep *nbhptre*" became the pharaoh of Egypt in the second millennium BC, 2011 to 2061 BC. At the time, Egypt was going through a critical period in its long history. For more than two centuries of civil strife and local sovereign struggles over power, the country was divided into small kingdoms with each region claiming its independence and private monarchy. Each of these ruling families claimed divine and historic rights and legitimacy to rule the entire country, which sparked continuous and spiteful civil wars. Disunity and regional conflicts had eradicated the older glory of Egypt's united monarchy and the foundations of the strong central government that had been established long ago by the pharaohs of the Old Kingdom.

Historians classified this dark period as the First Intermediate Period, when the country had split into two main kingdoms, the first in Upper Egypt with its capital the city of Thebes, capital of the 4th District, and the other in Middle Egypt in the area of Ihnasya. Beyond these two most powerful kingdoms were a number of smaller kingdoms in the Delta and way to the very south in Nubia. The war of atrocity between the two main conflicting kingdoms continued for a long time swinging between victory and defeat, until the kingdom in Upper Egypt achieved final triumph during the reign of its Pharaoh Montohotep.

Soon after he took rule of the Theban kingdom, King Montohotep strove to unite the entire country once again, to rebuild the united monarchy of Egypt and to establish a new royal dynasty with the power to govern the country from the new capital Thebes.

The rule of King Montohotep brought stability to the land and enabled him to resume the construction of great, religious buildings and large temples dedicated to the gods. He also built a massive funeral temple suitable for a great king who had united Egypt anew, the founder of a new era of a strong and powerful ruling family. King Montohotep built his tomb in the mountains of western Thebes by the edges of the escarpment of the sacred mountain, the bullhorn mountain peak. That holy area was highly venerated by the people of Thebes as the home of the mother Goddess Hathor, Mistress of the West. It was the perfect choice for the king's final resting place, his extravagant tomb. The king selected the beautiful, wide, western valley situated in the arms of the mountain and engulfed by Theban escarpments and hills on all sides, seeming to be a small crater in the heart of a mountain. The place the king chose was not an isolated, abandoned location. On the contrary, it had been used before for many centuries by earlier kings and nobles from the First Intermediate Period where several tombs and cave-like burial places could be found on the lower and upper hills in a full circle surrounding King Montohotep's Temple.

The site was thought to be under the protection of Goddess Hathor who, according to the myth of the daily rising and setting of the Sun God Re, swallowed the sun as it was setting behind the western hills of Thebes and at the same time, swallowed the souls of all the dead who were buried near her mountain. During the night hours, she was responsible for protecting their souls and securing their tombs in the heart of this divine mountain site. The myth goes further to explain that each morning the mighty Goddess Hathor assisted with the birth of the sun on the eastern horizon and caused the souls of all the dead that she had preserved from the previous day to be born again like the sun.

King Montohotep built his funeral temple in a unique architectural style, unprecedented in Egypt, blending together several local and traditional elements in a beautiful fusion and presenting traditional ideas in a fully new style. The temple-like grand tomb ascended gradually, level by level, as it approached the mountain face where the divine sanctuary of Goddess Hathor was thought to be located. It took the shape of a temple, gradually rising higher and higher as it approached its ultimate sanctuary and final sacred room. In addition, it embraced the shape and elements of pyramids, the ancient symbol of kingship inherited from the Old Kingdom times.

These new architectural elements featured by King Montohotep in western Thebes inspired later kings from the New Kingdom to use the same valley and build their funeral temples dedicated to the Cow Goddess Hathor. Sadly, out of all the New Kingdom temples and shrines, only one temple has survived. It is the Temple of El Deir El Bahari of Queen Hatshepsut, which stands next to the ruins of the older Temple of King "Montohotep *nbhbtre*." In its day, the temple of the king was the most famous building in the whole valley. For this reason, during the Middle Kingdom, Ancient Egyptians identified the place by the name of the king, the Valley of *nbhbtre*.

King Montohotep designed a lush green garden for the front of his temple and decorated it with more than 400 statues representing himself. In front of every statue, there was a small offering table but very few of the statues have survived; only two endure in front of the temple ruins. The statues were situated facing the Nile with their backs to the temple as if the funeral images of the king were welcoming visitors with their petitions. The temple itself, under the mountain and above the garden, was built on two different levels with a causeway connecting them. On the second level, a small pyramid, about 20 meters in height, was built in the center of the upper terrace, surrounded on all sides by a colonnade of pillars. The pillars connect the temple and its pyramid to King Montohotep's inner shrine carved like a deep cave into the heart of the mountains at the end of a long, deep and descending corridor.

The king also built a small symbolic tomb outside the temple in the front garden, and from this tomb, he built a long tunnel to reach the main burial chamber beneath the pyramid and the mountain face. This famous tomb would be known later as the Tomb of the Horse.

As time passed, the Temple of King Montohotep *nbhbtre* was neglected, forgotten and completely covered by sand, fallen rocks and gravel from the mountains above, to such an extent that the temple was invisible to the eye for many centuries. The amount of sand that covered the area was great enough to hide even the large Temple of Queen Hatshepsut. The obliteration occurred over centuries when no one in Egypt cared about monuments or preservation of any kind, up until the years of François Champollion. Champollion's ability to decipher and decode the signs and symbols of the Ancient Egyptian language marked the defining moment that heralded the beginning of a new era and opened the door to a new science, Egyptology and Egyptian archeology. The next story recounts the discovery of the Tomb of King Montohotep *nbhbtre,* one of the important milestones in the history of the rediscovery of Ancient Egypt.

Discovery Story

On a cold day in December 1898, after he finished his workday in the digs at El Deir El Bahari, as assistant to the famous archeologist Edward Neville, Howard Carter hurried to ride his horse back to his house in unusually rainy weather. Digging and managing archeological sites in rainy weather could be a very hard task with wet, sandy, muddy ground. It can be slippery and dangerous for the workers.

Carter was approaching his house when suddenly the all-day rain made a deep depression beneath the horse's feet, and the horse unexpectedly fell, sliding with Carter on its back into the resulting sinkhole. The horse became scared, and Carter wondered what had made the ground collapse suddenly and fall into itself. He peered down beneath the horse's feet where the ground had given way and observed that the hole seemed to be the opening to a tunnel. The rainwater had removed accumulated layers of mud and the thick dry layer of dirt that had covered this hole and tunnel for centuries, making it too weak to carry Carter and his horse. And so, they fell. When this accident happened, Carter's curiosity prompted him to further examination. There was a hall and a corridor, which he entered, finding in the long corridor limestone blocks that were set together in a way that indicated it was ancient and that it led to a much deeper structure beneath the ground, maybe a tomb or maybe something else. Bear in mind that, at that time, the Temple of King Montohotep was completely covered with sand and debris, and no one had seen it for centuries or even knew about its existence. Carter sensed the magnitude of his accidental discovery of this enigmatic underground tunnel and mysteriously, he refilled the hole with sand and mud to cover completely the entrance to the underground tunnel leaving no trace. He restored the place as it had been before the accident. Carter kept the secret to himself and never spoke to anyone about it, even to his manager Neville, particularly because the area he discovered had not been included in the concession of excavation given to the Egypt Exploration Society that owned the rights to dig in the area of El Deir El Bahari.

A few years later, Carter had been appointed the General Manager and Chief Inspector of Upper Egypt for the Egyptian Department of Antiquities, and his new job offered him the pleasing opportunity to return to his little secret near the Temple of Queen Hatshepsut. He prepared a team to help him excavate the hidden, underground hole and find out where it led. This mission, "he was saving for himself." He wrote to Gaston Maspero, the Head of the Department of Antiquities in Cairo, asking for special funds and financial aid to start his new project. On January 20, 1900, he started removing the dirt and sand above his secret hole. After a few days of digging, he found a wide, square underground hole, cut into the rock beneath the earth at almost a 90-degree angle. The eastern sidewall of this room opened onto a long corridor that ascended to the ground surface, exactly at the location where Carter and his horse had stumbled accidently a few years before. On the western side, he found another descending corridor, filled completely with big stone blocks that sealed its door and cut into the rock of the underground. When Carter reached this point, he started to develop a better understanding of the underground structure he was excavating. It was certainly an underground secret tomb that was carved out of the mother rock under the mountain of western

Thebes, and to enter the tomb, one needed to start at ground level and gradually descend into the heart of the mountain to the west.

On March 10, 1900, the team of excavation workers reached a distance of 17 meters below the ground where they reached the main entrance of the tomb, still perfectly sealed with rocks and mud brick. The original funeral and cemetery stamps made by the embalmers and priests could still be seen on the mud brick walls, which meant to Carter that the tomb that lay behind that door was intact and unlooted. Carter made a small hole in the mud brick doorway of the tomb, just large enough for him to slide through. He was surprised to find a much longer descending corridor that continued behind the mud brick door with an incredibly beautiful vaulted ceiling and a total length reaching 150 meters. At the beginning of the descending corridor, Carter found mummified parts of a sacrificed bull; the head and the thigh of a mummified bull lay on the floor. Carter brought in some light to see down the deep, dark, confined corridor and walked slowly to the end where he found a large room with another vaulted ceiling. In that room, he found a large statue of the king made of sandstone. Wrapped in linen like a mummy, it was lying on its side in the corner of the large room. Close to the statue, Carter found a wooden coffin covered on the outside with religious texts, but no royal names were found in the texts and the insides were void of any inscription. Also beside the statue and the coffin in the same inner room, Carter and his team found a number of pottery bowls and dishes, animal bones and many embalmed remains of animals all sacrificed to the unknown owner of the tomb. By the western wall, Carter found a vertical shaft cut in the rock going deep below the ground surface, but nothing was discovered there.

The leader of the Egyptian working team was Rayes Ahmed Korqar, who had worked very closely with Carter for several seasons and at various sites on the West Bank of the Luxor Necropolis. Rayes Ahmed had the full trust of Carter and was essentially Carter's advisor on all his digs. On March 11, 1900, Rayes Ahmed advised excavating the shaft and clearing the interior, too. He was forced to terminate the work on April 7th because he recognized the unusual depth of the shaft and consequently the obvious unsafe working conditions. With the hot summer months of Upper Egypt arriving soon (the usual resting season for all archeological teams and digs in Egypt), he commanded that work be stopped. Once the shaft was reinforced with scaffoldings and supporting beams, they resumed digging in the tomb again on December 7, 1900, with a clear goal to reach the bottom of the deep shaft hoping it might possibly lead to the true underground, well-hidden royal burial tomb of the mysterious king. Carter was desperate to pursue his alluring dream of finding an intact royal tomb of a well-known pharaoh full of artifacts and treasures. His ambition had taken him to the far horizon and induced him send a special letter to Lady Amherst on December 19, 1900, telling her:

> *"I am working hard to reach the end of the tomb that I discovered last year in the area of El Deir El Bahari, and I am quite sure that I am able to do so even though I am facing a lot of challenges and obstacles. My workers have reached deep in the shaft to 97 meters, and it is almost dangerous and vertically standing and we still do not see the bottom of it. My mind cannot think of anything else but a happy ending. We shall see soon. It is a wonderful possibility to find a nice discovery undisturbed and intact."*

Carter not only wrote that letter but he excitedly wrote other letters to Gaston Maspero and Lord Cromer, both in Cairo, updating them with the latest news about the upcoming significant discovery he was about to make in the mysterious royal tomb. His letters charged the Egyptological atmosphere in Egypt and abroad, and anticipation and expectations were rising by the day. People were waiting for news from the Luxor area, and finally Gaston Maspero, Head of Egypt's Department of Antiquities, was unable to wait anymore. He took his dahabia (sailboat) called Maryam up the Nile with Lord Cromer onboard to Luxor to attend the grand opening of Carter's great new discovery.

On December 25th, Carter unwrapped the linen shroud that covered the pharaoh's statue that had been found inside the large room of the tomb to reveal the statue to his guests, Maspero and Cromer, at Egypt's Department of Antiquities guesthouse near the area of Habu Temple.

The statue appeared to everyone as a royal seated figure made of sandstone. The king was wearing the red crown of Lower Egypt, and his body was covered with a white dress of jubilations that pharaohs would have worn during feasts and festivals. The king's hands were crossed over his chest in Osiris' mummy fashion. Everyone remarked that the statue had been executed in a poor, local fashion, and that the body of the king himself was painted all in black, indicating its funeral function. The height of the statue was 183 cm., and the legs of the statue were clearly much larger than the body proportion, another reason for Lord Cromer not liking it.

On December 31st, the workers reached the bottom of the shaft where they found a smaller room; its door had been hermetically sealed with large blocks of stones. On the following day, Carter open the sealed door of the last room in front of Maspero, but to their great surprise and utter disappointment they found the room empty except for a few small wooden funeral boat models and a number of pottery jars. Both searched the small room more carefully, helplessly trying to find something valuable or at least a clue to the tomb's owner, but they recognized this was the end of the tomb and the end of the beautiful dream.

Carter gave instructions to his assistant Rayes Ahmed to reexamine the long descending corridor once more, and Rayes Ahmed discovered a shaft in the middle of the long corridor vertically cut in the floor and about two meters deep. When the small, new shaft was completely cleared, there was a surprise for everyone. Carter and his team found at the end of the shaft a small wooden box in poor condition and of a very basic design, but on one of its sides, Carter was able to read a funeral text with a royal insignia, *htb di nso*. The text mentioned the name of the king and the tomb's owner, Montohotep *nbhbtre*. This box and text were the only evidence that mentioned the name of the owner of the tomb.

The discovery of the Tomb of King Montohotep from the 11th Dynasty, Middle Kingdom, circa 2050 BC, is very important from a historic and scientific viewpoint, but Carter was unable to hide his sadness and deep disappointment. His great expectation had been to find an intact royal tomb and he had reflected this in the letters he wrote to the Amherst family, Maspero and Cromer. The expectations on their side had been even greater. That had been the motivation for Lord Cromer to make the trip to Luxor. He was obviously unhappy with Carter's new find and he showed it clearly. On the other hand, Maspero realized Carter's mistake and even affirmed the great importance of the discovery as he wrote in a letter on January 8, 1901, to Edward Neville in Switzerland to tell him:

> *"Carter spoke about his new discovery too early to Lord Cromer and the lord travelled especially to Luxor to be a witness to his great success. Once there, he was greatly disappointed because Carter could not show him anything of what he promised. Carter stated: "I am doing my best to relieve his pain and entertain him as much as I can because he is truly a nice person, and he's doing all that he can to help us.""*

Even though it was empty, the new royal tomb's discovery in the Luxor area, helped Carter to retain his job for several more years as manager of the monuments of Upper Egypt in the Luxor area, despite having disappointed Lord Cromer, the powerful man who also dreamed of a wonderful find, full of gold and jewels. Cromer's clear intent was to have acquired a fabulous collection of pieces that could easily be smuggled out of Egypt and later sold for a higher price. In this discovery, Carter found no more than an ugly sandstone statue and valueless funeral boat models that Lord Cromer never liked at all.

However, Carter had learned a lot from this discovery, and his passion for making discoveries never faded. His ambition to find a complete, intact royal tomb in the Luxor area never waned. He also learned how to manage his public relations with the government and the sponsors—what should be told and when it should be announced. For this reason, this story was a great experience in the life and career of Howard Carter, who was on an appointment with fate 20 years later to make his dream discovery, or should I say, the greatest archeological discovery in the history of mankind, when he found the Tomb of Tutankhamun in the Valley of the Kings in 1922.

This interesting and unimaginable discovery has another story to tell.

CHAPTER 8

Catacombs of Kom el Shoqafa

ALEXANDRIA RESERVES A VERY SPECIAL place in ancient world history and particularly with respect to ancient Mediterranean civilizations and their relationships to Egypt. Founded by Alexander the Great and enhanced by the subsequent great Ptolemaic rulers of Egypt and other significant parts of the ancient Near East, Alexandria was expanded by the Ptolemys to have it serve as the capital of their New Kingdom. Alexandria was a rival to Athens and all other major towns of the old Greek world.

The inspiring hero, Alexander the Great, built the City of Alexandria to surpass Naucratis and act as the link between Greece and towns in the Nile Delta. However, the people who actually brought the town to its greater Hellenistic status through subsequent expansion were the Ptolemys, starting with the rise of Ptolemy I Soter (Savior) in 323 BC. The Ptolemaic rule from Alexandria continued into the days of the notorious Queen Cleopatra VII, 48 BC to 31 BC. The city was described thoroughly in the early Greek travelers' books and by Roman visitors' chronicles. It boasted impressive grandeur with great prosperity and featured wide streets, grand palaces, elegant gardens and a busy port with ships of all kinds, full of activity as boats came and went to and from all Mediterranean lands.

In addition, the early travelers' and visitors' books (e.g., Strabo's Geography) tell us about the rich cultural life in Alexandria, with its schools and museums. They often describe the town as the greatest city in the ancient world during the period from the 3rd century BC to the 3rd century AD. It was a rival to the glorious city of Rome, capital of the Roman Empire and residence of the great Roman emperors.

The ancient city of Alexandria was a melting pot for many races and religions and a true reflection of cultural diversity in the eastern Mediterranean world. Greeks, Egyptians and many other ethnic groups in smaller communities lived within the borders of Alexandria and practiced their own religions, common to the ancient Near East. There were shrines, temples and places of worship dedicated to Egyptian gods, Greek gods, Roman gods, the Jewish god and gods worshipped by the many ethnic communities associated with them. There were a number of cemeteries on the eastern and western edges of the town, Greek tombs in the area of Mustafa Kamal on the east and Roman tombs in the area of Kom el Shoqafa on the west. In Alexandria, ancient world gods and goddesses were worshiped and adored freely until the spark of Christianity spread the new faith into the city around the 3rd century AD.

Alexandria remained the capital of Egypt and one of the most important Mediterranean cities until the Arab conquest of Egypt in 641 AD. Near the beginning of the 8th century AD, a gradual shift of beliefs arose in the hearts and minds of most Egyptians, leading them from ancient pagan practices and Christianity toward the Islamic faith and Arabic language. The Arab invaders created a new capital and administrative center for themselves, called Fustat (known now as Old Cairo). They combined several smaller towns with Fustat, to make the new, large capital of greater Cairo, completed in the 10th century AD. (Cairo is still the capital today and is the political and financial center of Egypt.) Trade activities gradually diverted to the new capital of Cairo because of its proximity to the old trade roads and caravan routes running from the Arabian Desert, through the Sinai Peninsula and across the Red Sea. Eventually, Alexandria became neglected, disregarded by history, its lights faded and its palaces and great monuments ultimately vanished.

It is important to mention the ancient Lighthouse of Alexandria, one of the Seven Wonders of the Ancient World. From the times of Cleopatra VII, around 48 BC, the lighthouse was gradually ravaged during the civil war between Cleopatra, with Roman intervention supporting her, and her brother Ptolemy XIII. The remaining part of the lighthouse still functioned normally up to the 12th century AD, when a massive earthquake destroyed it. The location of the ancient Lighthouse of Alexandria has been recorded in a number of books by early Arab travelers, Al-Masoudi and others, who visited Alexandria at that time. Its materials were later recycled during the Mamluk period and used to build a massive fort in the 15th century AD, the period of Sultan Qaitbay, who used any remaining stones from the damaged, pancaked lighthouse structure to fortify the port of the town. This fort still exists in Alexandria, and the Egyptian government recently restored it. Most archeologists believe that the fort was built atop the ancient lighthouse site with its stone blocks.

Post-earthquake, Alexandria was no longer attractive and shrank to a small population, its inhabitants having chosen to abandon it. Only small scattered groups of people survived there, making their living by fishing and living in huts built mainly atop the ruins of ancient city monuments. Glory was gone and Alexandria vanished leaving only a few areas of broken stones and abandoned lifeless sites.

The situation in Alexandria remained unchanged for several centuries, until the French expedition to Egypt by Napoleon Bonaparte (1798–1801) and the landing of the French troops on the fallen city's western beaches. When Napoleon entered the city, he was shocked by the state of deterioration of the city's streets, homes and markets and the extremely poor conditions of life. This decrepitude was all that remained beside a very small harbor that could no longer accommodate large ships. Napoleon decided to restore the ancient city to its former glory and rebuild its old harbor, remodeling it to accommodate large ships rather than just small local fishing boats. He also built new roads and widened the narrow streets by demolishing old houses and little local marketplaces. From this point on, the revival of Alexandria's importance continued, carrying it toward modern times and the rediscovery of its ancient magnificence began to reveal hidden treasures lost for several long centuries.

Leaving this introduction of the importance of Alexandria in the history of Egypt, I would now like to introduce a brief history of the great city's construction and how the very idea of creating the city was born in the days of Alexander the Great.

The Old Town

Rakodit was a small, peaceful and neglected fishing village situated by the Mediterranean Sea when Alexander the Great entered it with his troops en route to the distant desert Siwa Oasis, in the western Libyan Desert on the edge of North Africa's great sandy sea. Sometime in 332 BC, as if fated, Alexander the Great chose the coastal road to search for the Siwa Oasis rather than trekking into the heart of Egypt's western desert, a route shorter in distance but with lifeless and dangerous terrain.

Alexander found Rakodit very charming, situated on a beautiful beach facing many small rocky islands that provided natural protection to its small harbor. He envisioned his new city being built right at Rakodit's small village site, a place that would carry Alexander's name forever. On April 7, 331 BC, the foundation stone of the new city was placed, and its construction officially began, designed by the well-known architect Dinocrates of Rhodes. Soon the new city buildings started to rise by the new harbor.

Later, the Ptolemys, who ruled Egypt after Alexander the Great, relocated their royal residences to Alexandria and made it the capital of Egypt from 320 BC on. They continued constructing and expanding Alexandria's important buildings, and it became the pearl of the ancient Mediterranean world.

During the Graeco-Roman period (the Ptolemys followed by the Romans), Alexandria gained so much power that it became a magnet that attracted people from surrounding countries to come to live and enjoy its grandeur. Groups hailed from various ethnic and cultural backgrounds. An early traveler, Dudorus Cicilius, who visited Alexandria in the 1st century AD, remarked that the population during the time of his visit reached 300,000, making it one of the largest cities in the ancient world, a reason that Roman emperors considered Alexandria the second most important city in the empire, after Rome, of course.

In his description of Alexandria toward the end of the 1st century AD, famous geographer and traveler, Strabo, indicated the five different districts were classified in the order of the Greek alphabet. He noted that the fifth district in town was reserved specifically for the Egyptian community and was called Rakotis, the name of the old fishing village and the nucleus of the new, Greek town. Strabo also indicated there was a fresh water canal that ran through the Egyptian district and that there was a large necropolis to serve the community and their funeral traditions. This necropolis was located southwest of the center of the old village and was separated from the new city by walls that had once surrounded the old town on all sides. The following is a small part that survived from the book of Strabo about his visit to Alexandria:

> *"Nothing remains behind the fresh water canal, Sechedia, except a very small part of the town's edge. Then one can see the necropolis area where you find a large number of gardens, funeral houses and tombs."*

This area of the town had a large temple dedicated to the local god of Alexandria, Serapes, and a large festival and sports auditorium. A long ditch surrounded the entire area for 5 km. to protect the town on its southwest side. The area also had a natural rocky stone cliff where Roman people interred their mummies in small tombs hewn into the rocky mound. They called it Lofus Kiramaikos, which means "the mounds of pottery shards." The mound had arisen due to the old burial ceremonies' tradition in the local community of breaking and shattering a number of funeral pots and jars after they had been offered to the dead person as a votive gift. Locals thought the tradition would protect them from death, curses and all sorts of evil spirits. (This superstitious tradition is still in practice in various parts of Egypt and the world today.)

The city of Alexandria retained its Hellenistic spirit, nature and culture with economic strength from Graeco-Roman times up to the Arab conquest of Egypt in the summer of 641 AD. As described before, the new invaders built a new capital in Fustat, instead of Alexandria, which led to the old capital's gradual decline in cultural glory and consequently, in population. That said, Alexandria had become an important Mediterranean port and the commercial gateway to Egypt, and it maintained its commercial status through the end of the 15th century when the Portuguese explorers began their surprising discoveries in the New World (1492–1497). Alexandria was negatively affected by new encounters once again and the importance of being at the crossroads of ancient world trade routes was diminished. The city took another hit in 1517 when Ottoman armies invaded Egypt and isolated the entire country along with its major ports from the outside world. Trade into and out of Alexandria was reduced substantially during the Ottoman period, while other commercial ports in Egypt, such as Damietta, and elsewhere on the Mediterranean began to capture more shipping activities from Alexandria.

For almost 300 years, Alexandria was trapped in history under the rule of the Ottomans, and the city lost much of its glory and appeal and sustained obvious damage to its main buildings. Historic neighborhoods eroded to mounds and ruins. Napoleon's French Expedition to Egypt at the end of the 18th century arrived to find a city whose total population did not exceed 8,000, according to the estimates of Gratin le Pere, one of the French historians who accompanied Napoleon to Egypt. He described the town in detail along with the monuments that could still be seen in his day. He noted the importance of the monuments and relics still in existence within the ruins of the old town of Rakotis just southwest of the modern town.

When Muhammad Ali ruled Egypt in 1805, he reserved a very special place for Alexandria in his modernizing plans for Egypt. He started with the area known as Al Max and Al Qabari, very poor neighborhoods that lay west of the modern town today, where the new main harbor was built. This western suburb of Alexandria was associated with the famous ancient site of Kom El Shoqafa, the necropolis of the catacombs. Muhammad Ali rebuilt the ancient city walls to reinforce security and built the famous Alexandria Arsenal as a shipbuilding dry dock. His development of the city succeeded in revitalizing the economy and raised its population to 60,000 by 1821.

His grandson Ismail ruled later from 1863–1879, and he continued the modernization of the town with widespread and significant construction. The result of Ismail's efforts completely changed the shape of life in Alexandria and made the city a true metropolis, an attractive industrial and financial center for Egypt. Ismail moved his government every summer to Alexandria for at least five months, from May to October. This meant more royal palaces were needed, e.g. Qasr El Tin Palace. The railway service connecting Alexandria to Cairo was developed, and the city's tram service, new roads, and infrastructure, such as the telegraph, were built.

Ismail also helped people who moved to Alexandria to buy land and build homes by encouraging land ownership in town and authorizing special permissions for foreign investors to work and build in the city freely. Alexandria gradually took on the look of a very modern, almost European, city. (Old Central Alexandria still bears witness to this building and its golden era.) This revitalization happened relatively quickly, and the population continued to grow as the town continued to attract more businesses from all over the Mediterranean. By the 1880s, the population had grown to 270,000 with the foreign communities representing one-third of this number.

It is important to note that urban development in Alexandria in the 1860s, 1870s and 1880s required a lot of land to allow for town expansion and to create new suburbs and neighborhoods, which meant real estate developers had to push the city limits eastward and westward. Eventually, as they expanded outward and built, they discovered and violated ancient city relics dating from the Greek and Roman times. Unfortunately, many investment companies working in Alexandria at the time were not inclined to worry about preserving monuments when they found them. They preferred to remove whatever they found and continue with their projects. The national law that protects monuments in Egypt had not yet been enacted, and the only government body responsible for archeological sites was Egypt's Department of Antiquities. And they were more interested in pharaonic monuments in the south of Egypt than in Hellenistic culture and finds near Alexandria. It seems archeologists and the government did not take Alexandria seriously at that time.

Between 1859 and 1880, the Institute of Egypt created a special committee to study the Hellenistic art and monuments of Egypt. Most of its members were foreigners who lived permanently in Alexandria: Italians, Maltese, Cypriots, Greeks, and French. In 1860, a committee of the Institute of Egypt made a profound affirmation to preserve all monuments and relics of Alexandria whenever they were found. The necessity of building an up-to-date art museum where all artifacts could be displayed and archived became clear. Consequently, another committee was formed called the Permanent Committee of Archeology, whose job it was to preserve Egypt's heritage and protect associated artifacts and relics from constant local, haphazard looting and against organized crime.

Discovery Story

In 1884, Giuseppe Botti, a young Italian, arrived in Alexandria to look for a job and live among the large Italian community in town, the largest foreign community in the city after the Greek community. (In 1927, the Italian community in Alexandria reached 27,000.) Soon after he settled in town, Botti found a job as an Italian language teacher in one of the many Italian schools. During his free time, he developed a special interest in the oldest neighborhood of Alexandria and enjoyed walking through the ancient sites of

Alexandria that remained from the Graeco-Roman period. He would collect artifacts whenever possible and sell them to art galleries and antique dealers.

In 1889, Archibald Sayce visited Alexandria, hosted by the British Consul in Alexandria, Sir Charles Cookson, who introduced him to Giuseppe Botti at a dinner. The three men held a very long discussion about Alexandria, its history, its remaining heritage and why it was imperative to preserve this heritage. They all recognized the importance of building an art museum for Alexandria where they could display and preserve all artifacts found in town.

Two years later, in 1891, Sir Charles Cookson successfully established the Athenian Society of Alexandria and raised enough funds from individual sponsors to build Alexandria's first museum, later known as the Graeco-Roman Museum. The Athenian Society chose the young Italian teacher Giuseppe Botti as its first manager of the new museum. The foundation stone of the new museum was placed on October 17, 1892.

Giuseppe Botti did not waste time waiting for the museum's construction to be completed. He actively launched a number of small, quick archeological missions in Alexandria to collect artifacts for his new museum and preserve as much as possible from threatened monuments in the old town, especially in those areas close to the crowded, poor, southwest area where the ancient necropolis once was.

In the following year, 1893, another new society was founded, the Alexandria Archeological Society, which continued to support technically and financially all excavations in Alexandria and aided in the building of the new museum until it was officially opened in 1895.

The field explorations Giuseppe Botti made in Alexandria enlightened his knowledge of the ancient and lost city of Alexandria and made him aware of the danger the new growing town would have on the ancient monuments. He realized the threat posed by the overcrowded, poor area of town, the southwestern neighborhoods of Karmouz, Alqabari, Wardian and Kom El Shoqafa, where many relics and artifacts had already been collected and subsequently sold. Botti highlighted the importance of this area during the golden era of Alexandria from 300 BC to 300 AD, and he concentrated his efforts on excavations in this area between 1892 and 1900.

His persistent efforts pushed for the continuation of work in the difficult conditions presented by the density of homes and people. Furthermore, the return value of his excavations was not as high as he had expected. He discovered remnants of ancient Alexandria's southwestern walls, a large number of funeral coffins (which indicated the existence of a large necropolis in the area) and a huge number of large and broken granite and marble columns. Millions of shards of shattered pottery were discovered in the mounds of mud and rocks in the area. However, the sad fact is, for eight unpromising years, Botti did not find anything special or significant until one special day when Ali Gebara visited him at the museum at 5 pm.

Ali Gebara, a local stone trader from Alexandria, was accustomed to roaming the city, especially in the old part of the town where ancient ruins existed, and collecting stones that he could sell later for other purposes. He had done this for years, and he liked the southwestern Alexandria area because he could collect large pieces of white marble scattered in and among the mounds.

On September 28, 1900, he went as usual to the city's ancient mounds to select rocks and load his donkeys. It was Friday, early morning, when most people were still sleeping because it was the weekend in Egypt, so he could work peacefully until the afternoon without being harassed by local children and antiquities people who kept watch over the mound as a protected archeological site. He chose a high mound, apparently with rocks easily seen in it, to start extracting the stones. Ali began hitting the rocks hard with a hand ax and suddenly found a large hole, deep and black, into which many of the stones fell making an incredible noise. He examined the hole closely in the sunlight, realized it was oddly rectangular and guessed it might hide something very important deep inside. He weighed his options and reached a simple conclusion: Alone, he could never go down to find out what lay beneath. Besides, the locals would soon hear about it and would loot whatever they found. Therefore, it was wiser to hide the hole, go to the authorities at the museum to report his discovery and obtain a solemn guarantee that he could continue taking rocks from the site whenever he wished.

When he met with Giuseppe Botti, the museum manager, he excitedly told him:

"While quarrying for stone, I broke open the vault of a subterranean tomb. Come see it. Take the antiquities if there are any and authorize me to get on with my work without delay."

Botti was used to meeting people like Ali Gebara, who claimed to find great monuments and were looking for rewards or government attention, almost every week. At first, he gave the man no attention, but Ali's excitement and persistence made him think twice about the story and give him more consideration. It was Friday afternoon, the weekend, and soon the museum would become busy with visitors and Alexandrian high society families. In addition, few Egyptian employees were working that day. Therefore, Botti could not leave the museum to go out looking at this new find in Kom El Shoqafa. He resolved to visit the site on the following day.

When Ali Gebara failed to convince Botti to go to check on his find, he told Botti that he would be obliged to go back to the area and continue taking rocks as if nothing happened, and he would meet the museum inspectors in the morning to show them his find.

The story occupied Botti's mind all afternoon. He changed his mind and before the museum closed at 5 pm, he dispatched one of his Italian assistants, Silvio Beghe, and one of the Egyptian museum workers, Abdo Dawoud, to the area of Kom El Shoqafa to check out Ali Gebara's story and report directly to him when they met again a few hours later on Friday night. The two men visited the site and met with Ali Gebara, who was still collecting rocks in the area nearby the mound with the hole. He guided them to his find, and they went together down the deep shaft to find a large cave-like tomb inside with lots of broken pottery and stones. Silvio Beghe immediately realized it was a great discovery, very different from other finds they had examined in the old town over the past few years. He prepared a full report and presented it to Botti when they all met later that night.

The following morning, Botti examined the shaft and the large underground catacomb and prepared for a large excavation campaign for the new discovery. He would lead the team that started in October 1900. They began by removing all of the debris from the main shaft and reached the main level of the tomb. At this point, Botti recognized the true size and scope of the tomb and noted the much lower, deeper levels it contained. He found a large number of pottery jars and human skeletal remains.

The cleaning of the tomb lasted almost three years, until 1903, when Giuseppe Botti died. His assistant, Evaristo Breccia (1876–1967), continued leading the expedition and worked inside the tomb. Breccia had studied ancient history at Roma University and first traveled to Egypt to work in the Italian excavation at El Shmoneen, in El Mynia in Middle Egypt, with the famous Egyptologist at that time Ernesto Schiaparelli, the man who ultimately discovered the famous Tomb of Queen Nefertari in the Valley of the Queens. Breccia had moved to Alexandria, where he had started a job at the newly opened museum of Alexandria working as assistant manager, so it was natural for him to lead the excavation team in the new tomb. It was deep inside the tomb that he found a complete banquet of boiled eggs, salted meat and grilled ducks all on pottery dishes, offered to the dead person as a gift, accompanied by a large number of wine jars and pots. All were found in the side banquet hall, which he named Triclinium.

For Breccia to continue working safely inside the underground tomb, he needed the help of a professional engineer to restore the badly damaged roof, rehabilitate the area surrounding the tomb, prepare the site for a proper archeological survey and prepare to host visitors later on. He hired Ehrlich, an independent engineer who lived and worked in Alexandria, and it is this man who is responsible for everything we see today when we visit the catacombs of Kom El Skoqafa. The entrance of the tomb was first marked and protected. Then, the collapsing parts of the underground tomb were reinforced. Next, all the dirt and sand removed were piled in huge mounds in the area above the tomb. Ehrlich also provided the underground tomb with electricity and protected the land above the tomb with a layer of asphalt. It became the open-air museum we see as we enter the site today. The entire area in front of the stairs down into the main shaft into the underground tomb is all Ehrlich's creation.

Breccia worked on the catacombs of Alexandria for a long time during his years as Manager of the Graeco-Roman Museum of Alexandria, until 1931, before returning to Italy to work as a professor of classical history, Graeco-Roman, at the University of Pisa. He left the management of his museum in Alexandria in the hands of another Italian, Achilli Adriani (1905–1982), who also worked for a few seasons in the catacombs area and continued the preservation and conservation of the tomb. Finally, came Alan Rowe who excavated the catacombs from 1939 to 1940 and discovered the remains of Roman burials of a number of upper class women, along with their jewels, gold necklaces, bracelets, rings and other accessories, in the style expected of wealthy women who lived in Alexandria some 1,800 years ago. All the jewels and decorative art indicated a connection between the buried women and the powerful Roman Goddess Nemeses, the Goddess of Revenge and Protection. Alan Rowe concluded that these women had likely served as priestesses in the shrines and caves of Goddess Nemeses and had therefore been buried together.

The catacombs of Kom El Shoqafa are a series of underground, connected burial places, originally started as a private tomb dedicated to a wealthy family who lived in the city sometime toward the end of the 1st century AD or the beginning of the 2nd century AD. Later, due to lack of burial space in the necropolis area, the tomb was reused many times as a public burial place with more than 300 tombs in various shapes and styles found inside. Today, it is still the largest tomb found in Egypt from the Roman period. It may have been used as recently as the 4th century AD, but no archeological surveys have provided evidence of any burials from the early Christian period.

The various styles of burial inside the catacombs, loculi (small coffins), sarcophagi, graves, clini (deathbeds), funerary urns, crematory amphora, indicate a wide range of social strata used this public tomb. The presence of amphorae provides evidence that the catacombs were used in Roman times, as cremation of the body and keeping only the bone and ashes was common then.

Originally, the tomb had a building above the ground that served as a small funeral temple to receive embalmed bodies, where families and priests performed the final funeral rituals before sending the mummy down into the underground tomb. This temple is now completely in ruins, and only a few pieces of rock remain at the site. From the temple, we find a large vertical, round shaft with a spiral stairway that takes us down to the underground tomb. It is 30 meters deep and descends to the bottom level of the tomb. Originally, it had 100 stone-cut steps that gradually increased in size descending toward the tomb's lowest level. (These original steps no longer exist, but Ehrlich created new, small, easy-to-use steps, about 245 in total.) The main shaft is provided with small windows, allowing sunlight to enter and penetrate the darkness of the inner part of the tomb. The shaft opens to the main level of the tomb, level one, and is almost round in shape, a rotunda, with a hall. In the middle, we find another shaft much smaller than the principal one with a short, 1-meter high, wall supporting six pillars, all cut in the mother rock of the underground cave-like tomb. The central shaft is connected to the deeper part of the tomb, level 3, with a large dome-like ceiling above it, all cut in stone.

To the left of the entrance room, we find a large square-shaped room with four massive pillars all cut from natural rock and connected with three long stone-cut tables that were used mainly as a family banquet and gathering room for various ritual ceremonies such as Father's Day, Spring Feast, and birthdays of the deceased. It should be noted that this is where Evaristo Breccia found the varied banquet offerings previously mentioned.

If we return to the central hall, we find to the left of the banquet room, steps leading down to the private family tomb with a small hall in front with two pillars stylized in Egyptian and Roman capitals. We also see the famous protection symbols of Egypt, the winged disc with small images of God Horus, above the two pillars. Beyond the two pillars, we see the large, round faces of Medusa, Greek Goddess of Protection, along with two large serpents wearing the double crowns of Upper and Lower Egypt, the white crown and red crown. The two snakes may represent other Greek deities, Hermes and Dionysus or the Guardian God Agathodemon.

Flanking the entrance to the tomb, there are two statues posed in Egyptian style dress and stance, with the left foot forward, but the faces are obviously Roman. The statue on the right before entering the tomb represents the male owner of the tomb, on the left his wife.

Through a small door, we enter the final burial chamber to see three stone sarcophagi styled in Roman fashion. The carved scenes above the sarcophagus are in typical Egyptian style, ritual and ceremony with an offering to the sacred bull Apis and traditional embalming scenes showing the dead person being embalmed by both God Anubis and God Thoth. In addition, we see images of God Ptah and Alexandria's God Osirapes (Serapes).

Walking out of the burial chamber, we find on both sides of the antechamber small entrances to the side galleries and long corridors, which were added later as an expansion to the main private tomb. This public tomb holds over 300 burials found in a maze of rooms, corridors and chambers. Many of these side galleries are still not fully explored or mapped. (Over the centuries, underground water has caused the collapse of some stones so researchers can find it hard today to navigate through all the side rooms of the public tomb.)

If we return to the central hall at the main entrance of the tomb, we find another side entrance to another side wing carved into the rock during the times of the Roman Caesar Caracalla. (It is not the original entrance, but a new door made in the 1930s excavation.) Many bones were found in this side wing, explained (it turns out, incorrectly) by the Massacre of Alexandria during the historic visit of Emperor Caracalla to the city in 215 AD. Upon closer examination of the bones, we have learned they were animal bones from horses, and for some unknown reason, they were buried in this wing of the grand tomb. Some scholars believe they were the special horses that died in the frequently held horse races in Alexandria, special enough to be buried under the protection of Goddess Nemeses in her underground tomb. Also in the same wing, Caracalla Hall, we find a large number of burial niches in the stone walls prepared for all kinds of burials, embalmed bodies, amphorae with ashes and urns of ashes.

In modern times, the catacombs have suffered greatly from the significant rise of underground water that has fully submerged the third level of the tomb and parts of the second level. The lower levels had been inaccessible to visitors for decades until the Antiquities Department started a project to lower and control the underground water inside the catacombs. This project was finished in 1995, and the tomb has once again reopened to visitors.

Alexandria began to reveal parts of its mystical history soon after the city's art museum, the Graeco-Roman Museum of Alexandria, opened. The new museum welcomed new finds and artifacts that had been found between the new museum and the site of the catacombs, dating back to the Golden Age of Alexandria. The distance between the two sites is not great, but it comprised virtually the busiest area in the modern city and sat exactly on top of Old Alexandria and its southwestern necropolis. Several discoveries were made after finding the great catacombs, and every few years, we hear about a new find dating back to the Greek or the Roman period. New discoveries commonly occur during the rebuilding of the old and rundown houses of the old town. There is much to be found beneath houses and streets in the old town, but very little of what people really find during the process of putting up a new building is ever reported. Consequently, we know very little about much of what the people of Alexandria find. If they do report their finds, they may lose their land to the government by eminent domain. Government compensation for confiscated, archeologically protected land has always been slow and bureaucratic, complicated and unfair, all good reasons for people to not report anything they find.

One can only imagine the number of artifacts still waiting to be revealed under homes and streets of Old Alexandria. Recently, the authorities managed to save a number of large, significant pieces from the Ptolemaic period, one of which was a house mosaic. It was removed from the ground, examined and restored, before the new home construction could take place. (These pieces, including the famous head of Medusa, are now on display in the newly opened Alexandria National Museum.)

Recently, two unique, large, mosaic pieces dating back to the Ptolemaic period were discovered accidently while digging the foundation for the modern library Alexandria Biblioteca. The two pieces, the mosaic of "the two wrestlers," and the breathtaking mosaic of "the dog," are now on display in the art museum annex of the new library, in the basement along with a number of other artifacts from other Egyptian periods. Additionally, many other small pieces and artifacts reach people's hands either by chance or through illegal digs here and there.

The question begs to be asked: Who will reach the hidden secrets of Alexandria first? The local people and treasure hunters or the professional archeological teams? It is important to understand that professional teams and art historians always face complications and difficulties when it comes to working inside a large and heavily populated city like Alexandria. We have a true story from Alexandria that occurred a few years ago as a Greek archeological team tried to excavate parts of the downtown area near Daniel Street, one of the busiest streets in the city, claiming they knew exactly where the tomb of legendary Alexander the Great was. Permission was issued, but practically speaking, the mission faced enormous obstacles working in the heart of Alexandria traffic and beneath old rundown buildings. The project had to be stopped, and the Greek mission was suspended in an obvious dilemma. Which is more important, finding and preserving monuments, or letting people keep their dilapidated homes and shops?

The great hope of finding the tombs of Ptolemy I to XIII, or even any one of them, and the biggest hope of all, finding the Tomb of Queen Cleopatra VII, seem sometimes close and sometimes far away. Zahi Hawass declared more than once that he was very close to locating the secret place where Queen Cleopatra was entombed. His excavation west of Alexandria, about 30 km. toward the town of Alamein, revealed an ancient necropolis dating back to the Ptolemaic period, and there are clues at the site of some royal burials. However, to this day (2015), nothing has been officially discovered.

The whole world is still waiting for another big discovery in Alexandria to help us understand more about life in what once was the greatest city in the world, even by accident.

CHAPTER 9

Tebtunis Papyrus

THE GREAT DISCOVERIES IN THE old necropolis area of Alexandria cast light on the history of Egypt during the Graeco-Roman period and the valuable artifacts that Egypt surely possessed from this era. Eventually, the circles of interested individuals and institutes focused on this period grew larger. The news that emanated from Alexandria and its new museum was very promising.

Over time, many papyrus scrolls have surfaced in the antiquities markets in Cairo and Alexandria dating back to that desirable Graeco-Roman era. Most Classical papyri have come from Middle Egypt, specifically from the areas of El Fayoum and Beni Swif, located south and southwest of Cairo about 100 km. All the new Graeco-Roman era papyrus discoveries fueled an excitement to find and collect more artifacts and materials from this era. A sudden rush developed to excavate throughout Egypt in the pursuit of all types of old Egyptian papyri from all parts of the country and from any historic period.

The two mentioned regions, El Fayoum and Beni Swif, first became the focus of in-depth research and subsequently became active dig sites, a great treasure hunting ground for those who were looking for papyri from the more recent times. These localities had never attracted the first generation of explorers and treasure hunters because they were simply not important in comparison to the West Bank of Luxor, the Giza Plateau and Saqqara Cemetery. No major monuments remained in the El Fayoum or Beni Swif areas except a few pyramids from the Middle Kingdom and cemeteries scattered here and there dating back to later days.

However, after the opening of the Graeco-Roman Museum and the establishment of the Archeological Society for Classical Studies in Alexandria, the passion to find more materials from the Classical Period, Egypt's Graeco-Roman times, amplified. Beni Swif, known earlier as Oxyrhynchus, and just south of El Fayoum Oasis, known earlier as Tebtunis, were the sources of many papyrus scrolls. Unexpectedly, some of them came into the antiquities market wrapped inside small, mummified crocodiles.

The area of Karanis in the southern part of El Fayoum, where the ruins of a Roman era city still exist, became a well-known source of artifacts. Consequently, numerous unauthorized excavations took place within the city's ruins; its convenient proximity to the main road leading to Cairo made it easily accessible to all the local villagers. If someone visits Karanis now, they will see the remains of the old guesthouse that was built inside the archeological site to serve the British Military Commissioner of Egypt, Lord Cromer, around the turn of the 20th century. Lord Cromer used to visit the area in the wintertime because he loved the sunny winters of El Fayoum and enjoyed digging on his own in the city's ruins, collecting whatever artifacts he could take away. These were the years of British power and hegemony in Egypt.

Our next story, about a great accidental discovery, occurred in the south of El Fayoum Oasis. The discovery is rated as one of the biggest discoveries ever made in the region, in a small, quiet and neglected village now called Om El Burigat. However, about 2,000 years ago, it was called Tebtunis.

Historic Background

When the sun set on Egypt, plunging it into its weakest period in the later days of the 26th Dynasty under the rule of Pharaoh Psamtik, the country welcomed many foreign communities that hailed from all over the eastern Mediterranean region. People favored Alexandria and Egypt in general, as a place to live and work. Ironically, despite political decay and weakness, the country still enjoyed relative stability and was attractive to foreign immigrants in various fields of work. Many of them joined the army as paid mercenaries. Some were employed in regional trade between Egypt and the surrounding countries and tribes, and still others found jobs in agriculture, especially in the newly reclaimed areas at the edges of the Delta or the Fayoum Oasis. So, during the 26th to 30th dynasties, there was a significant community of foreign immigrants living all over Egypt, many opting to live together in newly built towns and colonies, in particular, the Greek colonies mainly in the Nile Delta.

When Alexander the Great conquered Egypt in 331 BC, the country was ready to accept the new ruler who had arrived. There was already a large community of Greeks and Macedonians living in Egypt, and they helped promote Alexander and encouraged people to accept the new ruler without a fight. Due to the friendly relationship between the Egyptians and the Greeks over several preceding centuries, both joined together to face their common enemy, the Persians, who had conquered and ruled Egypt since around 500 BC. In 331 BC, Alexander freed Egypt from Persian tyranny and oppression.

Culturally, the Greek colonies in Egypt, with their obvious Greek flavor and nature, were considered true, principal, social features of Egypt. Greek dialects were common in streets and marketplaces, used by both Greeks and

Egyptians, who readily learned Greek for trade purposes. Later, the Ptolomys declared Greek as the official state language for all government administrations in Egypt, which also meant Greek became the language of the new era and the culture, science and intellect in Alexandria, as the capital, and throughout Egypt. However, the Ancient Egyptian language and its local dialects remained. For the common people, the local spoken language was used in all rituals in Egyptian temples and religious centers, and local dialects were still used in local government offices in small villages and the countryside.

During the Ptolemaic period, Fayoum Oasis and its surrounding fertile land was one of the important centers for Greek and Egyptian communities, separate and mixed. Records from these days indicate the exact number of farmer's villages in the Fayoum region to be 113, 15 of which were purely Greek. Tebtunis was a village in the region where a mixed community of Greeks and Egyptians co-existed, living in harmony. Tebtunis, known locally now as Om El Burigat, is situated in the southwestern corner of the Fayoum Oasis, an area that had been developed during the agriculture reforms demanded by the Middle Kingdom pharaohs (circa 2000 BC to 1800 BC). From the early days, the community depended on farming and fishing from the large lake just north of the village. The annual summer flood of the Nile provided the village with enough water to cultivate its lands, and the village achieved a certain amount of economic stability due to the introduction of innovative irrigation methods introduced by Middle Kingdom pharaohs. The village was built near the southwestern gate entrance to the Fayoum Oasis and controlled the fresh water canal (now called Joseph Canal) that linked the Nile with the desert oasis. The village dams could control the amount of water flowing into the wide oasis plains and the large natural lake to the north. Indeed, Tebtunis held a prominent economic and strategic position throughout the entire region until the 3rd century AD.

Archeological clues from the site have indicated that the original village Tebtunis covered a large area of land, and on its south side, we now see the surrounding walls and the village tombs in the historic necropolis. The main temple was in the middle of the ancient village, built on a high mound with a private ceremonial-roofed avenue to serve its main gate. The temple was dedicated to the local principal god of the village, Soknebtunis, who was one of the local manifestations of the God Sobek, the crocodile-shaped god, Master of the Fayoum region.

People of ancient Tebtunis worshipped God Sobek in the form of a living crocodile, and after its death, they followed a strict tradition of embalming the divine crocodile and providing an honorable burial that would be adequate for a god. They took the mummified crocodile to the specially reserved cemetery, near the people's tombs at the edge of the village. These practices were common in almost all villages in the El Fayoum region. People of the ancient Fayoum area were obsessed with all forms of crocodiles. They collected unhatched crocodile eggs and baby crocodiles, whom they fed, to honor before ritually embalming them and offering them to the temple during a special local feast as a votive gift to the Great Divine. They kept small crocodile models of wood and ivory at homes either for private worship or to accompany their own bodies to the afterlife as a protection emblem.

Tebtunis remained accessible and well populated and enjoyed significant stability and prosperity until the rise of Christianity in the region, from 300 AD to 350 AD. Furthering the decline, the water in Lake Qaroun (now known as Morris Lake), the largest lake in the region, fell to its lowest level in the 4th century AD, forcing the local community to leave the villages to relocate for a better life. (The reasons for the lake water level dropping so significantly are still unknown. But, this lake is formed by a natural salt-water spring situated 40 meters below sea level, and the annual flood of the Nile used to enter El Fayoum Oasis from the southwestern gate, near the Joseph Canal of the Nile, the only fresh water source for the region. The canal was used for irrigating all the lowlands, smaller canals and spillways until ultimately all waters reached the lake. Each summer the lake maintained its high salinity level despite the fresh waters of the Nile. Therefore, if the lake water level dropped sharply, it meant that either no Nile water was reaching it in the summer; or that the climate had become hotter, leading to a spike in the evaporation rate and causing an increase in the land salinity rates and the ruin of crops. Either way, farmers were forced to leave the area.) This may be why the village of Tebtunis was abandoned suddenly during the 4th century AD.

In the 1890s, small pieces of papyrus were appearing in Egypt's antiquities markets. The papyri available in the markets were small parts of larger pieces and included old texts written in Greek and Latin script. Because most dealers and collectors focused on Ancient Egyptian artifacts and papyri, these Classical papyri failed to attract dealers and buyers. Fortunately, some of these Classical papyri came to the notice of professional historians of the classical, Graeco-Roman period who found them very interesting and recognized that most of these pieces were mainly coming from the Fayoum and Beni Swif regions in Middle Egypt. Understandably, these two regions were known to have been places that had large Greek communities living close to Egyptians, sometimes mixing with them and adopting many of Egypt's traditions and religious costumes.

Discovery Story

Bernard Pyne Grenfell (1869–1926) and Arthur Surridge Hunt (1871–1934) were both leaders of a Queen's College, Oxford University, expedition to Egypt in 1896 to excavate the archeological site of Oxyrhynchus, now known as the El Bahnasa area, in the Beni Swif region, nearby El Fayoum. Oxyrhynchus had once been a very famous as a Greek settlement. Because most of the Classical papyri discovered in Egypt came from these two regions, the Queen's College team came to search the area's cemeteries and ruins for artifacts and papyri from the Classical period. For this mission, the Oxford University had selected Grenfell and Hunt for their previous knowledge and research in Classical texts and literature.

In the first few seasons of digs in Oxyrhynchus, Hunt and Grenfell discovered more than 100,000 pieces of papyrus from the classical Graeco-Roman period, the largest archive of Classical material ever to have been found.

After their resounding discoveries in Oxyrhynchus, Hunt and Grenfell became prominent names in Egyptology circles. Their discoveries were impressive enough that the important archeologist George Reisner from the University of California contacted them in England and requested they work for him. Reisner was preparing extensive plans to excavate in Egypt on behalf of the University of California. His plan was to focus on the small village called Om El Burigat, in the southwest El Fayoum region, not far from Oxyrhynchus, where Hunt and Grenfell had made their earlier discoveries.

A few years before, Reisner had purchased some papyri from Egypt, and after close examination, he determined the papyri had come from Om El Burigat, which had been the original site of the village of Tebtunis in Graeco-Roman times. Reisner sensed the importance of this village and committed to explore it. He was quite certain that more of this Classical papyrus would be found in the village. He convinced the university to act on his plans and managed to secure funding from California's Hearst family. (Hearst Castle, the family mansion, can be visited today high on a hill overlooking the Pacific Coast Highway #1 between Los Angeles and San Francisco. One can see many Egyptian artifacts in the palace garden. Most were gifted by University of California in Egypt to the Hearst family during excavations that the family had generously sponsored.)

The Om El Burigat expedition started on December 3, 1899, under the two leaders Hunt and Grenfell, with hopes of finding a good collection of artifacts, monuments and papyri in compensation for the inestimable hard work done by George Reisner to convince the University of California and the Hearst family of the validity of such a project. Hunt and Grenfell were under pressure before they even started.

They carefully surveyed the ruins of the village and located the mound that marked the ancient temple in its center. They began their excavation in this mound to explore the temple and all surrounding cemeteries. Surprisingly, within the first week of work, Hunt and Grenfell discovered nearly 50 human mummies, all unearthed from the cemetery behind the temple and numerous papyri written in Demotic script and some in Greek script. It was a very promising excavation to the extent that George Reisner, as supervisor, wrote a special letter to Lady Hearst in California on January 2, 1900, sharing with her the great news from the site of Tebtunis and affirming that discoveries made in one week likely equaled the efforts of one year's worth of work in other sites.

Hunt and Grenfell continued excavating the temple and its surroundings, then moved to the southern cemetery where they found another 50 human mummies all wrapped in papyrus shrouds, all covered with Demotic and Greek religious texts. The papyri were thought to be pieces that had been collected at some later point and used to provide dead people with additional protection after their death. They also found mummies' masks made of pottery, funeral accessories and jewelry.

The team moved to the southern edge of the cemetery where they found yet another cemetery dedicated solely to mummified crocodiles, representations of God Sobek, the local god of the Fayoum region and its lake. They found almost 1,000 crocodiles mummies of all ages and sizes. They had been buried and arranged in perfect order, reflecting the great importance of such divine creatures to the local community.

On January 16, 1900, one of the hired workers became frustrated and annoyed by being required to carry and remove mummified crocodiles all day long. To him, they seemed just useless, valueless objects. He had been dreaming about human mummies that normally included jewelry and accessories of high value that could bring substantial money on the market. (Supervisors had to closely watch local workers; otherwise, if a local worker found something of worth, he would quickly hide the object and sell it for his private gain.) The poor man, after a long day of tedious work, was utterly disappointed with all they found. He was angry and kicked the small crocodile mummy he was supposed to be removing from the cemetery. In his anger, he tried to crush the miserable 2,000-year-old crocodile.

The crocodile mummy broke into pieces, and the worker saw before him wrapped papyrus shrouds coming out of its belly. The mummy was filled with written papyrus texts, and only his angry kicking caused it to reveal its insides. The hired man immediately went to the tent where Hunt and Grenfell were sitting in their chairs, observing the site. He told them about his accidental discovery, and all work on the site stopped. Hunt and Grenfell ordered all the workers to concentrate on the crocodile cemetery and to check the insides of all the discovered crocodile mummies carefully. There were over 1,000 mummies but only 31 mummies were contained papyrus scrolls.

By the end of the first season, it was clear this was very fruitful work, and Hunt and Grenfell continued for two more seasons (1900 and 1901). The scientific publication of the work started in 1903 and is ongoing today, with release of new translations of the massive amount of materials discovered over the last century.

Hunt and Grenfell made the decision to split the collection of mummified crocodile manuscripts from the cemetery of Tebtunis and four other areas near the main temple with George Reisner, the professor who had hired them. Because he had obtained financial backing from the Hearst family, Reisner decided to gift his share of the papyri and manuscripts of Tebtunis to Lady Hearst. She later dedicated the entire collection to the University of California at Berkeley, where it is now catalogued and protected in its own special library and gallery.

The University of California was keen on collecting all the papyri and manuscripts of Tebtunis after learning of their age and understanding their paramount importance from an historical and religious perspective. These were religious texts that described rituals performed for God Sobek by high priests, as well as lay texts that related to local life issues of the time. They cataloged all of the materials to prepare for translation and in-depth examination all the while protecting the fragile manuscripts in archival condition.

During the 1920s, local people around the village of Om El Burigat actively launched waves of casual digs and their own excavations at the site where Hunt and Grenfell had surveyed a few years earlier. The discoveries made by the two Englishmen aroused the locals' dreams and lured trophy hunters to dig for ancient treasures. More manuscripts and papyrus materials were illegitimately discovered and sold in Egyptian antiquities markets and sent on their way to Europe. On the University of California's web page on the Tebtunis papyrus collection, it indicates another smaller collection from this set of papyri was sold in the 1920s to the University of Michigan; the University of Oslo and the University of Jessen in Denmark purchased other papyri; and finally, some are at the Carlsberg Foundation.

The rapid spread of Tebtunis papyri around the world further intrigued additional Classical period researchers and historians to examine the collection, its history and the village where it all originated. Thus, a special archeological expedition from Milan, Italy came to examine the village of Tebtunis and its surroundings, working under the French Archeological Institute in Cairo in the early 1930s. Italian archeologist, Anti Bagnani, the expedition leader, and his assistant, Vagliano, began at the same locations excavated by Hunt and Grenfell some 30 years before, the central mound, the ancient temple and the south cemetery.

Serendipity led to the Italian team's excavations becoming productive quickly, and they found even more papyrus manuscripts inside crocodile mummies. The new finds of Tebtunis material were once again divided, this time between the Italian team and the French Institute in Cairo (probably ending up in the Louvre Museum and Museo Igizio in Turin).

By the 1930s, the village of Tebtunis had become well-known as a source of great Classical manuscripts, and the original explorers, Hunt and Grenfell, were considered leading figures in their field. Their publications on the first two collections of papyri, which they had begun back in 1903, were translated and circulated in Europe and North America. Unhappily, their dream of publishing all the discovered materials was never fulfilled, as Grenfell suddenly became ill and died; shortly after that, his partner Hunt died as well. However, their illnesses and subsequent deaths did not prevent the publication and translation of the third and the fourth collections of Tebtunis papyri in 1933 and 1937.

In 1938, the University of California at Berkeley managed to gather all the scattered Tebtunis papyri from around the world. (The university's Tebtunis papyri web page does not mention how they were able to get this accomplished.) The collection was catalogued and displayed in a dedicated gallery, and a museum area was built at the Bancroft Library at University of California at Berkley to properly preserve the Tebtunis papyri, all this done with the great help of Professor Edmond Kase whose work was completed in 1940. The project of translating and publishing more of the vast Tebtunis papyri collection continued. Later, more manuscripts were translated and published by two other American scholars, also associated with the University of California at Berkley, John Shelton and James Keenan.

In 1996, the University of California launched a new project that comprised restoration of all damaged pieces, over 30,000, and provided microfilm images of the entire collection making it available for students and researchers.

In a final look at the vast collection of Tebtunis papyri and manuscripts, we find they were mainly written in Old Greek script and some were written in Demotic script. A few pieces were discovered written in Latin script.

The Tebtunis papyri were mainly religious writings including texts with special ties to rituals dedicated to the local deity of the village, God Sobek, Lord of the Fayoum region. Some papyri also included descriptions of the works and service conducted by the high priests of the ancient town. Some of the translated material showed letters of correspondence that touched on everyday life issues of the village and surrounding communities. Also discovered were parts of famous quotes from literature books known in the Classical period. Important to note: All the manuscripts were discovered inside the mummified crocodiles in the cemetery south of the temple. All translated and published materials are now available on the Tebtunis papyri web page of the University of California-Berkeley.

With this phenomenal discovery, Egypt entered the 20th century with solid cooperation between Britain, then the governing power in Egypt, and America, the rising power of the modern world. The first fruits of this joint-venture collaboration in the field of exploring Ancient Egypt were the Classical papyri and manuscripts of Tebtunis, work that was orchestrated by Professor George Reisner, who is considered the mastermind of the complete undertaking. The discovery marked a new era in Egyptology with wealthy families in America enthusiastically sponsoring archeological missions in Egypt for the sake of American universities.

Would we see more collaborations in the next few years?

The next few chapters will answer this question.

Jean François Champollion

Henry Sal

August Mariette

Gaston Maspero

Flinders Petrie

Akhenaten

El Dier El Bahari Temples

Alexandria Catacombs

Arthur S Hunt

Bernard P Grenfell

By Way of Accident

Hathor chapel

Lord Carnarvon

George Reisner

Pierre Montet

By Way of Accident

James Robinson

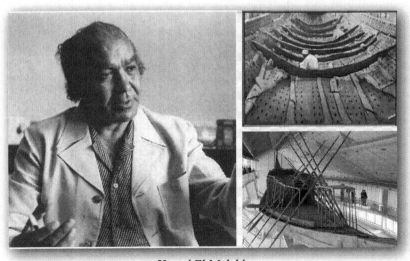

Kamal El Malakh

Gamal A. Nasser

Luxor Temple Cashe

By Way of Accident

Zahi Hawass

Valley of the golden Mummies, guard and his donkey

CHAPTER 10

Chapel of Hathor, Mistress of the West

EGYPT ENTERED THE 20TH CENTURY with solid, archeological collaboration between Britain and a number of wealthy families from the United States, who had a genuine interest in archeology and Egyptology and special ties with American universities and academia. I have described in previous chapters the extent to which Britain was in control of both Egypt and Egyptology and the methods Lord Cromer used to personally influence Egypt's Department of Antiquities' higher managerial posts, in particular the head of the department. Lord Cromer preferred Gaston Maspero because of his weak, malleable personality, which allowed Cromer to prevail over the Department of Antiquities and arrange for more English artists and surveyors to work with Maspero as assistants.

The previous chapter and its discovery have opened our eyes to the new links that developed between established academic institutions in Britain (Queen's College) and the rising universities in the United States (the University of California at Berkeley). The Hearst family provided the financing of this collaboration, with coordination by George Reisner, one of the greatest archeologists in the world at the time.

During this same period, the newly founded Egypt Exploration Fund, headquartered in London, was rapidly becoming the main player in Egypt's archeological excavations and explorations. It, too, sponsored many new dig projects. This period also introduced a number of young names in the field, some of which would later come to the forefront of Egyptology and archeology, names like Flinders Petrie and his Swiss assistant Edward Neville, who came to Egypt to learn and help Petrie. That said, Neville stayed in Egypt for almost half a century and recorded more discoveries in Upper Egypt and in the Delta than did any other Swiss scholar.

Edward Neville was apparently fated to find another great monument in the Theban cemetery, not far from the Valley of the Kings and the Mortuary Temple of Queen Hatshepsut. There, he accidently discovered the Chapel of Goddess Hathor, Mistress of the Western Hills and Gates of the Netherworld.

Religious Background

Since the early beginning of Egypt's long history, the Nile River cast the shape of life in the surrounding environment, and its annual flood regulated the everyday rhythm of Egyptian society, belief system, local culture and traditions that had developed over thousands of years. The Luxor area, with its wide valleys on both sides of the river, provided enough space for a large number of people to settle along both the east and west sides of the Nile. Their main activity was herding domesticated animals and limited seasonal cultivation.

The archeological deposits found in the southeastern corner of Karnak Temple clearly confirmed the existence of early Egyptian settlements in Luxor's valleys, as many stone hand tools discovered there dated back to the late Stone Age. Similar tools were also discovered near the western edge of the Theban Mountains. This confirmed the range of activity of the Stone Age people who used the wide valley of Luxor on both sides of the Nile.

The geography of the Luxor area and the mountains beyond the river valley helped to form the Ancient Egyptian mind and imagination, especially with respect to religion and superstitions regarding life after death, rebirth and resurrection. The Ancient Egyptians strongly believed in the return of the soul to its body after physical death: Free souls would accompany the disc of Re, the Sun God, in its eternal, cosmic journey each day from the moment of sunrise to sunset. They were accustomed to herding their animals as far as the edge of the western hills where they spent the night, waiting for the sunrise before herding the animals back again to their villages in the east. To the locals, the cycle of the sun in connection with the cycle of life made a strong link.

People imagined the sun disc traveled to the west with them every day toward the mountains, and they believed the sun disc entered one of the mountain's large, deep caves dominated by a powerful goddess who took the shape of a cow. They also imagined the Cow Goddess swallowed the sun disc every night as it entered the cave, and the sun disc traveled through the night within her body to reach the netherworld, where it was reborn again through her. She then delivered the disc as she would a baby, behind the eastern horizon and its hills with each new sunrise.

Locals had developed a very interesting connection between the daily sunrise and sunset and their funeral beliefs. They imagined the sun traveled every day beyond the western horizon carrying with it the souls of all the dead. The Divine Cow and Mistress of the Western Hills received them all, swallowing all dead souls into her cave. She protected them, fed and nursed them inside her womb until the morning light when she delivered them as newborns with the sunrise.

At some point in the historic times of Ancient Egypt, people united all the divine figures that took the shape of the cow (the Divine Sky Cow Goddess, the Western Cave Cow Goddess, and the Cow Goddess Hathor) and merged them all into one image, that of Hathor, daughter of God Re. She was his blazing eyes and force, protector of the cemetery to the west and divine guardian of Re's throne on his divine barque that traveled through the day and night. These were a few of her ascribed religious titles and powers.

Ancient Egyptians portrayed the sacred cow as yellow, having skin the color of gold, with black spots all over her body, spots that represented the night stars. Her eyes were black and wide, and her head was crowned with the disc of Re between her horns along with two feather plumes on each side of the disc.

People of Ancient Egypt had assigned a specific job to Goddess Hathor as the guardian mother who left her western cave every morning to greet the rising sun in the eastern horizon at the edge of the green Nile Valley. Every morning, she delivered the good souls of all dead people and received them into the netherworld as the sun went down every evening behind the western hills. She swallowed the sun disc together with the dead souls and secured their journey through the night until they were all reborn in the new morning, completing the daily life cycle of the Nile Valley.

El Deir El Bahari Valley, the widest of the area, was situated beneath the mountains of western Thebes and encompassed cultivated, flat land that extended to the edge of the mountains' escarpment just before the limestone hills and caves. The special nature and topography of El Deir El Bahari Valley was the main reason that Ancient Egyptians considered it the divine place where the cave of Goddess Hathor must exist. It was there that she resided and all the western mountains were under her protection and rule.

As early as the Old Kingdom period, they called the area generally "The Valley," without a specific name, and it wasn't until the next historic period, the First Intermediate Period, that the valley became actively used as a burial place for local governors and government high officials. The religious interest in this valley continued to grow into the early days of the Middle Kingdom with the pharaohs of the 11th and 12th dynasties, starting with the days of King Montohotep I who built his tomb and mortuary temple at the edge of the sacred valley. He also consecrated royal tombs for his family around his mortuary temple along with a number of tombs for his close entourage and high officials.

The Temple of Pharaoh Montohotep (as we learned in Chapter 7) has a special character and very innovative design. It was a wonderful combination of the classical design of the Egyptian temple and the traditional shape of the royal tombs, the pyramid. The unique architecture of the complex represented the ascendancy from earthly life toward the heavenly western cave of Goddess Hathor, standing at the gate of the mountain face. Therefore, the pharaoh was occupied with keeping the sanctuary and shrine of his mortuary complex beneath the mountain itself, to guarantee absolute unity and protection of the Mother Goddess Hathor.

In the days of Montohotep, the valley became known as the valley of "*nbh-btre*," the royal name of King Montohotep, and during the Middle Kingdom and the following historical period known as the Second Intermediate Period, all kings and local rulers showed great respect and paid homage to the divine valley and its growing cemetery.

With the rise of the New Kingdom (18th, 19th and 20th dynasties), the sacred valley experienced a fantastic architectural and constructional renaissance that started with the works of King Amunhotep I, followed by his granddaughter Queen Hatshepsut who built the most extravagant, breathtakingly designed mortuary temple in all Egypt, the Temple of El Deir El Bahari. Queen Hatshepsut's Temple was completed by her stepson and successor Thotmosis III, who built his own small, mortuary temple on a ridge located between the Temple of Hatshepsut and the older Temple of Montohotep. Thotmosis III designated his small, hanging temple the official resting place of God Amun's sacred barque during the seasonal Feast of Harvest on Luxor's West Bank. The king also cut a special chapel into the mountain's rock face dedicated to Goddess Hathor, above his small temple (instead of near the queen's temple), to symbolically represent the original cave of the sacred cow.

(Most mortuary temples located in the valley of El Deir El Bahari were originally comprised of a small manmade cave cut into the mountain, dedicated to the guardian mother cow Hathor, but most of these artificial cave chapels were destroyed, and only one chapel survives through the ages. It is the subject of this chapter.)

The cave chapels of Hathor were each designed to have a small, open courtyard in front with one or two small side rooms. A special causeway ascended from the wide-open valley up to the higher levels of the chapel courtyard and small gates, similar to the impressive stone causeway built for the mortuary Temple of Thotmosis III, and the Cow Chapel. The causeway was massive and dominated the view of all visitors to the edge of the mountain. It lay above and in between the Temple of Queen Hatshepsut and the Temple of Montohotep. Thotmosis III installed a life-sized statue of the divine cow Hathor inside the chapel cave, but it is important to note it is not the statue now displayed in the Cairo Museum. The one now in the museum was offered by Amunhotep II, the son of Thotmosis III. Perhaps the original cow statue of Thotmosis III was lost shortly after he died, so his son and successor Amunhotep II was obliged to erect another one. This hypothesis is supported by the discovery of the alabaster head of the Cow Goddess Hathor inside the same chapel of Thotmosis III, inscribed with his name. This head was found in the chapel by Edward Neville and is now in the British Museum.

Feasts and rituals continued to be held regularly for Goddess Hathor in El Deir El Bahari Valley until the later days of the Ramesside (Ramesses) period, the 20th Dynasty, when the resting place of Amun's barque was moved from El Deir El Bahari Valley to the Habu Temple complex. In the later days of the 20th Dynasty, a strong earthquake destroyed the third floor terrace of Hatshepsut's Temple, parts of the nearby temples of Montohotep and Thotmosis III, and eventually the small cave chapel of Hathor that had been located just above the temples. Stones and debris from the earthquake covered the temples' ruins and led to the subsequent collapse of the mountain. The earthquake's devastation hid forever the Chapel of Hathor, until the day of its accidental discovery.

In the Christian period, during the 4th century AD, the ruins of temples in the valley were reused as the monastery of a local saint called Phoebamonand and was locally known as the "Northern Monastery," which translates literally to El Deir El Bahari.

This area had attracted visitors to Egypt since the early Christian period through the times of Napoleon's Expedition to Egypt when French scientists visited El Deir El Bahari and recorded their observations. Additionally, the famous Italian explorer Belzoni had excavated in the valley looking for treasures. But it was the historic visit of Champollion, the Frenchman who deciphered the Rosetta Stone in 1824, to El Deir El Bahari that was remarkable, because it was Champollion who was first able to read two royal names on the ruins of the temples of Queen Hatshepsut, Thotmosis I and Thotmosis II, her father and her half-brother husband. By reading these names, Champollion accomplished a significant feat in decoding the secrets of the Ancient Egyptian language. A few years later came the Prussian archeologist Karl Richard Lepsius (1810–1884) who excavated in the valley and collected a large number of relics that he shipped to Berlin. The first true archeological survey ever made in the valley was the work of August Mariette between 1858 and 1862. Finally, the greatest expedition ever conducted in El Deir El Bahari was that of the Metropolitan Museum of New York from 1921 to 1926, led by the well-known American archeologist John Gardener Wilkinson, who actually gave the current name to the entire area as El Deir El Bahari, still in use today. (Visitors can still see the small guesthouse near the temples built in the 1920s for the New York Metropolitan Museum team. The wealthy New Yorker J. P. Morgan sponsored the house and the expedition, and the guesthouse still is called Morgan House.)

Edward Neville 1844–1926

June 14, 1844 was the day Henry Edward Neville, one of the true giants of Egyptology, was born in Geneva, Switzerland. Edward Neville studied ancient history and Egyptology in London and Paris. He was also educated in Berlin under his master and mentor Lepsius. He came to Egypt for the first time in 1865, and his first task was to copy the text from Edfu Temple that narrated the epic myth of gods Horus and Seth. Neville translated the text and published it in 1870. His work in Egypt was interrupted from 1870 to 1871 when he joined the Swiss army as a volunteer captain in his country's army in Europe's Prussian War. Soon after the war though, Neville resumed his studies and pursued his passion for Ancient Egypt. This time, he returned to study the magical, solar, religious texts in the tombs of the Valley of the Kings. He published his translated work in 1875.

The opportunity to launch a real archeological dig did not come until he joined the rising organization of the time, the Egypt Exploration Fund, based in London. He signed up to work for the organization in Egypt in 1882. As one of the early explorers in the organization, he led his first excavation and mission in the Delta area around 1883. He focused his digs in the area of Tell El Maskhouta (1885–1886), where the Hyksos rulers of Egypt had located their capital, in the Valley of Tumilat, and in the area of Bubastis (1886–1889) near the large Temple of Goddess Bastet, the Divine Cat. His work in the eastern Delta lasted until 1893. Later, he moved to work in Upper Egypt, starting in the famous valley of El Deir El Bahari to reexamine the places excavated by Mariette some 30 years earlier. His team included several assistants, D. G. I. Hogarth, the architect S. Clarke and the young painter and surveyor Howard Carter (the man who was destined later to make the greatest discovery of all time, the Tomb of Tutankhamun in 1922). Also joining the team later was H. Hall, who helped excavate the Temple of Montohotep.

Discovery Story

The extensive excavation by Edward Neville in El Deir El Bahari from 1893 to 1897 revealed the great Temple of Queen Hatshepsut after centuries of neglect and abandonment. Neville's archeological surveys in and around the mortuary Temple of Hatshepsut were published in a wonderful six-volume scholarly work under the name of *Excavation at El Deir El Bahari*. Later, in 1903, Neville began to focus his digs to the south of Hatshepsut's Temple, where the first level and ground foundation of the mortuary Temple of King Montohotep *nbhbtre* was discovered. In the middle of the first terrace, Neville exposed the remains of the pyramid base that was at the heart of the upper terrace of the mortuary temple. In addition, a large number of royal family side tombs and burials were found. Neville managed to identify them as the 11 princesses' tombs next to the king's tomb.

Neville and his team observed the western side, the mountain side, of the temple and noticed a large amount of debris and rocks piled behind the temple structure leading all the way toward the mountain face. It was dangerous to excavate this area because the rocks could collapse while digging. Therefore, Neville made a plan to very gradually remove all the sand and debris while securing the area around the dig to avoid further rock collapse from the deteriorated escarpment and ridges above the temple. He continued slowly, removing all the dirt and managed to lower the mound until it reached only 30 feet above the temple ground. At this point, Neville started to see what looked like a chapel or a cave hewn into the mountain face but it was still covered with debris.

On December 1, 1904, Neville discovered a stone platform, like an entrance to a room inside the mountain. The flat stone platform was the entrance hall of the Chapel of Hathor that had been hidden under debris. This was Neville's thought as his team examined the stone ground. On December 10th, he found remains of a doorjamb with obvious 18th Dynasty style work and decorations, but the royal name in the cartouche was badly damaged and it was impossible for Neville and the local workers to remove all the debris in their attempt to see what lay beneath the thick layers of dirt and rocks. Because of the danger and the workers' fears of sudden slides and ground collapses, Neville moved his team farther south of the Temple of Montohotep where they revealed the foundation of the 18th Dynasty, small, mortuary temple built right in front of the cave chapel that remained hidden.

In January 1906, the team successfully revealed the 18th Dynasty temple walls and foundations and a statue of the scribe *Nedjem* from the 20th Dynasty along with a number of ceremonial vessels and tablets from the 18th, 19th and 20th dynasties.

On the morning of February 7, 1906, as Neville recorded in his diary, one lucky worker of the 54 hired laborers was working on a large piece of stone that was stuck in the dirt. He was trying to remove it very slowly with the fear of having a sudden collapse of the rocks. It happened at that particular moment, as the worker removed the big stone from the debris, a larger stone fell suddenly, bringing with it more sand, some rocks and debris. As in a windstorm, the area became full of dust, and no one could see anything. After the dust had begun to settle, everyone could detect a big hole that had appeared in the debris. They tried to focus through the dust and waited impatiently to see what lay inside the dark cave hole.

The surprise was a large cow face in the dark room peering up at them! She was actually looking down toward the wide valley facing the mountain, the same famous valley that became crowded several times each year with priests and supporters celebrating the Cow Mother Goddess Hathor. She had lived in her cave shrine, cut above the mortuary temples, built adjacent to the mountain, for 3,400 years. Now, as the Divine Cow looked down on the same valley, she did not see priests or devotees; rather, she found the local workers and the Swiss archeologist Edward Neville. They were very happy to see the head of the cow appear to them through the dust. It was a special moment for Neville to release the Divine Cow and set her free from her chapel prison after thousands of years.

Neville cleaned the area in front of and around the Chapel of Hathor, finally to discover a large cave chapel cut into the mountain, beautifully decorated with colorful scenes and a vaulted ceiling, all painted with blue sky and golden stars. The life-sized statue of the cow was in the middle of the chapel standing on a moving pedestal built for festivals and offering ceremonies. Neville recognized the statue as the first example of a life-sized statue of the Divine Cow from Ancient Egypt. The cow was represented as she was emerging from the marches and wearing the crown of the two plumes and the disc of Re.

Under the head of the cow, a standing royal figure was found, under the protection of the Mother Goddess Hathor, and another royal figure was sitting beneath her large chest. The royal figure was nursing directly from her chest like a child. Neville was easily able to read the royal name of Amunhotep II inside a cartouche on the back of the cow statue, which made him believe the chapel and the statue of the cow were originally the work of King Amunhotep II, but Thotmosis III's name was shown throughout the chapel's religious scenes and walls. Again, to solve this puzzle, Neville concluded that Amonhotp II co-ruled with his father Thotmosis III (in the co-regency period) and that this was when the Chapel of Hathor had been built and decorated.

The chapel itself was 2.25 meters high, 4.04 meters long and 1.57 meters wide. On its walls, we see the colorful scenes of Thotmosis III and his wife *"meritre"* both offering libations to Goddess Hathor. In addition, there are other scenes showing the king offering holy oil in front of God Amun, the great God of Karnak. The king was also depicted on the sidewall with two of the royal princesses offered to Hathor.

Edward Neville and his teams decided to cut the chapel as one unit, and move it to the banks of the Nile where they shipped it by boat all the way to Cairo where it remains today, in the Cairo Museum's New Kingdom room. Neville thought if they kept the chapel where it was in the heart of the mountain and above the temples of Montohotep and Hatshepsut, it would likely end up covered with sand and debris again in a few years, lost again as before for another 3,400 years.

CHAPTER 11

Tomb of Tutankhamun

EGYPT WAS DIRECTLY INFLUENCED BY the First World War crisis and its subsequent outcome, and the general national atmosphere in Egypt was pushing toward the necessity of ending the British occupation of the country that had begun in 1882. Even the political frame of the relationship with Great Britain had changed after the war, and Egypt no longer felt they needed occupation even if it provided "protection." The picture was quite clear to most

Egyptians, in the cities as well as in the villages. The British army was still everywhere in Egypt, especially along the Suez Canal, and it was because of this presence that the fires of the war had reached Egypt unnecessarily. The British base in the Suez Canal area was its largest military base in the world, and its geographical location made it the most important, too. All major navigation lines for Britain's military and commercial shipping passed through the Suez Canal, from England's southern ports of Plymouth and Southampton all the way to India and southeast Asia.

The archeological situation in Egypt was not much different from its politics. Actually, it was a mirror reflection of the politics, with the British Consul's full control and domination over Egypt's Department of Antiquities. Young, ambitious English explorers were the official, government managers in the Antiquities Department, e.g. Howard Carter and others who had arrived with Flinders Petrie to assist him at his excavations and extensive digs.

Having arrived in Egypt when he was only 20 years old, by the age of 35 Carter had become the acting manager of the entire Upper Egypt region for the Department of Antiquities (1910 to 1922), a department that had spread its authoritative and restrictive control throughout most archeological areas in Egypt. He was in charge of the Luxor area, Karnak temples and the great cemetery of western Thebes. He was the one who gave authorization for digs. He was the one who personally supervised most of the active dig sites. As a result, many of the known discoveries in the area of Luxor were recorded under the name of Howard Carter between 1910 and 1920.

Carter was professionally a governmental department manager, and it was certainly odd and only because of his English nationality that an exception was made allowing him to also work independently as a hired archeologist for several missions at the same time. He was available for hire by collectors and adventurers who were seeking great wealth and fame. These people invested in excavations in the Luxor area by acquiring permission from the authorities of Egypt's Antiquities Department, hired the team leader to direct the work and covered all costs. The permission normally designated the specific area permitted for digs and according to the details of the signed agreement; it determined the number of discovered relics permitted to be taken away or to be shared between the permission holder and the Egyptian government. However, the whole permission game was shrouded in political mediation and the consideration of powerful international individuals.

Preferred people obtained the greatest number of authorizations, the best dig locations and at outstanding prices. Sometimes, there was no price. The split of discovered artifacts with the authorities covered the cost of work. It was not so much a purely scientific process as it was a political game. At the very least, the authorization game was a scientific operation shrouded in political cover. Therefore, Cairo's largest hotel lobbies, especially the one at Shepherd's Hotel, at that time attracted a great number of antique collectors and treasure hunters from all over the world, all seeking their way to Egyptian artifacts and ancient treasures. They knew the way to reach such ancient treasures must start and end in Cairo with a few influential persons who enjoyed powerful contacts within the authority. There was a need for all types of mediators, who offered their services to make connections with important government employees, especially within the Antiquities Department, who could facilitate the issuing of permissions for excavations. At the very least, they would try to help in acquiring a special concession to dig exclusively at a specific site, but as a rule, these types of authorizations were provided only after advanced project plans had been approved for accredited archeologists who were working in Egypt and had experience with excavations. To reach one of the known celebrities in the field of Egyptian archeology and employ him could be almost prohibitively expensive, as one was required to hire the archeologist to perform the work on the ground and solely lead his team. Famous archeologists always wanted to finagle more money to finance and sponsor their own future projects. Almost all had archeological dream projects, and their biggest challenge was always sponsorship. Therefore, in the early days of the 20th century, archeologists were the focus of rich families and art collectors and vice versa. It was a fair equation: One was looking for a trophy, and the other was looking for glory.

This was the equilibrium in the antiquities market at the time, and everyone involved in issuing new authorizations for digs in Egypt was an element in such an equation, with obvious and clear goals for some, and ambiguous, secret agendas for others. So it was not surprising that Lord Carnarvon, a wealthy English businessman, acquired special permission to dig inside the Valley of the Kings; and equally, it was not a surprise that Howard Carter, the most famous and experienced archeologist of the time, facilitated all permissions with the Egyptian authority. Carter himself signed all of the permissions, authorizations and dig concessions for Lord Carnarvon because he was the Manager of the Upper Egypt region in Egypt's Antiquities Department. At the same time, Carter was Carnarvon's appointed, hired archeologist to lead the expedition for seven continuous years in a circle of power, corruption, ignorance and greed.

It is important to note here that Lord Carnarvon was facing serious financial difficulties back in England, and bank loans had started to close in on him from all sides. He was about to declare bankruptcy and about to sell his farms and estates in the midlands of England, so the adventure of digging in the desert of Egypt came exactly at the right moment for him. Obtaining the very special authorization to dig inside the Valley of the Kings was a lifeline for the sinking man. It was his final gamble and his last opportunity to save his name, wealth and image. The hope was to find something big inside the Valley of the Kings, something worth vast sums of money, enough to pay off all his debts. It was a real gamble, but Howard Carter repeatedly assured him that the Valley of the Kings had not yet revealed all of its secrets. Missing still were many royal tombs and one of them was that of Pharaoh Tutankhamun. Carter promised his lordship that finding a 3,500-year-old pharaoh's tomb with intact artifacts would be more than enough for both of them. After selling his share of whatever they found in the tombs, the lord could save his life, pay all of his loans and leave his long, dark tunnel of financial troubles behind. Moreover, the ambitious archeologist would become eternal, achieving the highest level of immortality in Egyptology.

In his desperation and hopes for financial salvation, the lord invested far away from home, dreaming about the ancient treasures he would return with. Carter, too, was desperate in his pursuit of his alluring, unfound pharaoh called Tutankhamun.

Carnarvon and Carter's adventure started when Egypt was in the midst of serious political and social turmoil. In 1915, a few years before the discovery, the first university was opened in Egypt, the University of King Fouad, now Cairo University. The school was responsible for delivering awareness and nationalism to a large circle of middle-class Egyptians, and the university students were eagerly seeking modern science, modernity in general and independence for Egypt from the Turkish palace and the British mandate.

The rhythm of the changes in Egypt took on two different styles. In Cairo, the educated modern society, almost European in its lifestyle, was pushing for independence and modernization. In the countryside, most people were looking for justice and services. The new atmosphere created new cultural streams, especially in Cairo with its university students, lecturers, and professors in various fields of research. Altogether, it contributed to the birth of a new movement: the realization of the paramount importance of preserving Egyptian heritage and protecting artifacts from all periods of Egypt's history from looting and being smuggled abroad.

In 1919, the nationwide revolution against the Turkish palace and the British occupation began. The leader was Saad Zagloul, the famous politician and lawyer. He was a wealthy nationalist who took the initiative to defend Egypt's rights for independence. The 1919 Revolution was the official declaration of the birth of a new, free and patriotic Egypt. The new atmosphere put pressure on all government departments, especially the Antiquities Department, which for several decades had been the symbol of subordination and submission to European colonialism.

It is certain that Egypt's archeology and Egyptology developments were strongly tied to European colonial growth since the early years of the 19th century. From the days of Napoleon and the discovery of Rosetta Stone to the days of Lord Carnarvon and the Tutankhamun discovery, the 1919 Revolution in Egypt was the spark of awakening after years of slow, national identity search, which began in the 1880s. Thanks to a large number of university graduates and postgraduate students, the chain of Egypt's modern, intellectual movement grew stronger than ever before, featuring a long line of great names that helped to form the basis of the new national identity. From Refaa El Tahtawy, the forerunner of Egyptian modernization, to Kasem Amin, preeminent judge and reformer, the rise of many bright names, appeared during the revolution's process of modernizing the country, based on independence through political parties in the 1920s.

The voice of Egypt became clearer and louder, and public awareness became perfectly attuned to the political leaders like Saad Zagloul. The populace was crying for independence, and other voices were demanding the termination of all digging concessions for foreigners in Egypt to prevent further plundering of Egyptian monuments. The constant bleeding of Egyptian antiquities and artifacts had to end. For many Egyptians, the authorizations of digging in Egypt were nothing but a political cover to loot and export Egypt's heritage unethically, a tragedy that had been happening since the days of Muhammad Ali Pasha through the 1919 Revolution.

Let's return now to Howard Carter and his exciting discovery in the Valley of the Kings. Carter said in his book about Tutankhamun, that it was not an easy task to obtain permission to dig inside the Valley of the Kings. Earlier, in 1902, Theodore Davies, a wealthy American collector, had obtained exclusive permission to dig inside the Valley of the Kings for 12 continuous years. For that time, no one else, individual or archeological team, could enter the valley or start any sort of excavation. Davies had obtained strict exclusivity for himself.

Davies' 12-year expedition in the Valley of the Kings explored a number of great tombs between 1902 and 1914. The Davies team discovered and revealed the tombs of Thotmosis IV, Hatshepsut, Saptah, Yuya and Tuya, Horemheb, and the Amarna Caches Tomb 55. The fascinating discoveries of Davies' teams in the valley had made news for several seasons, and the world started to look again at the desert valley across the Nile from Luxor. The new interest attracted people such as Lord Carnarvon to seek permission to dig again in the Valley of the Kings. Carnarvon was able to start in 1914 and continued for seven years with Carter as the hired expert for the mission.

Before Howard Carter set his digging plans for that first season, he had relied on tangible clues to support the true existence of Tutankhamun's Tomb somewhere in the Valley of the Kings. The clues already existed from the time of Davies' work. The name of Tutankhamun had been discovered on a broken glazed pottery wine cup, but the name had not rung any bells for Davies. The second clue was the name found on a wooden box discovered in the valley, but again, it hadn't attracted enough attention to look seriously for the mystery name and his tomb. To Howard Carter, it seemed very strange to see Theodore Davies and his team completely ignore the royal name Tutankhamun. As Davies was leaving Egypt in 1914 at the end of his mission, he proclaimed that his teams had excavated the valley inside out for 12 years, and he was utterly convinced that the Valley of the Kings had yielded all its secrets and that there was nothing more to search for in the valley. More emphatically, he advised archeologists to look elsewhere because the valley was empty. It was interesting to hear that from Davies because Belzoni, the Italian explorer, had said exactly the same words when he was ready to leave the Valley of the Kings after the discovery of Seti I's tomb in 1819. However, it was a lucky turn of the spade, and Carter had an appointment with fate—once again.

Carnarvon and Carter's seven-year excavation inside the Valley of the Kings was a tiring and excruciating operation, with costly and endless expenses. A look at Carter's daily diaries shows a long list of names of hired workers from the villages nearby the Valley of the Kings. The diaries note that Carter was keen to pay them their wages daily to ensure they returned the following day and to encourage them to work hard and achieve more digging. Sometimes the digging ran on for weeks without finding anything important or of any value (at least for the workers). The issue was in keeping the workers motivated and therefore, when they found something special or valuable, they would get extra payment as a reward from the manager.

It was a difficult and expensive gamble, at least for Lord Carnarvon, who was starting to lose his passion for archeological work and his patience with Carter after six years of spending large sums of money every winter. They were in the very last season in 1922, and still there was nothing to celebrate. It was the closing year of his permission in the Valley of the Kings and the hope to find something important was fading quickly. Carnarvon was running out of time and money, but fate and coincidence were to be merciful to him and his team in the Valley of the Kings, and to Carter, too. Carter wanted to close his great 35 years of work in Egypt with something unforgettable. He wished to end his career with a radiant discovery the world would talk about forever. Everything happened quickly when one of his workers in the heart of the valley suddenly shouted, "HAGAR…….. It's a stone!"

Discovery Story

The truth is that Howard Carter had previously found the royal name of young King Tutankhamun in several places in the Luxor area, on the walls of the Karnak and Luxor temples, and inside the Valley of the Kings. The name was found buried along with a number of mummification materials and tools. His name was written on an ink linen docket stored high in the mountains, not far from the tomb location in the Valley of the Kings, thought to be a cache for royal embalming materials from the days of Tutankhamun. Carter was quite certain of the existence of the king called Tutankhamun. He truly believed his tomb was still undiscovered in the Valley of the Kings. For seven years, Carter had been digging in the valley and looking for his mysterious royal tomb until the very last authorized season. It was the season of Carter's final hope as an archeologist to celebrate the climax of his career with an unforgettable discovery. For Lord Carnarvon, it was the last chance to survive financially.

On October 28, 1922, Carter arrived early in the morning in the Valley of the Kings and gathered his team of local workers. He arranged the daily work plan and assigned small groups. The main mission was to clear the huge amount of sand and debris in the middle of the Valley of the Kings that nearly blocked the heart of the valley, prohibiting tourists from walking freely among of the tombs. Mounds of debris had accumulated in the valley's heart during Carter's previous seasons of excavation and the wonderful discovery of the Tomb of Ramses V. It had been an enormous tomb, and an enormous mound of sand and debris had resulted from its clearance. (The Tomb of Ramses V was located literally above the Tomb of Tutankhamun, the sand and debris that came out of it thereby obliterated Tutankhamun's Tomb.)

Carter also intended to clear all the mud brick workers' huts that still remained from Ancient Egyptian times on the hillsides in the Valley of the

Kings. These were the only locations that had not yet been carefully examined. Therefore, it was time to remove them all and examine the rocks and sand beneath. Carter set up his tent to supervise his team right in front of previously discovered Tomb 55, which was located opposite the Tomb of Ramses V (and beneath it the Tomb of Tutankhamun).

On November 4th, only one week after the expedition had commenced, one of the workers had a moment of providence. After removing all the ancient mud brick workers' huts, the workers focused next on removing all the sand and debris in front of and around the Tomb of Ramses V. When they had nearly reached the bedrock of the valley floor trying to level the entrance of the valley area for tourists, one worker hit something hard with his hand axe. It sounded like a hard stone right beneath the sandy surface of the valley floor. He carefully cleaned and checked the rock he had hit. To his amazement, it looked like a clean, flat-surfaced step, cut into the natural rocks of the valley floor, and it became clear the step was the first of a descending hidden passageway. The workers gathered and checked the stone step closely as excitement overtook the whole gang and they began running and shouting to their manager, Carter.

Carter was sitting astride his usual chair smoking a cigarette when he heard the workers shouting and hurrying toward his tent. He spoke and understood Arabic very well, so he could understand his workers' excitement. Something intriguing had been found. When they told him about the solid step found under the debris, he amused himself and said to himself:

"I almost dare to hope, we have found our tomb at last."

Carter's knowledge of the tombs and the valley was impeccable, and he was familiar with such situations when workers became suddenly excited about something they thought might be important. He had learned not to jump to any conclusions before having examined the object, as he did with this newly found mystery step.

The short distance between the tombs of Ramses V, Ramses II and his tent area next to Tomb 55 was the only spot in the heart of the valley that had never been carefully excavated, and this small triangle was his final hope. When the workers pointed to the spot where they had hit the solid stone, it was exactly beneath the Tomb of Rameses V and in the southern corner of his imaginary triangle. It would be difficult to dig in this small piece of land. It was right at the entrance of the tourist area and excavating it would prevent the tourists' seasonal winter traffic from reaching into the Valley of the Kings where there were a large number of beautiful tombs to visit, such as those of Thotmosis III, Saptah, Seti II, Amunhotep II, Horemheb and others. Therefore, the challenge became a surgical digging operation.

In his book about the discovery of Tutankhamun's Tomb, Carter never mentioned the story of the water boy, but it is a poignant one, which I will relate for you here. A young boy, a worker's son, usually accompanied his father to work every morning. His job was to tote water for workers to refresh with when it became hot. Since they started shortly before sunrise when it was still cooler, this normally happened after two to three hours of working. Upper Egypt's sun was strong even in the winter season and workers needed to drink cool water whenever it was possible. This was the boy's job. The first two hours of the day, the boy was free from toting water, so he sat somewhere near his father watching men digging and singing. He amused himself by acting as a real worker and digging in the sand where he sat and placed his pottery jar full of water. To keep the water cool and away from the beating sun, he searched for a nice spot where he could bury his jar in the sand and put small rocks he collected around it on all sides. That way, he prevented his jar and water from being exposed to the hot sun. On one special day, as he was burying his jar, he found a solid, flat, natural rock step just where he was sitting. He marked the spot with stones, ran to Carter and revealed his secret discovery.

Here we have two very interesting stories about the accidental discovery of Tutankhamun's Tomb: the worker's and the water boy's. Both are recorded in various sources, but the official diary of Howard Carter never mentioned the story of the water boy. The truth is, the greatest tomb ever discovered in Egypt strangely had steps to its entrance that gave it away lying only three feet beneath the sand, and people had been digging for centuries around it and

By Way of Accident

above it. However, it had had to wait several decades until the day it was joyfully revealed by either a worker or a poor child.

The discovery of the stone step has changed many histories. First, it led to the greatest archeological find in all of Egyptology, and maybe in all of archeological history. Second, it was an unforgettable happy ending to the more than 30 years Howard Carter spent in Egypt, where he made great discoveries, but this last one would be forever, the special one.

Enthusiastically, Carter ordered his men to dig further at the single step and see where it went. Soon, more steps were revealed leading deeper into the bedrock, ten feet or more beneath the entrance of the Rameses V Tomb. Carter had worked in the valley long enough to understand that this was the type of stairwell normally associated with general construction of tombs, essentially a giveaway to the main entrance of the tomb itself.

The following day, the frantic pace of digging in the descending corridor that led down to the supposed tomb entrance excitedly resumed, but Carter started the second day with muted fear and many worries that he would find another robbed tomb or unfinished burial place for an unimportant person from ancient Thebes. His worst nightmare of all would be to find a royal tomb but totally looted.

At the end of the day, on November 5th, Carter reached the bottom of the lower staircase; it was ten feet high and six feet wide. After they had cleared 12 steps, they could see the upper part of a door. Carter described this moment happily:

"The door is blocked, plastered and sealed."

It was a positive sign and all his hopes now appeared before his eyes. He resisted the rising tide within him to continue digging and to break down the sealed door to see what lay beyond, but he was a professional hired archeologist. Instead, he ordered his men to fill in the stairwell once again!

He wrote to Lord Carnarvon, telling him about his recent discovery in the Valley of the Kings and asked him to travel to Luxor as soon as possible, so they could open the sealed door together and celebrate the unimaginable wealth they would soon gain. Carnarvon wrote back quickly to inform Carter of his arrival in Alexandria on November 20th and that he would proceed straight to Luxor as soon as he landed.

Carter began to prepare professional help to assist with the important work coming ahead. He hired his friend, Arthur Calendar, to be his assistant and set the stage for the grand opening of the tomb.

On November 23rd, Lord Carnarvon and his daughter, 21-year-old Lady Evelyn, arrived at Luxor by train from Cairo. The Lord was ill and so tired he needed to rest before going to the Valley of the Kings on the following day. They arrived at the site early, and soon Carter's men began removing the dirt and clearing the steps of the staircase. Moments followed that were full of hopes and fears, as Carter examined the dirt shoveled from the staircase. He found shards and broken artifacts with royal names of 18th Dynasty pharaohs Amunhotep, Akhenaten and Tuthmosis. Carter was less than pleased to meet such names in a new tomb because it only meant that this tomb was nothing but a cache for 18th Dynasty pharaohs with miscellaneous objects neglected outside its door. Carter's heart started to pound harder. His name and the recent fame he gained because of all the media coverage he had enjoyed for the last three weeks was about to shatter now, especially when workers finished clearing the sealed door. He realized the door was not intact; someone had been here before him.

Only one thing gave Carter hope, the seal of Tutankhamun was stamped on the door. His lost dream pharaoh... he was finally about to see him face-to-face.

Arriving on the same morning, Rex Engelback, the Manager of the Department of Antiquities insisted on attending the opening of the tomb. (Carter had never liked Engelback, nor did Lord Carnarvon. They called him Trout, describing his demeanor.)

On November 25th, everyone was ready to open the door. Cameras were ready and focused on the lord who would officially make the opening but, to everyone's surprise, they saw nothing behind the door except another descending corridor, completely filled with stone and rubble. At that point, it was impossible for Carter to determine how far the second, lower corridor would go. However, one thing Carter was quite sure of, someone had been here before.

The second door was almost an exact replica of the first one, with Tutankhamun's seal also stamped on it, but this door had the royal necropolis seal stamped on it, a very promising sign. Carter's fever of anticipation was racing, and his emotion was swinging between optimism and pessimism moment by moment.

On November 26th, Carter broke open a small portion of the second door using an iron rod handed to him by his assistant, Calendar. Behind the door, there was nothing. It was very dark. His eyes strained to adjust to the faint light coming from behind. He peered into the little hole he made. There was only air.

At this moment, Carter was supposed to wait for Engelback, who was officially to open the tomb himself, but that morning Engelback had gone to inspect another dig site not far from the Valley of the Kings. During his remarkable absence, Carter took a brave step. He made a small hole in the door, big enough for everyone who stood behind to see, Lord Carnarvon, his beautiful daughter Evelyn and his assistant Calendar, who handed him a small candle that flickered as the air trapped inside the tomb whooshed and escaped from the chamber.

After a few seconds, the candle's flame became stable, and Carter's eyes grew accustomed to the faint light. He was able to see. The three people standing impatiently behind asked in one voice,

"Can you see anything?"

Carter waited a nerve-wracking moment, then replied calmly,

*"Yes. Wonderful thi*ngs!"

AFTER THE DISCOVERY

There are more books written about the Boy King Tutankhamun than any other pharaoh in Ancient Egypt or the entire ancient world. His mysterious origin and very short reign, his sudden death for obscure reasons, the finding of his small tomb with its unimaginably beautiful artifacts, has all increased the fever linked to this Boy King.

Without a doubt, the discovery of Tutankhamun's Tomb had opened a profound, new chapter in Egyptology, and the large number of artifacts discovered inside his tiny tomb in the Valley of the Kings has essentially modified our knowledge about life in the times of the pharaohs. Their clothes, shoes, sandals, underwear, jewels, accessories, umbrellas, wigs, beds, musical instruments, fans, gloves, home furnishings, chariots, knives, daggers, decorative vases, thrones, and chairs are truly astounding! This is all aside from the enormous number of funeral objects made especially for the king's burial ceremonies in the later days of his life or shortly after his death and subsequent mummification.

The discovery of the tomb and its intact contents created new political complications regarding the splitting of the treasures between the Egyptian government and Lord Carnarvon who should have been entitled to some split because of the previous authorization. There arose a great fear of losing such priceless treasures. Through newspapers, nationalistic voices in Egypt launched a campaign to press the government in early 1923 to immediately issue new laws to prevent any permissions to dig in Egypt that consequently allowed sponsors to take any part of the finds. However, as increased awareness of the Tutankhamun case grew in public media, the issue resolved itself only three months later with the sudden and mysterious death of Lord Carnarvon in Cairo's old Shepherd's Hotel. Most records mention the cause of death as malarial fever, but it has never been confirmed. The body was found dead in the hotel room after three days! Media pressure ended as the rights to split Tutankhamun's treasures died with the lord.

Nationalistic feelings in Egyptian society had started to grow notably stronger with the end of the First World War and the 1919 Revolution. In the case of Tutankhamun, Egyptians found a reason to escalate ill will against the politicians in Egypt who were biased toward the Turkish king and the British mandate. The discovery also was an important turning point for the Antiquities Department, its management, and its authorizations and dig permissions. All protocol was reviewed and revised because of the Tutankhamun Tomb.

On another shore, English newspapers wrote extensively about the sudden and mysterious death of Lord Carnarvon and belief in the pharaoh's curse that haunted the man who paid to open the tomb after 3,400 years. Indeed, this charged atmosphere made Tutankhamun even more intriguing, popular and famous.

A bit of schadenfreude in the discovery story led to a number of problems that emanated soon after the tomb's discovery. Engelback and the Antiquities Department had wanted to take full control the tomb and its artifacts. Engelback had appointed a French assistant, Pierre Lacau, and another Egyptian as deputy manager, Ibrahim Effendi. Both were waiting in the city of Luxor for news from Carter, but Carter and Carnarvon had decided to keep the tomb opening solely to themselves. For them, it was now a private matter, and they felt the antiquities managers should stay out of it, at least the first night. Carter was encouraged by the lord to write a note to Ibrahim Effendi in Luxor notifying him of the time for opening the tomb. However, the note was sent late at night. While Carter, Carnarvon, Evelyn and Calendar were opening and searching the artifacts in the main chamber and antechamber, under the madness of curiosity and treasure hunting fever, they broke into the side room and the burial chamber to find the large gilded wooden shrines. Carter opened the four shrines and entered through to the smallest one to see the golden coffin of the pharaoh that was sleeping inside the stone quartzite sarcophagus. It was very late, almost early morning the following day, November 27th, and no one had "officially" entered the tomb on the previous day.

Many questions arose from their unauthorized entry. How many artifacts had been handpicked by those four persons before they left the tomb at dawn? (Carter himself admitted in his book that he slipped into his pocket a rosette from one of the gilded wooden shrines' doors when he opened it.) One can only imagine that crazy night and what may have transpired inside the tomb with the four individuals who had decided not to tell anyone about their adventure.

If we don't have answers to all of our questions, we have some clues to help us imagine the answers. A few years ago, the grandson of Howard Carter confessed that he accidentally found a small museum with Tutankhamun artifacts in the basement of his grandfather's house. The interview was published in English newspapers and is no longer a secret.

On the other side of the spectrum, Howard Carter tried to persuade his British government, through the ambassador in Cairo, to negotiate with the Egyptian government in order to retain Lord Carnarvon's share in the Tutankhamun treasures. He thought they should at least be entitled to a small part of the collection as compensation for the work Carter and the deceased lord had done for Egypt. But, the matter of the split was growing in significance every day in Egypt; pressure inside Egypt had become alarming; and any negotiation on this subject might have led to the rise of a huge wave of violence and demonstration against the British army in Egypt. As Carter became less and less satisfied with the controversial working conditions, he slowed down the work process inside the tomb. He moved the artifacts inside the tomb into the larger Tomb of Set II for better examination and photographs, until finally, all the objects (in theory) could be transported to the Cairo Museum where they were to occupy half of the second floor.

Finally, the great discovery of Tutankhamun's tomb was a real game-changer for Egyptology. The new constitution of Egypt, drafted and approved in 1923, clearly stated enactment of required protection of antiquities to preserve Egyptian heritage. In addition, it provided a platform for new rules and regulations on dig work in Egypt to prevent theft by treasure hunters and art collectors who sought only wealth through excavation. The general archeological movement in Egypt took a sharp turn after that, taking on a purely nationalistic approach, something we will see in the next few chapters.

CHAPTER 12

Tomb of Queen Hetebheres in Giza

AFTER THE GREAT DISCOVERY OF Tutankhamun's Tomb in the Valley of the Kings in 1922, the allure of the royal necropolis of ancient Thebes again gripped large museums, universities and institutes with strong ties to Ancient Egypt. At the same time, the lucrative revenues that Lord Carnarvon would have collected from his share of the Tutankhamun treasures seduced the minds of collectors from all around the world, heralding the entry of new players into Egyptology and archeology.

In faraway lands beyond the Atlantic Ocean, there were many affluent American families, private universities and growing American art museums. All aspired to possessing some of Egypt's wealth of artifacts and unique treasures, like those of Tutankhamun, and sought to strengthen their chances to dig in Egypt's deserts and discover new hidden secrets. Ultimately, the discovery of Tutankhamun wildly fueled imaginations and expanded the horizon of possible similar finds.

While the discovery of Tutankhamun's Tomb attracted attention, at the same time it opened Egyptians' eyes to the necessity of preserving discovered artifacts and Egypt's heritage. This eventually had implications on laws regarding permissions to work in Egypt and terms of agreements on splitting the discovered artifacts. Intentions toward prevention of theft did not completely stop the bleeding of lost artifacts, but it was a vital step toward changing the terms of authorizations.

In the early 1920s, the wealthy American executive J. P. Morgan from New York was very interested in sponsoring an important American archeological campaign to dig in Egypt, in particular, in the area of Luxor. This mission was orchestrated by the Metropolitan Museum in New York in 1921 under the leadership of the famous archeologist, Wilkinson. The mission selected the area of El Deir El Bahari, near the mortuary Temple of Queen Hatshepsut as the center for their digs and research. To that end, Morgan built a special house for the New York team in one of the southern corners of the valley of El Deir El Bahari, to be their guesthouse and research center at the same time. It is now called Morgan House and is still used as a guesthouse by archeologists who occasionally work the area.

(The last tour group I guided for the Metropolitan Museum in New York paid a visit to Morgan House, and we talked about Wilkinson's work in the area and Morgan's generous contribution to this mission. It was very special to have Charles Morgan, the grandson of J. P. Morgan, as a guest traveling with the group, a very kind person who was exceptionally proud of his grandfather's guesthouse and of his family's association with the great expedition in Luxor back in the 1920s.)

The Metropolitan Museum expedition in the area of El Deir El Bahari discovered many interesting tombs in the surrounding mountains above the valley: nobles' rock-hewn tombs from the Middle Kingdom 2000 BC–1850 BC. Inside the Tomb of Prince Meketra, Wilkinson's team discovered the many wooden models and miniatures of daily life images and activities representing lifestyle in Ancient Egypt in the times of the prince. Some remain in Egypt on the upper floor of Cairo's Egyptian Museum while the rest of the collection resides now in the Egyptian Gallery at the Metropolitan Museum in New York.

Simultaneously, on the eastern side of the Nile in Luxor, there was another American team from the University of Chicago actively working in the large complex of the Karnak and the Luxor temples. The Oriental Institute sent the well-known orientalist James Henry Breasted to lead that mission in Luxor. The team comprised of art historians and archeologists came to Luxor and began examining the decaying walls of the labyrinthine complex of the Karnak and Luxor temples, and initiated a wonderful, undeniable legacy of preservation and conservation of the temples' art and texts. They established a guesthouse and research facility within the town of Luxor, on the banks of the Nile. They called it Chicago House, which still exists, providing services to University of Chicago art historians and archeologists. It houses one of the best Egyptology libraries in Luxor and maybe in all Egypt. The members of the University of Chicago team have written their names in golden letters on Egyptology research and preservation of Ancient Egyptian art. Well known today, the University of Chicago's Department of Egyptology is the best in the field in the United States. For more than 80 years, the City of Chicago has developed a special bond with Ancient Egypt and ancient Thebes along the eternal Nile. Artists and art historians associated with Chicago House in Luxor continue to contribute to the preservation of art at Luxor's various sites. They are pushing forward with efforts toward restoration, conservation, renovation and preservation of all related scientific documentation of monuments in the Luxor area.

(When I guide groups from University of Chicago, and occasionally groups with National Geographic Expeditions, we always visit Chicago House. I take the opportunity to walk between the many library shelves intrigued by the great volumes on Egyptology, some dating back to the late 19th century. It is a genuine pleasure to be able to touch and smell the history of Egyptology, strong in the nostrils.)

The third and last element in this picture is another American team that worked in Egypt around the same period: the Boston Museum of Fine Arts and Harvard University co-expedition. It was an important campaign under the leadership of the George Reisner, the professor from the University of California, who had been hired to survey the Giza Plateau and reveal its secrets hidden beneath the desert sands. The team was very academic and systematic in their research, influenced by their team leader. Having worked extensively since the beginning of the 1920s in the Nubian region, Reisner had made a number of resounding discoveries in the Qustol area, among them the royal tombs of the Ancient Nubian kingdom in Kerma, circa 1700 BC–1800 BC.

The Boston Fine Arts Museum and Harvard University hired this man of stature for his experience in archeological research, to perhaps find priceless treasures similar to those of Tutankhamun. If such finds were to occur, the city's museum would become one of the richest in the world. The actively digging, sponsored expeditions from New York and Chicago in Luxor factored into the decision to stage Boston's archeological campaign in the Giza area. The logical place to start the work was Giza, nearby the three great pyramids and not far from the Sphinx. At this point, Giza was the only choice with two other American teams already working in Luxor.

Timing was critical for several reasons: 1) Egypt's political turmoil had been increasing every week since the 1919 Revolution; 2) the Egyptian nationalists' pressure was growing against the British political mandate over Egypt and British influence over Egypt's cultural matters; and 3) the Department of Antiquities' affairs and related games of permission and authorization were in obvious jeopardy. Everyone in Egypt suspected illegal cover-ups of the plundering of artifacts and their removal from the country. The atmosphere was changing quickly, and dark clouds were hovering with news of a new constitution and protection laws regarding antiquities.

These were the general circumstances in Egypt in the 1920s when a number of great discoveries were made in Giza near the great pyramids. Toward the end of their mission in Giza, Reisner and his team came across one interesting accidental discovery behind the Great Pyramid of King Khufu, from 2600 BC.

However, before I tell the story of this interesting discovery of the Tomb of Queen Hetebheres, Khufu's mother, I would like to take you on a quick journey back 4,600 years ago.

Historical Background

In the middle of the 27th century BC, King Huni ruled Egypt as the country was undergoing major political changes. Egypt was steadily becoming more politically stable, and social development allowed people to embark on a cultural renaissance. The fruits of domestic stability were evident throughout the country. Upper and Lower Egypt were now firmly united under the rule of the king. He declared a central government with administrative states that now had full authority over the cultivated lands, water resources and general natural resources (e.g., copper, turquoise, granite, and limestone).

This new age and control of resources by the powerful central government enabled the king to proceed economically with a number of great construction projects, such as his pyramid and royal tombs at Maydoum. The ultimate purpose of the king's royal tomb was to secure his eternal life and to guarantee his son and successor would rule the country after him. (Records from this early historic period never mention the name of the pharoah's son, who died during his father's reign and was buried next to his father's pyramid in the large mysterious mastaba, Tomb 17 in the area of Maydoum.)

During the construction of his own tomb, King Huni had had to bury his only son and successor to the throne. A premature death always became a complicated matter in Ancient Egypt, as the question of new succession arose. In the case of King Huni, he had fathered a large number of royal princesses but no other sons. The oldest daughter was Princess Hetebheres. Her name means "the one with happy face." After 24 years on Egypt's throne, Huni decided to select a strong prince as a husband for his oldest daughter; his name was Senefru, a prince of unknown royal lineage with no blood relations to the king. Senefru was a fine choice for the old king and for Egypt as he would be the heir to the throne as the son-in-law to the pharaoh.

When Senefru ruled Egypt, he continued the long period of stability and prosperity. His wisdom and power enabled him to solidify the unity of Upper and Lower Egypt and continue the renaissance era started by his father-in-law. Later, when scholars and historians were researching Ancient Egyptian history, they chose to start a new dynasty with Senefru, the 4th Dynasty, which witnessed the great days of pyramid building. He finished what his father-in-law had begun (he was likely the one who finished Huni's pyramid in Maydoum) and embarked on a huge pyramid construction project in the area south of Saqqara. His first large project was the Bent Pyramid at Dahshur. It was a harsh learning experience for both the king and for his chief engineer. It seemed a fatal mistake had been made with the pyramid's foundation and reinforcement of its interior galleries, along with another error with the inclination angle of the outer surface of the structure. These mistakes affected the total height of the structure and the incurable deflection of the pyramid's summit. As a result of such problems, the master architect and chief engineer were forced to make inevitable changes to the design and crop the inclination angle of the outer surface from 54 degrees to 45 degrees. This made the pyramid much shorter and gave it an obvious bend on its outer faces leading to the name the Bent Pyramid.

One may imagine the unhappy Pharaoh Senefru with the unappealing shape of his royal tomb. Senefru decided to build another pyramid, only three km. north of the Bent Pyramid in the desert area of Dahshur, not far from Memphis, Egypt's capital in the days of Huni and Senefru. Built on a much better foundation and avoiding previous mistakes, the Red Pyramid of King Senefru was the first true, complete pyramid in Egypt. (Petrie called it the Red Pyramid when he surveyed the structure in the 1890s, pointing to the reddish color of its stone in the later hours of the day and at sunset.)

Modern pyramidologists Zahi Hawass and Mark Lehner consider Senefru the greatest pyramid builder of all time. During his reign, he built many satellite pyramids, small and symbolic, all over Egypt to represent his immortal spirit. The royal spirit of the divine King in the Ancient Egyptian language is called *"hut ka,"* which literally means spirit house. Scholars think the number of symbolic pyramids of Senefru may have reached seven, but we can see the remains of only two: the Pyramid of Kom El Sultan at El Mynia and the Pyramid of Seila at El Fayoum.

Senefru never forgot his wife who gave him the throne, Queen Hetebheres. He ordered a tomb built for her next to one of his two pyramids at Dahshur, but this mysterious tomb has never been found. That said, the queen certainly died during Senefru's reign, and she was buried somewhere in the Dahshur area.

When King Senefru died, his son and successor Khufu ruled the country. He did not waste time in starting the construction of his royal tomb and pyramid, but he chose a new area suitable for his ambitious dream project. He moved some thirty km. north of Dahshur where his father's two pyramids were located, to an area that in Ancient Egypt was called Rostau. He decided to build his tomb high on a solid limestone plateau and to connect the remote area with the Nile Valley. Designers provided the plateau with a lake and a port for transportation and a small workers village to accommodate the laborers of Khufu's dream, to build the largest and most beautiful pyramid in the country, far exceeding his father's two pyramids. (He had likely learned firsthand where and how to construct his own during the years of construction of the two pyramids at Dahshur.)

Here we ask a puzzling question: How were the funeral artifacts of Queen Hetebheres, Khufu's mother, which were lost in her original tomb in Dahshur (at least it was never found) discovered in Giza? It is one of the mysteries of modern Egyptology, and scholars trying to answer the vexing question have posited several scenarios. If the queen was originally buried in Dahshur, why did we find her tomb and funeral objects in Giza? And, if we have the tomb and all its burial accessories, why do we have no mummy inside the coffin?

George Reisner tried to solve the puzzle

George Andrew Reisner, 1867–1942, was born in Indianapolis, Indiana. His parents were of German origin. He studied at Harvard Law School and was granted a scholarship from 1893 to 1896 to study Semite languages at Berlin University. It was the gateway for his love of Ancient Near East history and archeology and later, his passion for Egyptology. Flinders Petrie's fame and finds in Egypt ignited Reisner's desire to further study Ancient Egypt and walk in Petrie's footsteps, as a true founder of modern archeological methods.

The modern archeological methods George Reisner practiced, wherever he excavated, in Nubia or in Egypt, have marked his name as a pioneer archeologist who used modern and innovative methods of work. He established a new school of dig work on grounds that rivaled the categorical and unique style of Petrie's school of work. Reisner was commonly known for his remarkable attention to the finest details during dig work and his incomparable manner of excavation. He would divide the area of work into small squares. He numbered everything and focused on every detail of his scheme of work. Many other archeologists around the world have adapted his methods of excavation.

In 1902, Harvard University managed to obtain permission for excavation in the Giza necropolis, to reexamine once more the ancient cemeteries around the Great Pyramid of Khufu. The Harvard-Boston expedition sought to employ the innovative, scientific excavation methods introduced by Reisner and the new generation of archeologists that differed from traditional dig methods practiced in Egypt for most of the 19th century.

The authorization to dig in Giza was extended a number of times, and the areas in Giza included in the permission were enlarged considerably as well. During the 1920s, the authorization covered almost one-third of the entire Giza necropolis. The space extended from the western side of Khufu's Pyramid to the western cemetery of Menkaure's Pyramid and from the eastern side of Khufu's Pyramid to the southern areas of the Sphinx statue.

For more than 20 years, Reisner's systematic excavation and documentation of all his Giza digs revealed many valuable discoveries within the royal cemetery and the surrounding mastabas, but the interesting accidental discovery of King Khufu's mother's mysterious tomb on the south side of the Great Pyramid was the special one. Its uniqueness, depth, royal artifacts and furniture all add to the mystery shrouding the discovery. The missing mummy

By Way of Accident

in the coffin remained an enigmatic situation, and Reisner tried to solve the dilemma by suggesting the following story:

"When King Senefru died, his son and successor Khufu ruled the country and began the preparation for building his eternal home in his afterlife. He chose the remote area of Giza, at the far northern edge of the western plateau of the Saqqara necropolis. During the construction of Khufu's pyramids in Giza, the chief of police, the head of guards of the royal cemetery at Dahshur, and pharaoh's personal advisers reported some bad news about the robbery of Queen Hetebheres tomb at Dahshur, where she was buried near her husband, King Senefru. Khufu's advisers never told the king the whole truth. They only told him it was a minor break in and very little looting occurred, amounting to few insignificant artifacts. The purpose of the decoy was to avoid pharaoh's rage and expected wrath. They probably continued lying to their master and told him that all of the criminals were arrested and severely punished, and his mother's mummy and all other personal funeral furniture and accessories were in perfect safety but the adviser strongly recommended relocating the royal tomb furniture and accessories along with the queen mother's coffin and mummy to a safer place and to be closer to her beloved son, right behind his Great Pyramid. At once, Khufu ordered preparation of the new home for his mother's mummy to be her tomb on the eastern side of his pyramid. Very close to the three small pyramids of the queens (the great royal wives). The workers began cutting into the limestone bedrock of Giza a deep shaft, almost 15 meters, to end with a single small room where all of the funeral furniture and accessories of the queen were relocated and reburied, along with the beautiful alabaster coffin, canopic jars and other objects, the new tomb was sealed and well-hidden with rocks and sands above it. The queen mother could now safely travel to the netherworld along with her son in his eternal celestial journey with God Re."

The tomb was neglected and subsequently disappeared until 1924 when Reisner's team accidentally discovered the shaft.

Discovery Story

On November 1, 1924, George Reisner's excavation team in Giza was ready to start a new survey in the southeastern corner of the Great Pyramid of Khufu. The first task was to remove a huge amount of dirt and the debris piles on top of what looked like rocky edges. Reisner was eager to find out about this solid rock beneath the dirt.

On December 2nd, workers completed the removal of the dirt and debris and reached the bedrock. They found the remains of a small, unfinished pyramid base from the time of Khufu. The newly discovered small pyramid base was very close to the three-sided Queens' Pyramids that lay at the southeastern corner of Khufu's pyramid. As excavation continued, they realized the site was an ancient limestone quarry used during the construction of the Great Pyramid and much of the soil and debris piled in the area was what had been left behind from the quarrying operation to cut large stones from the rocky edges for building pyramids and mastabas.

At the end of January 1925, Reisner returned to Boston to start his winter semester and lectures at Harvard University leaving the Giza mission to his assistant and workers with the trusted Egyptian chief of workers Rayes Mahmoud Ahmed Said, and professional mission photographer Abdou, who took daily pictures of all procedures, as per Reisner's instructions. This way, George Reisner documented the entire work process while he was conducting his lectures at Harvard until he returned to Giza to lead the mission himself.

On a cloudy February morning, Abdou was setting up his photography gear somewhere close to the newly excavated areas of the stone edges of the ancient quarry near the small pyramid base. His task was simple. He was to photograph everything they excavated before, during and after the dig. Abdou always started earlier than the other workers, preferring the early morning sunlight, and by the time workers and inspectors arrived at the site around 8 am, he had photographed the entire area before they started removing the soil. He stayed with the crew for a few hours until noon, taking pictures of the actual digging process. In the middle of the day, Abdou normally avoided taking photographs, returning later in the afternoon, as the workers were leaving the site, to photograph the site once again documenting what they had achieved during the day. This had been his daily operation until that morning.

He carried his camera and tripod and intended to set it up somewhere on the eastern side of the Great Pyramid, close to the Queens' Pyramids and the nobles' mastabas cemetery. He picked out higher ground to set up his gear, ground made of soil that was still unexcavated, a little north of the area where the workers were currently digging. Suddenly his tripod slipped forward, and he had to grab the heavy camera to stop it from hitting the ground. The spot he had chosen to set up had appeared to be a smooth, sandy surface where the tripod could stand stably, so Abdou moved his gear a few steps northward. Again, it was a sandy spot but the ground was less smooth but he still thought he could fix his tripod securely. But, as he began to set it up again, he saw the tripod was again sinking deep into the soft sands. He also noticed a solid pack of soil and debris just beneath the sand layer. He was curious to find out why his tripod's legs kept sinking.

Abdou recognized a soft layer of ancient mortar, very smooth and just beneath the sand that the tripod had slid into. These remnants of gesso mortar compelled Abdou to examine the spot further. He immediately rushed to Reisner's assistant, the site manager, Alan Rowe, who had previous experience with excavations in Alexandria. Rowe examined the ground and found a rectangular hole in the sand, sealed with the thick layer of white gesso mortar. They both sensed the importance of this discovery even though they were unable to judge its true nature, but Rowe's and Abdou's experience allowed them to realize that this small, rectangular, sealed hole in the ground could be nothing but a side entrance to a tunnel or underground tomb.

On February 23rd, the site was excavated, and the large limestone blocks that filled the entryway were removed. Now it was clear that they were about to discover a new tomb probably never touched before. Enthusiastically, workers removed all the dirt from the descending corridor and they found 12 steps cut into the bedrock from the northern side of the descending corridor leading directly to a deep narrow vertical shaft. The shaft was filled with rocks and debris. It was standard practice in Ancient Egypt to fill the main shafts leading to inner burial chambers and tombs with rocks, soil and rough stones to act as a decoy to grave robbers and create a type of natural setting to make it appear not worth digging there, a misdirection of tomb raiders of Ancient Egypt. This ploy did not work with all the tombs in Giza. However, it had worked with this tomb!

Excitement built as the workers began to clean the vertical shaft. Generally, in Giza, shafts were eight or nine meters deep, and exactly at nine meters, the workers found a large square piece of flat stone on the wall. Everyone imagined this must be the entrance to the burial chamber. When they removed the large stone, the workers found a niche behind it, cut in the bedrock, and buried in it, a human skull and three sacrificed bull legs (an offering in a hidden chapel). The workers next realized the shaft was much deeper than typical Giza tomb shafts. They were forced to dig deeper, and it began to get harder to clean the shaft as feelings of suffocation and terrible heat grew. Finally, the workers reached a level 25 meters. Next to the wall, one of the workers found a large block of stone that they managed to remove to find a small dark room behind it. They saw nothing, as the bottom of the shaft was very dark, and they had no light to help them see.

They asked for light, and workers above provided mirrors to reflect sunlight into the vertical shaft, and reflect it again at the bottom into the dark side room. It was an amazing moment of excitement for everyone as the rays of sunlight shone in the side room. It reflected gold over wooden furniture, and the floor of this room was completely covered with gold beads. Many royal artifacts were stockpiled in the side chamber, an alabaster coffin; jars and bowls; dismantled, gold-leaf furniture with the name of Queen Hetebheres clearly inscribed on it. The name of King Senefru was also found. They found the queen's royal canopy, personal bed and two wonderful chairs, all pieces adorned with the royal names of the king and the queen, Senefru and Hetebheres. A large, gilded wooden box was found; inside were eight small alabaster jars for the selected oils and perfumery of the queen. Each jar was labeled with the type of oil it contained (e.g. feast oil, which is the best oil of Libya), and there was green malachite for eye shadow and a beautiful collection of ornate silver with precious stone bracelets and bangles encrusted with butterfly images.

The general condition of artifacts in the burial chamber was very fragile and in an advanced state of disrepair. The wooden objects had mostly disintegrated and decayed with thousands of their gold leaf shards scattered on the floor of the room. Through meticulous restoration work performed on the wooden objects, the team was able to make out the tomb's owner and read her royal honorary titles "the Mother of the King of Upper and Lower Egypt," "Follower of God Horus," "Hetebheres." With this discovery, Reisner and his team had found the oldest royal tomb from the 4th Dynasty to be discovered with its original artifacts intact.

When George Reisner returned to Egypt in the spring to get back to leading the mission and continue examining the royal tomb and its numerous artifacts, he made a few observations on the collection. The first curiosity was the finding of a large number of objects in the tomb that had nothing to do with the queen mother and her personal accessories, such as large jars to collect dirt and sand, copper needles, uncarved large stone stelae, and original tomb-making tools from Ancient Egypt. All were a question mark for Reisner. The second point he wondered about was the chaotic fashion in which the tomb furniture and artifacts had been deposited and cached, with little order and only the slightest care or attention, as was normally required for royal artifacts and burial ceremonies. The treasures had been stored in such a way that many of the small and fragile artifacts were broken into pieces. Reisner arrived at a hypothetical conclusion about this situation; everything was buried very quickly. But why?

He made one last, very important observation inside the tomb: Reisner noticed that the alabaster coffin of the queen inside the burial chamber was still sealed and looked in very good condition, along with the four canopic jars found next to it. Reisner was certain that the royal mummy of Queen Hetebheres was still inside, but an unexpected surprise came when Reisner opened the coffin on March 3, 1927 with his assistants at the time, Wheeler and Dunham, and the chief of workers Mahmoud Ahmed Said and four of his workers. They found the coffin empty, no mummy inside, not even a trace of a mummy.

It was a jolting shock to everyone to have the mummy of the queen missing. No one could fathom where the mummy was if the tomb was intact. This question pressed Reisner to present his theory about the reburial of Queen

Hetebheres (the theory presented earlier). It was the only logical scenario possible as far as Reisner and his team could imagine. The mummy was originally lost in the first tomb in the Dahshur area, but for their own preservation, guards had lied to Khufu. Everything had been relocated, but there was no mummy, and the king knew nothing. That also explained the chaotic way the objects had been cached. One more compelling fact is that Reisner found some basalt stone still on the floor of the inner chamber that was identical to the stone used for the floor of the nearby eastern mortuary temple of Khufu's Pyramid, implying the reburial of Queen Hetebheres had taken place at the same time as the construction of Khufu's Mortuary Temple.

When Reisner began the restoration of the tomb's deteriorating objects, he consulted a number of world experts to find the best and safest method of restoration, but it was to be very difficult, such that some experts said it would even be impossible to assemble the shards of gold leaf and replace them on the decayed wooden objects. Finally, Reisner was advised to pour liquid wax on the floor to pick up all the small pieces of gold shards and return with the wax board to the museum. Before he executed his plans, the Department of Antiquities sent Ahmed Yousef, an Egyptian expert in restoration and renovation of ancient relics, to help with the task. When Reisner met Ahmed Yousef, he did not give him much courtesy, and Ahmed Yousef remained quiet for several days. He carefully watched Reisner's restoration technique and the method he was using to solve the problem of the gold shards on the tomb floor. Finally, to Reisner's astonishment, Ahmed Yousef said suddenly, *"I can restore it for you."*

Reisner actually laughed and nearly made fun of the man, but the challenge was putting the two men on edge and Ahmed Yousef told him, *"Give me only one hour; leave me alone in the tomb."*

Ahmed Yousef photographed the objects that needed to be restored inside the tomb. First, he started to rearrange all the pieces according to his photographs using models he had made of all of the objects. The small box that contained the linen curtain and canopy covers of the queen was almost in pieces and seemed the most difficult to restore, but Ahmed Yousef decided to start with it. Reisner skeptically gave him one week to try, but after only six days, Ahmed Yousef returned to him with the box intact and restored. Reisner was shocked and extremely happy with the results and hired him to be the chief restorer of the tomb and the mission. They worked together for several seasons until all of the objects were restored. The pieces are now on display in the Cairo Museum with a replica authorized to be on display in the Museum of Fine Arts in Boston.

However, the missing mummy of the queen remains a puzzle for many scholars today, and they present new theories and hypotheses to answer the dilemma. Recently, Mark Lehner came up with another new theory. He suggested the discovered tomb in Giza was the original tomb for the queen, and that she had never been buried in Dhashur as most scholars previously believed. Lehner also alleged the mummy of the queen was reburied inside one of the three small subsidiary pyramids behind Khufu's pyramid, and later, the smaller pyramids had been raided and entirely looted. That said, Lehner has never explained the existence of the canopic jars inside the tomb, very close to the coffin. Their proximity to the coffin serves as an important sign of a real burial ceremony next to its mummy.

This great discovery in Giza was not Reisner's greatest find in the area. He made some astounding discoveries near the third pyramid in Giza, at the Mortuary Temple of King Menkaure (or Mekerynus). Reisner found an exquisite collection of black basalt statues of the king along with gods and goddesses of Ancient Egypt. Scholars have rated them as some of the best examples of sculpture from the Old Kingdom and possibly from all Ancient Egypt. The statues now are now divided between the Cairo Museum and Museum of Fine Arts in Boston.

Finally, the accidental discovery of Queen Hetebheres' Tomb in Giza marked the end of an era of rediscovery of Ancient Egypt, as foreign missions could no longer operate in Egypt as freely as they had been. After 1925, due to major political changes in Egypt, attitudes changed and Egyptians themselves wanted to lead Ancient Egyptian research and excavations.

George Reisner concluded his career as an archeologist in Egypt with great finds in Giza, and he was generously rewarded as these discoveries made his name eternal and reserved a special seat for him in the history of Egyptology as a pioneering figure and a true scholar.

CHAPTER 13

Royal Tombs of Tanis

THE HARVARD-BOSTON EXPEDITION IN GIZA under the leadership of George Reisner was the last of the great foreign missions in Egypt in the 1920s and for a long time after. Due to constant political unrest and turmoil in Egypt and Palestine, the archeological atmosphere in the Near East, specifically Egypt, was not encouraging at all. In those days, two contradicting elements blew through Egyptian society: the need for European modernization to change Egypt's traditional customs and outdated lifestyle; and paradoxically, the necessity for independence from British colonialism after more than 40 years of occupation. The birth of these contradicting ideas was a difficult one, but Egypt's first modern constitution was nevertheless approved in 1923. The country took its first legal steps toward the new modern state and rule of law, and little by little, powerful national institutions arose that would provide the stability needed to run the country and represent the nation of Egypt well in the eyes of the outside world. We witnessed the birth of new social classes, liberal, if I may use the term in a cultural context. A strong wave of change grew, mainly in the cities of Cairo and Alexandria rather than in the countryside.

The rising nationalistic power in Egypt climaxed with a number of political leaders who aspired to the national dream of both independence and modernity. The famous lawyer and politician Saad Zagloul was the leading symbol. Statues commemorating him still stand in major squares in Cairo and Alexandria and a number of other major Egyptian cities. In the heart of this political topography, we see that King Fouad's weak and indecisive leadership was plainly unable to steer the rocking ship of Egypt through the rough, political seas. Saad Zagloul was the main orchestrator in political negotiations with the British government as he was the Chair of Egypt's Parliament and the leader of Egypt's most influential political party at that time, El Wafd (the modern Liberal party). After a long, complicated process of negotiations in the 1920s and early 1930s, an agreement was finally hammered out in 1936 between the two countries, announcing the independence of Egypt from British occupation and the ending of the British mandate in Egypt. The treaty was considered by many Egyptian politicians a glowing victory and was celebrated nationwide for many weeks, but the aftermath brought bad news not just to Egypt, but to the entire Middle East. It was a small piece of happy news for several weeks followed by a flood of truly horrible news for several years, continuing up to the present.

The 1936 Anglo-Egyptian Treaty sparked a series of major crises in Egypt and the Middle East. The continued volatile political events in Egypt and Palestine shaped both the political and military topography of the area around

Egypt. The modern political history of Egypt is not my main concern in this book, but I would like to shed light on the events that followed the 1936 Treaty that was signed by El Nahaas Pasha as Prime Minister. Many of the actions that occurred subsequent to the treaty directly affected every aspect of life in Egypt, including Egyptology.

In 1936, the Arab-Palestinian revolts against Jewish settlers cast a very uncertain shadow on the British evacuation and the independence treaty. The daily news from Palestine, along with the rising death toll emanating from clashes and atrocities between Palestinian and Jewish settlers, provoked the already charged atmosphere in Egypt against England, as Egyptians believed Britain to be solely responsible for the complicated situation in Palestine. Since the Balfour Declaration in 1917, the British state promised to secure a home in Palestine for Jewish settlers, immigrants from Europe and any subsequent waves of large numbers of Jewish immigrants, allowing them to settle in the Promised Land. Bloodshed and clashes pushed Egypt and England's relationship to a critical edge and destroyed the credibility of the signed treaty ensuring British evacuation.

King Fouad died in 1936, and Farouk, his son and successor, was crowned. He was only 18 years old, a person obsessed with his Turkish blood and proud of his royal lineage, but with no real political experience. With this change, the country faced the Second World War with a treaty yet to be executed and alarming border problems, rising due of the rapid increase of Jewish settlers in Palestine coupled with escalating violence between the new settlers and native population.

Ironically, in spite of all the difficulties Egypt was enduring under the young King Farouk, the country did help England during wartime and was assuredly a vital ally even when parts of Egypt were officially declared war zones, such as the Suez Canal area and the desert area of Al Alamein near the Libyan border. England promised, during the war, to execute the Treaty of Independence, signed some ten years earlier. The whole country lived for this moment.

In this charged atmosphere, the field of Egyptian archeology was not a focus for anyone, and digging and excavation went unmentioned. The country was at war and no one had any extra money to spend on exploration in some dry, Egyptian desert. In the meantime, the United States was facing a devastating economic catastrophe during most of the 1930s, the period known in America as the Great Depression. With this crisis, Egypt lost one of its great sources for financing research and sponsorship of digging missions in the country, as the usually incomparable and limitless American enthusiasm to explore Ancient Egypt had ebbed.

However, and against all odds, there remained indeed a few archeologists quietly working in Egypt, without much financial support or media coverage. They chose to dig in remote areas away from Egypt's complicated politics and ever-changing society. One of them was the French scholar Pierre Montet.

Pierre Montet was a professor of Near East Studies at Strasburg University in France. He led the university's mission to excavate the famous Baalbek Temple site in Lebanon from 1921 to 1924. During his years of work and research, Montet unveiled the strong ties between Ancient Egypt and the Phoenician coast and its ancient kingdoms, especially in the later period between 1000 BC and 300 AD. Accordingly, the professor was determined to seize his first opportunity to go to Egypt and try to organize a mission to excavate and research in the area of Tanis, the site of Egypt's political capital in the later days. What was so special about Tanis?

Historical Background

The death of Pharaoh Rameses XI marked the end of the royal lineage of the Ramesside family and opened the door for new, fresh blood to enter Egypt's royal dynastic chain of rulers. At that time, Prince Smendes declared himself king and pharaoh of all Egypt, affirming his intimate ties with the Ramesside royal house (most scholars agree about his obscure origin and surmise that he probably gained his legitimacy from marriage to one of the pharaoh's daughters. Marriage was a convenient, albeit devious, back door that enabled powerful princesses to mount the royal throne in the absence of powerful royal male successors).

The political situation in Egypt finally stabilized in his hands, and Thebes finally approved him as the new Pharaoh Smendes, Ruler of Upper and Lower Egypt. He began a series of constructions in the Karnak complex of temples, rebuilt some of its ancient walls and reinforced it to face the annual flood of the Nile. His remarkable political move was to transfer the capital and his royal residence from *"pr-ramses"* (the state capital of Egypt since the later days of Rameses II, circa 1250 BC) to another city only a few km. north of the site. His new capital was known in history as Tanis, where he moved to rule the country for about 25 years and subsequently died and was buried there.

In the days of Pharaoh Smendes, Egypt saw the birth and rise of a new political system with new royal blood, dynasty and capital. The true power and authority in Egypt was practically divided between the pharaoh and the High Priest of God Amun in Thebes and the complex of Karnak temples (symbolizing the political and religious authority of Egypt). Many records and historical materials collected from this period (late 20th and early 21st dynasties) reflect clearly the dual power struggle in Egypt. The High Priest of the Karnak temples was considered the true practical governor and ruler of all of south Egypt (Upper Egypt), while the pharaoh in the far north in the Delta was isolated and ruled only the northern part of the country (Lower Egypt) from his palace in Tanis.

Pharaoh Smendes' death brought about political turmoil in Egypt, and with the coronation of the new Pharaoh Psusennes I, the country was effectively divided between the two struggling authorities. The religious authority ruled over the south, the capital of which was Thebes, and the political authority ruled from the north with its capital in Tanis. The rift was not a surprise but it felt like a declaration of two new states in Egypt, the creed of the priests in the south versus the blood of the monarchs in the north.

Psusennes I, the rising star in town, was a great builder in Tanis. During his reign, the great complex of Amun temples in Tanis was enlarged. The remains of the wall surrounding the Temple of Amun and the Temple of Khonsu north of it are still visible. These great pharaohs of the 21st Dynasty were perhaps responsible for relocating many of the royal burials and tomb objects from the threatened tombs of Thebes, which were no longer safe from lootings and raiding that seemingly occurred on a daily basis. Therefore, the new royal family preferred to build their tombs away from the ancient necropolis of Thebes and establish their own tombs right where they lived, in Tanis.

During the times of Pharaoh Panedjem, raiding and robbery of the tombs in Thebes had become a truly alarming matter. Many of the tombs of the 18th and 19th dynasties had already been raided in the Valley of the Kings, and a rescue mission to relocate and re-embalm some of the badly damaged mummies had to be executed immediately before the loss all of the tombs and their funeral artifacts occurred. Acknowledging these problems, the new rulers insisted on giving up the Theban necropolis, and they chose a new place that was safer and better guarded. The Tanis tombs, smaller and more humble in design and art, were not as magnificent or large as the Theban ones, but they were safe.

Tanis

The site of Tanis today fails to preserve much of the 21st Dynasty works and buildings. Much of its stone was recycled a number of times over the course of centuries, starting from the days of Pharaoh Sheshonk III (22nd Dynasty). Also, the massive construction modifications that took place during the 30th Dynasty and the Ptolemaic period resulted in the disappearance of the original works of the true founders of Psusennes' family.

The 21st Dynasty ended with the death of Psusennes II, circa 950 BC. A family of new blood and obscure Libyan origin came to power and ruled the northern kingdom from Tanis. The 22nd Dynasty period began with rulers with obviously strange, un-Egyptian names, pharaohs such as Sheshonk, Takelot, Pami, and Osorkon. All lived, died and were buried in Tanis in the new royal cemetery, close to the Temple of Amun. The cemetery boasted great perimeter walls to guard the pharaohs' tombs. Earlier, during the 19th Dynasty, Rameses II had built his new capital, *"pi rameses,"* near the cemetery location, and later, with pharaohs of the 21st and 22nd dynasties, it became Tanis. Montet had originally thought the site was the ancient capital of the Hyksos rulers called Awaris, but after years of excavation and research from

1929 to 1946, Montet recognized that it was not in fact the same as the Hyksos' Awaris.

In the far northeastern part of the Delta, visitors to the Tanis site today see the ruins of an ancient city, now called Sa El Hagar. Taking the first few steps climbing up the hill to enter the vast temple complex, one is overwhelmed by a feeling of awe and respect for the magnificent view. Hundreds of gigantic, broken, red granite obelisks lie on the ground, and parts of shattered pharaohs' statues are scattered all over the place, dating back to the New Kingdom and the subsequent 21st through 30th dynasties.

The site certainly provides one with a clear picture of the several construction layers and historic style changes from one period to the next. It is a wonderful example of recycling building materials in Ancient Egypt, as rulers throughout the centuries often took previous rulers' stones and built with them. One gets mixed feelings of wonder and amazement with just a little stroll between the broken obelisks and shattered statues. For example, when we enter through the massive gates of the Amun Temple in Tanis, which had been restored and remodeled during the 22nd Dynasty by Pharaoh Sheshonk III, we see a great number of blocks and stones originally belonging to the earlier temples. Now, they are covered with engraved hieroglyphs celebrating the 22nd Dynasty pharaohs, many of them in odd upside down positions.

The ancient city of Tanis was a flourishing town for more than 2,000 years, from the rise of the 21st Dynasty until the Roman period. Later, it was neglected and forgotten. For ages, local farmers from the surrounding villages reused most of its blocks, the small and easy-to-move ones, but thankfully, the large pieces, some several tons in weight, obelisks and statues, remain at the site along with other mounds of debris and soil, degraded to a gigantic heap of dirt. For nearly two millennia, this well-known archeological mound summoned people to dig in it and find its buried ancient treasures. Finally, in the second half of the 19th century, August Mariette, the French archeologist, came to Tanis and set up his tent for digs to research the ancient mound. It was really the first mission to dig at the site but opened the way for several later missions to continue exploring the mystery of Tanis. Flinders Petrie worked in Tanis for one season in 1884. Pierre Montet launched his mission in the area in 1929, but it was not until 1939 that Tanis revealed its best-kept secrets and hidden treasures.

Professor Montet came to Tanis along with his wife and four assistants; they hired several dozen local villagers to work on the mission as daily paid diggers. Montet worked in the area for ten years from 1929 to 1939, and in his very last season, Pierre Montet was destined to accidentally find the Royal Tombs of Tanis, with their marvelous treasures and unique jewels that rival the treasures of Tutankhamun. From both the historic and artistic perspectives, it was a wonderful discovery that occurred on a special night that the world will never forget as Montet and his four assistants were entering a 3,000-year-old tomb on the night the Second World War began.

(Pierre Montet found the first of the Royal Tombs in February 1939. He entered the Tomb of Psusennes II in March 1939 and found the hidden shaft that led to the original owner of the Tomb of Psusennes I on September 1, 1939, the night the Second World War officially was declared.)

Discovery Story

When he started in 1929, Pierre Montet's ultimate excavation goal in the Tanis area had been to find more clues about the relationship between Egypt and the Phoenician coast during the period when Tanis was Egypt's state capital, from the later days of Rameses II through the end of the pharaonic period and the conquest of Alexander the Great. After almost ten seasons in the area, toward the end of his mission, Montet and his team unearthed much of the main Temple of Tanis, the Temple of God Amun, his consort and family, Goddess Mut and their son Khonsu. In February 1939, Montet began clearing dirt that had collected in the heart of the excavated site. Much of this soil had accumulated since the days of August Mariette and Flinders Petrie, and it now looked like a large, imposing mound of dirt and debris. Montet decided to remove it all before he left the site for good.

The team began excavating the mound at the eastern corner of Amun Temple, close to Goddess Mut's small, side temple, known as the Temple of

Anta. Beneath the soil, Montet found a large number of Ptolemaic period workshops and artisans' factories, but no one had really thought about what might lie beneath the factories and the workshops until Rayes Ibrahim, the chief of workers, noticed some remains of stone deposits mixed in with the dirt they were removing. He suspected some large pieces of stone might exist beneath the workshops. He advised continuing excavation of the mound deeper beneath the workshops and factories from the Ptolemaic period with the hopes that something older from an earlier period might be hiding.

First, in order to test the underground, Rayes Ibrahim used a long stick of wood inserted into the soil as deep as it could go. To everyone's surprise, the long stick seemed to hit something hard just beneath the soft layer of debris. It was some kind of a ceiling of underground building, and it obviously was made of hard stones. Based on Rayes Ibrahim's suspicions, Montet ordered the removal of all dirt and reached the mysterious stone building buried under the mound. After removing a large part of the dirt mound, they could see something like a stone bunker completely buried in the ground with only a small part visible. Montet managed to make a hole in one of the large stone blocks big enough for his assistant Georges Goyon to enter the underground building and see what it was exactly. After a long, silent minute, George Goyon screamed from inside with only one word, "Osorkon!" It was the Royal Tomb of Pharaoh Osorkon.

Compared to the tombs in the Valley of the Kings, the Royal Tombs in Tanis are extremely small, and we know of no good reason why the pharaohs that built them created such small tombs without great art or the usual funeral scenes and religious texts of Ancient Egypt. Tanis tombs are void of any colorful scenes or even great hieroglyphs. As Montet entered the tombs after his assistant, he found himself standing in a very small, rectangular room measuring four meters by two meters. The walls were covered with crude scenes, but the royal names in cartouches were clearly visible on the walls, and he was able to read the name *kakhbrre* Psusennes. In a room next to it, they found the coffin belonging to Pharaoh Sheshonk II and inside it, Montet found the famous royal treasure buried with the king, some of the highest quality of all

Ancient Egyptian jewelry. Montet described the wonderful moment of the discovery like this:

> "Around 2 o'clock, shortly after noontime, the debris and the stones covering the entrance of the tomb were removed. I entered a relatively square room, its walls covered and decorated with religious funeral scenes and hieroglyphs connected with it another room with a large stone coffin in its middle almost occupying three quarters of the space, and engraved on its surface the name of King Osorkon. Everyone was exceptionally happy and I called for Reyes Ibrahim to start immediately clearing and cleaning the tomb from inside. This wonderful discovery was worth all the years of hard work in the site of Tanis."

On February 27th, Montet entered all the side rooms that were connected to one another, where he found large stone coffins. Inside the tombs of Psusennes I and Sheshonk II, he found silver coffins and a large amount of royal jewelry (the famous Tanis treasure now in the Cairo Museum). The news of the great new discoveries in Tanis traveled quickly to Cairo and beyond, all over the world. King Farouk paid a visit to the Royal Tombs of Tanis to see the place where all the great jewels of the pharaohs had been found. On March 21, 1939, Farouk visited the site and entered the Tomb of Psusennes to look at the solid silver coffin of the pharaoh and the marvelous treasures found with the mummy.

(Selim Hassan mentioned, in his Ancient Egypt encyclopedia, that the granite sarcophagus of Psusennes originally had belonged to a much earlier period, from the times of Merenptah, son of Ramses II, but it had been taken and reused by Psusennes' workers in the 21st Dynasty).

The royal jewels of the Tanis tombs were discovered within the pharaohs' coffins and around their mummies, in particular, near the incredibly well preserved, falcon-headed, silver coffin of Pharaoh Psusennes and the human-headed coffin of Pharaoh Sheshonk. In with the pharaohs' mummies, Montet and his team found a golden pectoral that covered the chest and head of the mummy, with six ornate golden necklaces bejeweled with precious stones, and a large number of precious stone scarabs and bracelets. (Pharaoh Psusennes' mummy broke records among all pharaoh mummies with the large number of golden bracelets the mummy was wearing: more than 20 golden bracelets, 12 on his right arm, and ten on his left, two more on his left thigh, and two around his heel. His fingers on both hands were covered with a large number of rings and he wore a pair of pure gold shoes.)

In the room next to the Tomb of Psusennes, Montet discovered the stone coffin of King Amenemope. Montet thought it was a small, rather unimportant tomb already looted by grave robbers but after he opened the lid of the heavy stone coffin, he found the remains of the pharaoh's mummy (remnants of the legs only) and a number of small stone statues with a low degree of quality. At this time, Montet confirmed his thoughts on the tomb having been savagely robbed and its mummy utterly violated through a small hole found in the ceiling above the coffin, just large enough to allow tomb raiders to enter and rob the tomb.

Nevertheless, a beautiful surprise came when Montet entered the room next door. It was officially the burial place of Queen *"Mutnedjemet"/"Ankhefenmut."* Unexpectedly, another coffin was found inside the room beside the queen's coffin. When Montet opened the other coffin, he found the badly damaged remains of Pharaoh Amenemope's mummy, but the face was covered with a solid golden mask, similar to that of Tutankhamun. Two large necklaces of gold and precious stones were found with the mummy along with scarabs, bracelets and rings, and most beautiful of all, a golden falcon with its wings spread wide.

Pierre Montet was unable to continue exploring the Royal Tombs of Tanis because the Second World War that swept across Europe had now arrived in North Africa. He was forced to suspend his operations at the site and return to France to wait for conditions to improve. He had to wait until the end of the war when he prepared another French mission after the war ended in 1945. This time he brought with him an architect who specialized in mapping and drawing excavated sites. His name was Alexander Lezine, who worked very closely with Montet mapping and architecturally surveying the Royal Tombs of Tanis. It was a very complicated tomb design as all the royal tombs were attached to one another in a most bizarre fashion. The strange and unusual shape of Royal Tombs of Tanis inspired the genius architect Alexander Lezine to imagine more hidden tombs in small enclaves without entrances or connection to the large rooms. It was a crazy hypothesis based on one theory that all the tombs were truly made to be like one giant tomb, divided from the inside into smaller sided sections and private rooms and burial places. If this were the case, there might be other rooms hidden behind the walls.

The next big surprise came when the workers removed a number of large blocks of stone from the rear walls of Psusennes I's Tomb, to find a tomb of the military commander of Egypt's army in the days of Psusennes, General "*Winjebpauendjedet.*" He was very close to the king and one of his leading advisers so it was no wonder he was buried right behind his master's tomb. Many of this new tomb's funeral accessories were also discovered and are now all on display in the Cairo Museum in the Tanis jewelry room.

Today's visitors to the site, in the very northern part of Egypt's Delta, can visit the Royal Tombs of Tanis from the 21st and 22nd dynasties, all built of large and medium sized blocks of limestone and appearing as one large underground structure, half sunken in the earth. But, when one sees them up close, they show themselves to be different compartments and smaller tombs that were combined. To enter the tombs now, one has to get down on knees to be able to slip through the narrow short entrance. Inside, it is very small and the large coffins occupy almost all the space. One can barely walk around the coffins to see the poorly decorated walls, but the royal names are clearly written in their cartouches on the walls. Eventually, the Cairo Museum's discovered treasures of Tanis remain the second most beautiful royal jewels from Ancient Egypt after Tutankhamun's collection.

Before leaving this chapter, it is important to note that the unearthing of the Royal Tombs of Tanis was the greatest discovery of the 1930s, and with the spread of the Second World War, Egypt found itself obliged to support England. Egypt then remained under the British mandate. The 1936 Treaty of Independence had not yet been executed, but Egypt determinedly aspired to freedom after the war.

Because of WW II, all archeological missions in Egypt stopped, and all digging permission and teams were suspended for nearly ten years. In the meantime, domestic, political and social strife in Egypt was increasing to the point of eruption. The war was over and yet, independence had not been achieved. On the contrary, the results of the war and its aftermath were not good for Egypt nor for the Middle East.

In the next chapter, we will learn about the crisis in Egypt and surrounding countries and seek to understand the connection to the next accidental discovery that occurred in Egypt in 1947.

CHAPTER 14

Nag Hammadi Manuscripts

THE BATTLE OF EL ALAMEIN Desert signaled a decisive victory for the allies in the Second World War. Because of this battle, the war had become a tangible turmoil and the scale tipped in favor of the allies. England and its allies were now surely gaining steady momentum toward victory. Egypt, as one of its subsidiary allies, came out of the war with much hope for independence and modernity, but instead Egypt was afflicted by a suspicious delay in the implementation of the Treaty of 1936 as England refused to leave Egypt or their major military base in the Suez Canal area. The news that continued to trickle in from Palestine about the atrocities between the Jewish settlers and local population was not promising either since Palestine was also under the British mandate.

In such a charged atmosphere filled with dark clouds heralding heavy political storms, Egypt, along with the entire region, was on the brink of war, and the near horizon foreshadowed the very hard times that were about to begin.

In 1945, Taha Hussein (one of the greatest figureheads in Egypt at the time, and a leading literary figure, intellectual, critic, and thinker) was appointed Minister of Education in the newly formed government. Taha Hussein was born in Middle Egypt in the province of El Mynia and was educated in Egypt and France where he earned his PhD in Arabic literature. He came from one of the poorest villages in Middle and Upper Egypt where historic poverty had existed for several millennia. The neglected and ignored villages in the south of Egypt, ironically, contributed beautifully to Egypt's modern cultural development through the works of many pioneers who came from the south (Refaa El Tahtawi, Abbas El Akkad, and Taha Hussein). These three individuals helped shape the cultural, modern life of Egypt during the later years of the 19th century continuing through most of the 20th century.

In addition, Middle and Upper Egypt also generously gifted some of the greatest pharaohs' best-kept treasures, monuments and artifacts from the Coptic Christian period and the later Islamic era. Egypt's modern museums bear witness to the merit and graciousness of Upper Egypt. I argue that Upper Egypt, a region that deserves to be viewed differently after decades of neglect and ignorance, can solve most of Egypt's current economic challenges if we can only determine the best way to utilize its resources and qualities.

Every so often, Upper Egypt still presents us with great treasures and incredible finds. Our next story occurred in a small village in the deep south of Egypt. Accidently, a couple of poor, uneducated farmers discovered one of the most important written materials in the history of Christianity, not far from the village of Al Qasr, close to the town of Naga Hammadi, in the state of Qena (north of Luxor some 110 km.).

Two brothers were searching for sabakh, a natural, salty, soft, summer soil used to fertilize fields. It was normally deposited at the edge of cultivated areas and in the desert after the flooding season, the waters of the Nile having receded leaving a thick blanket of the soft soil on the ground, delivered to the fields annually. This rich soil of Africa was important to all farmers, and before the planting season, it was essential to spread the organic, natural fertilizer. At the edge of the desert behind their village, the brothers found a large pottery jar (one meter high) buried beneath the surface of the soil. They picked it up and saw it was perfectly sealed with bituminous linen. They were confused. What to do? Smash the jar and perhaps win the hidden treasure, or smash the jar and set free the evil spirit of the captured genie?

Historical Background

To understand the importance of the find of the Naga Hammadi books, we should go back to the people who really wrote them, some 19 centuries ago. In the very early days of Christianity, there was a group of people called Gnostics living in the Eastern Mediterranean region. They belonged to a large community who followed the Gnostic spirituality. This religious, philosophical movement's name stems from the Greek word *gnosis* meaning knowledge. The Christian Gnostic community originated in the first century after Christ and continued to exist, through various developments, until the fifth century AD. However, with the decisive victory of the new Christian religion over most forms of ancient religions and practices, many thinkers at the time considered the Gnostic movement a moderate view of religion. It explained the modern philosophical teachings of platonic thought with its material interpretations of life and the teachings of Christ and its spiritual view of life.

Gnostic groups see themselves as the true Christian believers. They firmly believe in God and his existence from the beginning of creation, but God's existence can only be acknowledged through knowledge and awareness, the principal core of the Gnostic esoteric teachings. From their perspective, it is a much deeper and higher set of teachings than the classical teachings of the church. It is the fate of the Gnostic person to know God through his secret teachings, teachings that explain inspirations, revelations and the true origin of the universe. Gnosticism explains that human life began with original sin, and the principal element in life as evil is thought to be the principal motive of human nature. Therefore, being a Gnostic with such awareness is the only way to avoid such evil through understanding its shapes, mutations and changes inside us. Gnostics eventually move beyond evil to gain salvation of the soul and reach a oneness with God. Higher Gnostic teachers or saints have a much deeper faith and knowledge of life than most Christians do.

Gnosticism sees the universe and the material world we live in as a completely different matter for God, whom they view as ultimate goodness. This particular notion of the duality, God versus matter, is one of the principal elements in Gnostic thinking. Understanding the fine line between the two concepts is a vital part of the esoteric teachings of Gnosticism.

The Gnostic teachings refer to Jesus Christ as being only human with the spirit of the Son of God incarnate in him during his baptism and disincarnate (departed) when he was crucified. They see Jesus the infant, the child, and later the adult only as a man and not as the Son of God. The true Son of God could not have died on the cross. However, they do believe everything that happened in his life happened to Jesus *the man* and that the divine spirit disengaged from him just before he was tortured and crucified.

Gnosticism as a movement was regarded as secretive, private, philosophical teachings in early Christianity. However, many of its ideas came directly from the Old Testament, and some teachings were derived from Greek philosophy and the discipline of Hermes; still others come from the Persian teachings of Mani. In wonderful and often confusing fashion, all these different teachings were incorporated and blended together to become the Gnostic teachings, one reason that provoked early Christian fathers to deny the Gnostic teachings, books and lectures wherever they were found. Due to these objections, the early Christian fathers saw Gnosticism to be an evil and extreme threat to mainstream Christianity, perhaps the most dangerous among all other philosophical heretical teachings known at the time.

The manuscripts of Nag Hammadi were a collection of lectures and books written in Coptic script as translations from a much older Greek text, lost now. The papyri discovered within the leather-bound folders included some letters. Two of them were precisely dated, one 341 AD, and the other 348 AD, giving us a clear picture about the dating of the Gnostic library.

What was discovered in Nag Hammadi was a small library of pure Gnostic texts, astonishing texts, ranging from poems, quasi-philosophical descriptions of the origin of the universe, secret gospels to myths, mystical practices, teachings and even texts on magic. They were likely collected by one of the Gnostic Christian monks in Upper Egypt, who may have lived in the place where the texts were found, near El Tarif Mountain. Above the discovery location on the mountain, there were a number of tombs cut into the rock dating back to the 6th Dynasty of Ancient Egypt (2300 BC–2200 BC). The tombs had been reused many times for burials during later pharaonic periods, the Graeco–Roman era of Egypt and early Christianity. On their walls, we find many scenes depicting early saints and images with Coptic crosses and texts from the Bible written in Coptic script. This confirms that the mountain was a well-known cemetery in the early Coptic period and that the monastic movement in Upper Egypt in this region was very popular and active on both sides of the Nile. The area was known in early Christianity as Chenoboskia, and many scholars think it was here that Father Bakhomious started his famous monastic order. The Bakhomious monastic movement (community monasticism versus the solitary monasticism established earlier by St. Paul and St. Anthony, also in Egypt) spread from this place throughout Upper Egypt, and in its early years, its monks were closely tied to the Gnostic teachings common in the area. They peacefully collected the teachings and books within their monasteries until the remarkable year 367 AD, when the Egyptian Christian patriarch, Father Athanasius, issued his famous historic church edict banning all unauthorized gospels related to the Christian faith and all teachings that could be seen as heretical, and therefore considered absolute blasphemy. Naturally, the Gnostic books, gospels and teachings were at the top of the banned list, so it made perfect sense that all bishops of monasteries in Egypt took action against the Gnostic teachings and books wherever they were found.

Father Theodor, the bishop of Bakhomious monasteries in Upper Egypt at the time of the declaration, translated the church edict from Greek to Coptic and distributed it officially to all the small churches and monasteries in the south, presenting it as church law to protect the faith from the spreading Gnostic ideas between the monks. In light of such a scenario, we may imagine one of the Gnostic priests in the area of Jebel El Tarif collected all his Gnostic texts (a small personal library) and decided to bury all of them, in order to cover up his crime. It was a perfect plan of action considering the unusual ideas and philosophical teachings contained in the texts. Hence, the library would have to wait for almost 1,500 years to be unearthed in 1945—accidently.

Discovery Story

May 7, 1945, was just another workday for Ali El Samman. He picked up his rifle and left his mud brick house in his village, Al Qasr, Nag Hammadi, Qena state, north of the city of Luxor. He was a night guard watching over the fields and the irrigation machines, water pumping gear and generators. It was a beautiful night and the air was fresh and cool when Ali El Samman heard a strange commotion near the hut where he was stationed in the middle of the field. In the dark, someone was trying to steal the irrigation machine. It was pitch black and impossible to see the man's face to recognize the thief. So, he shot the man who dropped dead at once.

The single gunshot was the spark that ignited a vicious feudal fight between two families. The murdered man was from a nearby village called Homret Dom, situated directly below Jebel El Tarif at the edge of the western desert. The village was the home of the powerful and large Arabian tribe of Hawara. Therefore, revenge was imminent and the following day witnessed the murder of Ali El Samman, the guard. Now it became a classic revenge story of Upper Egyptian villages, and Ali El Samman's family had to avenge their father. The male children of Ali El Samman were seven and one of them must retaliate for their father. It was only a matter of time.

In December 1945, Muhammad and Khalifa El Samman, two of the seven sons, left the family home at El Qasr to collect sabakh, the natural soft fertilizer that had to be spread on the fields annually. The two brothers took their camels and headed to Jebel El Tarif. They chose a large boulder and Muhammad decided to smash it with his mattock and collect the natural salt fertilizer that they hoped existed beneath it. They were bewildered with what they found under the ground beneath where the boulder had been sitting. It was a large pottery jar, almost one meter high, which looked very old from its rustic colors and style. The two brothers were excited but confused. What should they do with it? Khalifa, the older brother, was a skeptical, superstitious person and was reluctant to smash the jar to see what was inside. He thought it might hold a jinni, but Muhammad was a young, vigorous and brave person. His mind was lured by the notion that ancient treasures and gold coins might be inside.

Muhammad held his mattock and smashed the pottery jar. He and his brother found neither treasure nor did they set the jinni free. Instead, they found papyri wrapped inside old, leather covers that comprised many books with many pages. They appeared to be useless. "Let's go home and give it all to our mother," Khalifa said. "She might use it to kindle the fire of her mud oven inside our house." Um Ahmed, their mother, used some of the papers, but they did not burn well, and she dumped the books in the corner of the house, ready to throw them all away.

A few weeks later, a person named Ahmed, son of Ismail Hussein, the person accused of killing Ali El Samman, was walking by the edge of the village, Al Qasr, and selling molasses to village people from a large pottery pot he carried on his shoulder. He was tired, having walked his route selling all day, so he rested under an acacia tree not far from the El Samman house. The village people knew the person and his family, and they immediately informed the El Samman family about the stranger and identified him as son of the man who had killed their father a few months before. It was the perfect moment for the seven brothers of El Samman to take revenge for their murdered father. They attacked the man and killed him quickly. They cut him into pieces, pulled his heart out savagely and ate it raw as a sign of revenge. Now their father could rest in peace.

The seven brothers returned home to celebrate with their mother, knowing the police would arrive at any moment, search the house and possibly take into custody one or two of the brothers to investigate the crime. In the meantime, the whole village had witnessed the savage crime but no one would provide witness against them because everyone in the village of Al Qasr hated the Hawara tribe. At this point, Muhammad was ready for interrogation and a period of detention, but without witnesses, the police could not prove him or any of his brothers guilty. Muhammad looked for the sack of the old books and papyri he and Khalifa had found a few weeks earlier. Their mother had dumped it in the corner of the room near the oven, and Muhammad said to his brothers, "If the police come to search the house, they must not find these old books." Possession of them would be considered yet another crime, so he decided to give a portion of the books to each of his village neighbors until he and his brothers could decide later what should be done with them. He understood from some village people that his newly found books had a connection with old Christian texts and Coptic origin. They were indeed extremely old.

The only person in the village whom he trusted was the village Christian priest Basiliyus Abd Al Masih. His house would never be searched and the priest was certainly not involved in any feudal revenge. Muhammad asked the priest to keep some of the books with him. The priest was married to a woman whose brother, a history teacher named Raghib Andrawes, worked at one of the Christian missionary schools in Upper Egypt belonging to the Coptic Church of Egypt.

The teacher, Raghib Andrawes, later made a courtesy visit to his sister. During his stay, the priest, Basiliyus, showed him some of the books he was keeping for the El Samman family. (One was the third book of the collection, later classified by scientists as Codex III.) Raghib understood at once the importance and age of such materials from both a religious and historic perspective. He insisted on taking the books, or at least some of them, to further examine the texts and the materials. Under pressure, Father Basiliyus acquiesced and gave all of the books to him. Raghib took the books to Cairo where he met with a friend and family member, Dr. George Sobhy, a well-known physician in the city who had great interest in Old Coptic texts and language structure. Being a well-educated Coptic man, he was the right choice to have started with. When Dr. Sobhy examined the books and read some of the texts, he immediately realized their intrinsic value and knew that such unique materials needed to be in a museum, not in villagers' hands. Dr. Sobhy contacted the Department of Antiquities and reported the existence of the books. They confiscated the materials with the promise to pay a generous reward of 300 Egyptian pounds to Raghib Andrawes. It was a huge amount of money at the time for most Egyptians. They also convinced the teacher to donate 50 pounds from the reward to help the Coptic Museum that would hold the precious collection he had just donated.

On October 4, 1946, the first collection of Nag Hammadi materials was deposited in the Coptic Museum and the hunt to collect the rest of the books and papyri began. Recovering the texts was a national security mission for the Coptic Museum's manager, Dr. Togo Mina, who was determined to find and collect all the Nag Hammadi books so they could be preserved in his Coptic Museum collection.

In the meantime, the mother of the El Samman brothers had never liked the old papers and books her sons had found and brought home. She thought it to be evil material, and she wanted to get rid of all of it. She cut out several pages, used some to kindle the oven fire, gave away some to neighbors and may have sold a few others to local antique dealers (most of what she sold or damaged or burned was from Book XII).

Tracing even one of the pieces she had given away or sold for a few pounds proved to require interesting detective work. Someone in the village of Al Qasr, Nashid Besada, had bought one of the books from the mother and had given it to a well-known jeweler in the city of Nag Hammadi, who happened to work (illegally) as a part-time middle man for antique dealers. He sold the book (to an unknown buyer) and split the profit with Nashid Besada.

Another story from the village recalls that the mother sold one of the books to another merchant in town of Nag Hammadi, the merchant Fekry Gebrail.

He then sold it in Cairo for a very high price and used the money to establish the famous merchandise stores in Cairo called the Nag Hammadi Stores. The merchant, when investigated later, denied ownership of the famous chain of stores, but he was unable to deny his connection with the books.

However, the true maverick of the Nag Hammadi stories is Bahieg, a man from the village El Qasr, who somehow had managed to acquire the greatest number of books and papyrus materials from the mother or the brothers. Bahieg made a deal with a well-known antique dealer in the town of Nag Hammadi, Zaki Basta. Bahieg and Basta took the books to Cairo and marketed them for the highest possible price. They started with Mansour Shops and the art gallery at Cairo's old Shepheard Hotel, but in the end, they sold the books to the famous stores of Phokion J. Tano, a famous antique dealer from Cyprus who lived in Cairo, who paid them generously after they promised to bring the rest of the books that remained in the village.

By now, the manuscripts had attracted the attention of high officials in the Egyptian government, Taha Hussein, Minister of Culture and Education; and Togo Mina, Manager of the Coptic Museum. Togo Mina, with the honest and constant support of Taha Hussein, and under circumstances of high drama, worked tirelessly to acquire the missing books. The government of Egypt bought one book and confiscated ten and a half others from Cairo's illegal antique traders and from tourist shops, depositing them in the Coptic Museum in Cairo. The government ended up paying a settlement of 400 Egyptian pounds to the Tano stores for other books, for a total of 12 books. All were archived at the Coptic Museum.

That said, a large part of Codex XIII, which contained five extraordinary texts, was smuggled out of Egypt by the famous Belgian antique dealer Albert Eid, who offered it for sale in New York in 1949. This did not work.

Professor Gilles Quispel, distinguished historian of religion at Utrecht University in Holland, was excited with the news that was spreading about the groundbreaking contents of Codex XIII, now on the market and looking for a buyer, through Albert Eid's wife, Simone. He urged the rich Jung Foundation in Zurich to purchase the codex from Simone; the deal took place in Brussels on May 10, 1952. It then became known as the Jung Codex.

After examining the precious material, Gilles Quispel discovered that a few pages from the book were missing. He came to Egypt in the spring of 1955 to search for the missing pages in the Coptic Museum. He was authorized to take some photographs of the collection in the museum. He took the photos and remained at his hotel in Cairo to examine them. Gilles Quispel jumped out of his seat when he began reading the opening verse of the codex, which says:

"These are the secret words, which the living Jesus spoke, and which the twin Judas Thomas, wrote down."

It is important to note that the library discovered by the two El Samman brothers consisted of 13 leather-bound books (codices) with papyrus papers hand sewn together between their covers. The book covers were reinforced from inside with several old papyrus papers, which later were identified as older letters and personal texts. As mentioned, 12 of the books were mostly intact and are held in the Coptic Museum, but the separate book, called Codex XIII (the Jung Codex, not in Egypt now) was missing several pages. Eight pages of it were discovered as part of Codex VI. No one knows precisely why or how these pages became attached to a different book.

The books cover a wide range of subjects, 52 different topics in total. Forty subjects were new and only 12 subjects were found to be repeated in all of the books. The texts, written over a long period of time, reflected various distinctive styles of many writers who came from various geographical locations in Egypt, distinguished by their handwriting styles. There were not only Gnostic teachings; some of the books included other secular material such as parts from *The Republic* by Plato.

The total number of leaves is 1,240 pages; all are held in the Coptic Museum in Cairo except for the pages purchased by Jung Foundation in Zurich in 1952. Zurich is in possession of most of Codex XIII, but the first pages of this book remain in the Coptic Museum. We have a complete list of all the subjects and classifications of Nag Hammadi manuscripts made by the scholar J. M. Robinson, who dedicated much of the last 30 years of his life to studying the manuscripts starting in 1967.

Analysis of the Nag Hammadi manuscripts sheds light on early forms of Christian teachings and shows that early Christianity was far more diverse than we have thought. The manuscripts have given us a number of new gospels, like the Gospel of Thomas, and, most scholars date them to an earlier period than the common gospels.

The Nag Hammadi books have created a prickly debate about the history of early Christianity and the philosophical aspects of early Christian doctrine, especially in Egypt. Most profoundly, the new material and astounding texts essentially present a different view of Jesus, his disciples and the originality and dating of the various gospels that have been discovered so far.

In a visit to the magnificent Coptic Museum in Old Cairo, on the second floor in Room 16, one can see two or three of the original leather covers of the books, and just two pages from the large collection on display. The pages shown are the most important papers of all: the opening page, and first chapter of the newly discovered Gospel of Thomas.

This important discovery in Nag Hammadi took place during very difficult times for Egypt. On the horizon were political crises, crises that would storm, not only Egypt, but also throughout the entire Middle East. In May 1947, the news of splitting Palestine between the Jewish settlers and the Palestinians had accelerated domestic deterioration to the extent that Egypt decided to go to war.

Is there any connection between the rapid political crackdown in Egypt and the Middle East and exploring Ancient Egypt?

Let us find out.

CHAPTER 15

Solar Boat

———

1947 WAS AN OMINOUS YEAR for Egypt and the countries throughout the Middle East. It was a year of conflicts, atrocities and devastating wars between Arabs and Jews after the United Nations Security Council's Declaration 338

that divided historic Palestine between Jewish settlers and the Palestinian people. King Farouk of Egypt found himself in an abysmal political situation and was forced to send the Egyptian army to Palestine to fight the Jewish settlers in an act that was a rejection of the UN Security Council resolution. This was the first of many wars Egypt fought for the sake of Palestinian rights.

In 1948, the humiliating defeat of all the organized Arab armies in Palestine by a few thousand Jewish settlers and kibbutz farmers put further responsibility onto Egypt. As the largest and oldest Arab country, Egypt needed to understand how it happened that a few thousand settlers were able to defeat large, supposedly organized armies, and how this catastrophe could be prevented in the future. The consequences of the 1948 war and the subsequent declaration of the State of Israel, which occupied a large part of historic Palestine, discredited King Farouk as the leader of all joint Arab armies. The joint Arab armies were disgraced in their defeat, which had lost Palestine forever.

Sadness, desperation and disbelief were the overwhelming feelings among Egyptians in the 1950s, brought about by the loss of Palestine in only a few weeks. The atmosphere in Egypt was that of rising discontent and resentment against the King of Egypt. People pointed fingers at the corrupt king and the decay of his rule. Moreover, a flood of scandals emanating from inside Farouk's royal residences touched derisively on the behavior of his mother and other female members of his family. With shocking graphic details about the erotic adventures of Farouk's mother with multiple lovers inside the royal courts, pressure rose and inundated King Farouk. Such news became a typical hot topic in all the scandal and rumor magazines throughout Europe and America. The defeated army and its young officers were despondent about Farouk's failure while the common Egyptian felt utter rage at losing Palestine and the establishment of the State of Israel.

Like a powerful river current, events propelled Egypt toward a military revolution against Farouk. In July 1952, a group of nationalistic, mostly young, military officers calling themselves the Free Officers, formed under the leadership of a high-ranking officer, General Mohamed Naguib. Their goal since the 1948 catastrophe was to change the dreadful situation in Egypt and remove the king as soon as possible. July 23, 1952 was the day the army moved against the king, surrounding his palace in Cairo and forcing him into exile within a few hours. It happened quickly, and the army now controlled Egypt and drove the show. Egyptians nationwide showed enthusiastic support for the military move that was seen as an inevitable and necessary move against domestic and regional decay. The era began with the Presidency of General Naguib who was soon followed by the charismatic young Officer Nasser who ruled until 1970. Following him were two other officers, President Sadat and President Mubarak. Up until the 2011 Revolution, a long period of successive military leaders established their rule based on the principles of the 1952 Revolution and its legitimacy.

Certainly, the movement and the changes were met with great support from the vast majority of Egyptians. For farmers and laborers in particular, Nasser became a hero and a savior, and little by little, Nasser became the star of Egypt, his fame and legacy reaching throughout Arab countries, African countries and generally, poor world nations that aspired to liberate themselves from colonialism. Nasser became a hero symbol.

During the early years of his presidency, Nasser faced many challenges, and the exploding growth of Egypt's population was foremost. Other related challenges, such as generating enough energy and providing fresh drinking water to every village in the country, were all strongly linked to the River Nile. The immediate obligation became to build more dams to better manage resources. The Aswan High Dam project in the south soon became a national project and dream, equal in importance to the other dream from 1936 of liberation and independence from British occupation.

1954 was the year of Egyptian-American negotiations to finance the building of the dam south of Aswan. Talks were running smoothly in a promising atmosphere until discussions between the two countries took certain political turns and began to deteriorate. The United States government at the time was seeking to extract a major political price from Nasser to facilitate the financial plans of the Aswan High Dam through the World Bank. The price was… to sign a Peace Agreement with Israel.

Nasser was not ready for such a move. Negotiations fell apart and eventually ceased, and the consequences were rapid and shocking as Nasser, later in 1956, declared the nationalization of the Suez Canal and took it back from the private Suez Canal Company. The Suez Canal was to be run by Egyptians (the Suez Canal Company had been established in the 1850s with a lease contract of 99 years, to end in 1969). Nasser's move pushed the situation to the edge of war, and a crackdown was instituted to regain the canal by force. The 1956 Suez Crisis ensued, and English, French and, unexpectedly, Israeli armies attacked Egypt. This war was another turning point for Egypt and for Egyptology, too.

The war took place at the height of the Egyptian nationalistic movement, a movement that overshadowed all aspects of Egyptian life with obvious patriotic notions against "western colonialism, imperialism and capitalism" (as Nasser's regime had always described it).

As a result, the Department of Antiquities fired most of the foreign employees and forced others to submit their resignations whether they were in technical fieldwork or administrative positions. Gradually, Egyptian employees were taking control of the archeological digs in the country. The Antiquities Department followed in the footsteps of Nasser's revolution by Egyptianzing all aspects of archeological work in Egypt. The fruit of their new plans was the discovery of the Solar Boat beneath the Great Pyramid of Khufu in Giza during the summer of 1954. The discovery is a true reflection of the spirit of Nasser's days in witnessing the first big archeological discovery in Egypt since the revolution.

However, before we move on and tell the story of this wonderful accidental discovery, I would like to present a brief introduction on the religious importance of funeral boats in Ancient Egypt and the reasons that Old Kingdom pharaohs were keen on burying such boats, now called solar boats, next to their pyramids.

The Religious Significance of the Funeral Boats in Ancient Egypt

Egyptian geography and environment played a vital role in shaping Ancient Egypt's belief system and way of life along the Nile, since the very beginning of early settlement in the valley. Constant observation and contemplation of the surroundings were the usual everyday practice. The simple Egyptian dweller in the valley became accustomed to the clear sky year-round and the eternal flow of the Nile River with its annual flooding every summer. It was likely the principal challenge for the mind of the individual to find a logical and convenient explanation for all natural phenomena that occurred seasonally and annually. Eventually, the Ancient Egyptian mind worked to cast all interpretations into religious and mythical codes that provided a level of comfort in facing the biggest questions of life and death.

The Ancient Egyptians carefully watched the sun travelling every day across the clear, blue sky. From the moment it rose to its setting on the western horizon, powerful and shining in the morning, weak and waning toward twilight, they imagined the sun taking different shapes every hour as it traveled from the east to west. They even imagined the blue sky above Egypt as a huge, celestial, blue water lake, surrounding earth, through which the deities navigated every day using divine boats.

This mythical interpretation harmonized with the Ancient Egyptians' vision on life after death because, when they imagined the afterlife, they wished to join the gods on the divine boats traveling daily across the sky in their daytime journey from east to west, and in their nighttime journey from west back to east again. The resurrection of the Sun God every morning also represented the resurrection of the deceased every morning, young, healthy and powerful like the sun. For this reason, the early Egyptians took with them a number of small funeral boats made of wood or papyrus reeds into their own tombs.

In the 1st Dynasty tombs at Saqqara and Abydos, we can see that archaic period pharaohs took funeral boats, buried beside their tombs ready to use for their afterlife journey following the sun. We have found the boat pits, but unfortunately have not found the actual boats themselves.

However, from the 4th Dynasty, we have found a unique, royal funeral boat in incredibly well preserved condition. The story of this great find is our subject for this chapter.

Discovery Story

Mohamed Zaki Nour, a brilliant Egyptian archeologist, was born in Cairo in 1905 and graduated from Cairo University (then known as University of Fouad

I) in 1935 with a degree from the High Institute of Egyptian Archeology. After graduation, he joined Egypt's Department of Antiquities and served as Inspector in El Fayoum, Beni Swif and various other sites in the Delta. Next, he moved to work in the Luxor area until 1945, when he moved once again to work in the great necropolis of the Giza Plateau.

Dr. Mostafa Amer, Head of Egypt's Department of Antiquities at the time, appointed Mohamed Zaki Nour to be head of archeologists in Giza. He launched several digging missions in Giza, Abu Sir and Heliopolis.

In the winter of 1954, Mohamed Zaki was leading a small excavation team on the south side of the Great Pyramid of Khufu. The goal was only to remove the huge amount of debris and sand remaining from earlier excavation missions in the Giza area (the earliest big mission in Giza had been the Boston-Harvard expedition in the 1920s under the leadership of George Reisner). Because of the huge amount of debris requiring excavation, the Antiquities Department sent two teams to work at the Great Pyramid. The main team was Mohamed Zaki's team (the Department of Antiquities team), and the second was led by Dr. Abdel Moniem Abu Bakr (Cairo University's School of Archeology team).

While the two teams were working, they received news about a probable visit from King Abdel Aziz of Saudi Arabia to Egypt, his first visit to Egypt since the 1952 Revolution, and he wanted to visit the pyramid area in the afternoon.

The Antiquities Department and its Giza office began to prepare for this important visit, concentrating their efforts on the Great Pyramid area, which King Abdel Aziz intended to visit. In order to speed the work, the two missions were merged to allow faster excavation and preparation of the area south of the Great Pyramid. Mohamed Zaki enthusiastically removed the debris with the help of two young architects, Salah Osman and Kamal El Malakh.

Kamal El Malakh, born in Upper Egypt in the city of Assyut in 1920, graduated from Cairo University with a degree in architecture, and later a degree in Egyptian archeology. He worked for a short time as a teacher in a fine art school and later as an architectural restoration specialist for the Antiquities Department in Giza and in Philae in Aswan. He was a multi-talented person who developed a skill in photography and worked as a part-time reporter for *Al Akhbar Daily News* and for the *New York Times'* Cairo office.

On April 24, 1954, Mohamed Zaki, and his team (Kamal El Malakh and Garas Yanni, the chief of workers and masons) removed a large amount of sand from the south side of the Great Pyramid of Khufu and unearthed a small part of a large limestone block. After clearing the area around it, they measured it as 2.35 meters by 1.50 meters. However, to everyone's surprise, they also found several other blocks of similar stone monoliths arranged next to one another with a small stone in the eastern corner as a stopper piece. The stones clearly delineated the shape of an underground pit and certainly indicated something was buried underneath it. Excitedly, Mohamed Zaki and his team found the name of Pharaoh "*Jedefre*," Khufu's son and successor, written on the blocks in 18 places. The team became convinced that the blocks of stone certainly hid something important underneath them. Later, it revealed itself to be a large, wooden, funeral boat for King Khufu that had been buried and dedicated to him by his son "*Jedefre*."

Mohamed Zaki decided not to remove any stone blocks to reveal what was below until the team had completely finished removing all sand and debris from the south side of Khufu's pyramid. This way they could work in a clean space and provide maximum protection for the boat when it was revealed. It took them until May 25, 1954 to clear all the sand. On that same day, something happened that forced the unlucky archeologist, Mohamed Zaki, to leave the site and rush to one of the Cairo hospitals. A sudden illness and severe fever had attacked his little daughter, Wafaa. He spent all night with her at the hospital but sadly, she died. Bereft on the following day, he did not go to work as usual in Giza, instead going to bury his daughter.

In the meantime, excavation work in Giza was proceeding under the leadership of Rayes Garas Yanni, who managed to clear the area around all the blocks to prepare for removal of the small stopper rock at the corner of the pit. But who was going to do so?

Rayes Garas Yanni searched everywhere for Mohamed Zaki. Not aware of the death of his daughter, he searched for any other higher employee in the Antiquities Department who was part of the team. He found Kamal El

Malakh having an afternoon lunch in central Cairo at the well-known restaurant Excelsior, with a famous journalist, Anis Mansour (who later became one of the famous writers and journalists in Egypt in the 1960s, 1970s and 1980s). Rayes Garas Yanni pleaded for help. He had completed his work and removed all the sand. The blocks were cleaned and ready to be removed. The news of the discovery had traveled through the village close to the pyramids, and everyone was talking about the treasures that might be under the rocks. He urged Kamal El Malakh to rush with him to Giza to start the final step without delay, hoping still to hear from the manager, Mohamed Zaki.

They both went to Giza where the workers were waiting and on that May 26th afternoon, one of the workers, Mohamed Abdel Aal, broke open the small cornerstone and made a small hole through the blocks so everyone could see what lay beneath. In the large pit, they easily recognized the large oar of a huge boat, and then they found the actual boat, dismantled and buried inside the pit, several layers on top of each other.

Kamal El Malakh, as a part-time reporter, immediately reported the discovery of Khufu's boat that night to the *New York Times* and claimed he was the discoverer. The following day, the news about the Giza discovery had shaken Egypt, and all the Egyptian news agencies knew about it from the *New York Times*. The news coming from the press fell like an earthquake on the Department of Antiquities. There was rage and resentment against Kamal El Malakh who attributed the discovery only to himself and ignored the true hero and archeologist Mohamed Zaki, most especially on the day he was burying his daughter. It was a travesty and many managers resigned in objection and dismay. (Dr. Abdel Monem Abu Bakr tendered his resignation as an objection to Kamal El Malakh's report.)

That said, the work of removing all stone blocks resumed, and 48 blocks were removed to reveal beneath them a total of 1,224 pieces of the dismantled wooden boat without a single metal pin.

The boat was made of the famous cedar wood of Lebanon. It was 42 meters long with two decks. The lower deck, the heart of the ship, was used for sailors, service and storage purposes, and the upper deck was reserved for the pharaoh's private double cabins and chapels at the stern of the boat.

Toward the bow, they found the small canopy of the boat captain (the bridge). In addition, ten large rowing oars were discovered, and two smaller oars to be used at the rear as steering oars. Close examination of the boat and its wood clearly indicated that it had actually been used before, perhaps during the pharaoh's life for his journeys on the Nile.

The biggest challenge faced by the archeologists and restorers then became how to rebuild the boat, knowing that it depended only on ropes, sailor's knots, and no metal pins. There was also another big problem: 30% of the wood discovered in the pit was in such an advanced state of disrepair, it was unrecoverable, having disintegrated with age. For this technical mission, the Antiquities Department called for the professional wood restorer, Ahmed Yousef (the same expert who helped George Reisner in the 1920s' restoration of the contents of Queen Hetebheres tomb in Giza–Chapter 13), who then became the chief restoration specialist for the Antiquities Department. His task was to restore all damaged parts and rebuild the boat.

Ahmed Yousef's impressive success story of how he managed to rebuild the boat is another chapter in the history of modern restoration of ancient relics, full of exciting details and wonderful dedication. Ahmed Yousef started with a small model of the real ship at a 1:10 scale. He began a meticulous examination of all of the wooden pieces, restoring each one separately and replacing the severely disintegrated ones with new pieces of exact replication. To better understand how the different pieces of wood fit and joined so tightly, he invited Upper Egyptian experts in wooden boat building who had been using similar construction techniques for years, and they knew better than anyone else how to rebuild such wooden parts. In just over 20 years, Ahmed Yousef was able to assemble the wooden boat and restore all the damaged parts. Finally, in 1982, a special museum was established at the site exclusively for the assembled Solar Boat. The museum is in the shape of a boat, and visitors now enter the museum to see the boat hanging in the middle of an atrium three stories high. Visitors can walk around the boat and view it from three different levels. The Solar Boat Museum actually spoils the ancient panoramic view of the pyramids area, but it is perhaps the only way to preserve such an old relic and be able to see it presented in such as interesting and intriguing way.

Finally, it is important to know about the recent exploration and fieldwork being conducted in Giza by the University of Waseda, Tokyo, Japan. A Japanese team has scanned the entire Giza Plateau with a satellite remote-sensing program to explore the remains of buildings and monuments that are still covered within sands. The new project started in 1987 and continues today. One of the greatest discoveries made with this new technology has been to precisely locate another solar boat still under large blocks of limestone, located just south of where the first discovered boat was found in 1954. The team was excited and eager to start removing all the blocks that cover the underground burial pit of the second boat of Khufu, but the Egyptian government decided to postpone the work for several seasons. However, the Giza desert ants had a different point of view.

A large number of desert ants and other insects penetrated the underground pit where the wooden pieces of the second boat were hidden. The ants entered the boat pit through the small hole that had been drilled by the explorers to insert a tiny camera to photograph the wooden parts of the buried boat. When the project was suspended, they sealed the hole but not with strong enough material to block the ants. They ate the seal and the ancient boat wood became the main menu for the desert insects, eating happily and enthusiastically. The University of Waseda rushed to the authorities pleading for permission to intervene and save the boat before it was too late. The rescue mission began by fumigating the underground pit before removing the large stone blocks and recovering the wooden parts to restore them.

Today's visitors to Giza see a large tent just south of the existing Solar Boat Museum. Inside the tent, they began removing and clearing the sand and debris above the large limestone blocks that sit atop the second funeral boat of Khufu. The project is a joint collaboration between the University of Waseda, under the leadership of Sakuji Yoshimura, Director of Egyptology at Waseda University, and Egypt's Antiquities Department. The protocol of the five-year mission is to completely remove all blocks and begin restoring the wooden pieces. This new discovery began in April 2009. The Japanese professor and Zahi Hawass witnessed the removal of 41 large limestone blocks, each an average of 16 tons, which were sitting side by side on top of the boat pit.

There were numerous interesting surprises for everyone, such as a cartouche of King Khufu. In this location, no cartouche was found for his son and successor Jedefre, confirming to Zahi Hawass that Khufu had actually buried this boat during his own reign, without any royal designation to his son who was still only a crown prince.

Zahi Hawass has also mentioned on his personal website that the new boat, after all necessary restoration and preservation, will be displayed in a specially designed hall in the Grand Egyptian Museum under construction not far from the pyramids of Giza. Everyone in Egypt is anxiously awaiting this museum's opening in two or three more years. In the meantime, the restoration of the new boat of Khufu still carries on, and another large original solar boat from the days of Khufu, circa 2600 BC is about to be celebrated.

Before we leave this chapter, it is important to note that the discovery of the Khufu's funeral boat in 1954 was a very special find for a new Egypt. After the 1952 Revolution and the new era of nationalistic Egyptian rulers, the discovery heralded a new spirit in the field of Egyptology and archeological work. The 1952 Revolution propelled young Egyptian archeologists toward leading all field excavations in Egypt and avoiding foreign missions whenever possible. That opened the door for a large number of Egyptian archeologists to gain experience and fame in the 1950s and 1960s, the years when Egyptian politics directly overshadowed archeological planning and missions on the ground.

CHAPTER 16

Sunken Monuments of Alexandria

IN THE SUMMER OF 1956, President Gamal Abdel Nasser announced the nationalization of the Suez Canal ending the Suez Canal Company's 99-year canal lease contract that had been in effect since its foundation in the late 1850s. Nasser established a new Egyptian-owned Suez Canal Authority to be responsible for managing the strategic water corridor using only Egyptian pilot guides and employees. This declaration from Egypt was essentially a declaration of war against England and France because it was primarily English and French investors and institutions who owned the Suez Canal Company's stocks. The nationalization by Egypt was considered an act of hostility and an illegal step of escalation. Therefore, the two countries, with help from Israel, decided to wage war on Egypt to regain control of the critical canal. Nor was the United States government exempt from this complicated situation.

American-Egyptian negotiations to finance Egypt's new high dam in Upper Egypt were progressing smoothly and the situation seemed promising between the two sides. The project and all related plans were ready to be signed between the two countries and the World Bank when suddenly the American–Egyptian political relationship became muddled, complicated by Middle East politics. The American administration, represented by Secretary of State Dulles, saw an opportunity in this interdependent atmosphere to urge Nasser to publicly accept the new State of Israel, acknowledge its existence and perhaps go even further to hammer out a peace agreement between the two countries.

Unfortunately, but not surprisingly, negotiations melted down. Nasser went his own way and nationalized the canal to provide financing to his dam. The Aswan High Dam eventually became a hot political issue after the United States government refused the finance plans, withdrew from the project and urged the World Bank to pull out, too, thereby pushing Nasser into a corner and putting him under tremendous pressure. The consequences were catastrophic for all.

Late in 1956, the circumstances that surrounded the Suez crisis and the results of Nasser's crackdown were important not only to Egypt but also arguably to the whole world. Nasser shone as a hero and a leader not only to poor Egyptians, but also to many other nations in the world. Nasser became an iconic figure of resistance and struggle against the colonial powers of England and France, especially as the attacking armies of England, France and Israel were unable to break Egypt's resistance during the four-month war. On another front, the United States government realized their mistake in letting Egypt, and Nasser, elude them by walking away from their proposed financing for the Aswan High Dam project. President Eisenhower intervened to stop the war against Egypt and forced the armies of England, France and Israel to back off, but it was perhaps too late.

On the domestic side, the Suez War had finally freed Egypt from its 74 years of British occupation and protection. At the same time, Nasser's image in the Western media was becoming tarnished, and he was likened to the typical third world, nationalistic, military leader who gained his publicity through propaganda and anti-West public speeches.

After the war, Nasser changed his international political compass and steered his country toward Eastern Europe and the Soviet Union, embracing socialist ideas and practices. During this period, Egypt became one of the many important elements at the start of the Cold War between East and West (capitalism vs. socialism), even though the country officially was a founding member of the international, neutral states movements.

The time was right for the Egyptian-Russian honeymoon that began with the building of the Aswan High Dam with Russian engineering and technology. In little time, the two countries became strategic allies with extensive military collaboration and armed training. During this time, Russians were seen everywhere throughout Egypt: in construction, in military training, armed forces and naturally in culture. The cultural relationship between Egypt and the Eastern European countries that were associated with the Russians became very warm and very strong. These cultural ties were most remarkable in the field of Egyptology.

During the 1960s, a number of Eastern European archeological institutes opened large branches in Cairo and became actively involved in large excavation missions throughout Egypt. Numerous discoveries occurred, made by the new faces in the field of discovering Ancient Egypt. In the early 1960s, Egypt was destined once again to encounter another major discovery that certainly would reveal a significant part of its hidden secrets. It took place in the ancient, lost city of Alexandria that had been the cultural capital of the civilized world from the 3rd century BC until the 3rd century AD, Alexandria of the great Ptolemys, the magical Cleopatra and the invincible Caesars.

By sweet way of accident, the sunken monuments of the ancient, lost city of Alexandria were re-explored as an urban diver from the city, in one of his free dives in the Old Bay area, met a great stone Sphinx sitting on the sea floor, having waited for nearly 2,000 years to be spotted and retrieved. This led to the great discovery of the underwater remains of the Lighthouse of Alexandria, one of the Seven Wonders of the Ancient World. This is one of the best stories about Egyptian discoveries, but before we enjoy the story behind the interesting discovery, I would like to present a short historic background about the city of Alexandria and its foundation by Alexander the Great.

The History of Ancient Alexandria

Alexander the Great conquered Egypt in 331 BC and took the country from the Persians after a long period of civil strife. Thus began a new era in Alexandria's long history of experiencing new foreign rulers who came from the Aegean Sea islands. Little by little, Hellenistic culture spread in Egypt, and the Greek language became common in major Egyptian cities and markets because the Ptolemys made it the official language of culture, state correspondence and administration. Naturally, the capital city of Alexandria became not only the political center of Egypt, but it also became the cultural center of the entire Mediterranean world. Altogether, its design, buildings and spirit were pure Greek in flavor.

The twilight of Ancient Egyptian culture had begun. Except for the old, major cult centers in Upper Egypt and the Delta, around the large temples of the great gods and goddesses of Egypt, with ancient rituals, festivals and feasts reserved only for the temples and their surroundings, the glory of Ancient Egypt had become a local legacy, remaining solely in people's reverential accounts. In other words, Egypt, land of the pharaohs, was in total cultural decline.

The glory of the new capital Alexandria was growing quickly with its superb geographic location with the Mediterranean Sea on one side and close to the western branch of the Nile on the other side. It was located far enough from the mouth of the Nile such that the city's river trade and navigation was not blocked by the huge silt deposits left annually on its banks as the swollen river made its summertime trip to the sea. The new city was conveniently connected with Egypt via the Nile and the Mediterranean world through the two new harbors that had been built for all sizes of ships. The eastern harbor was reserved for the royal ship fleet. It faced the palaces and royal residences of the Ptolemys and other landmarks of the ancient city, and the western harbor was the main commercial port and economic center of activity with a large part of Alexandria's population living nearby. The city attracted many people from the Nile Valley and from all Mediterranean nations and many religions. The spirit of a town with a metropolitan multi-ethnic culture was born in Alexandria in its early years.

Against odds, the city of Alexandria remained the capital of Egypt for nearly 1,000 years, from approximately 300 BC to 700 AD. However, as soon as the new Arab invaders and rulers of Egypt conquered the land, they built a new capital on the Nile to be the center of political and economic activities, especially trade with Arabia, their homeland. The new capital, Al Fustat (located just south of modern-day Cairo, in the Old Cairo neighborhood), seized the light and power from the old capital Alexandria. Rapid deterioration ensued in Alexandria as people abandoned the city and the harbor became empty and neglected (in the early years of ruling Egypt, Arabs had no interest in trade with the Mediterranean countries, something that changed in later centuries). For several centuries, Alexandria was abandoned and its palaces and major buildings fell to ruin. The sea rose several times and swallowed many of the city's ancient coastal buildings. (Due to several recorded earthquakes, the seawater rose at least 15 meters above the old town.) Moreover, in the 17th, 18th and 19th centuries, new buildings were constructed on top of what had previously been the ancient city's landmarks, and this completely changed the glorious image of royal Alexandria. It was described only in somber stories in travelers' accounts.

We have been lucky enough to find a few parts of the ancient city here and there in the southwestern part of the modern city, the area where the ancient necropolis existed. This area is situated beyond the crowded areas of the growing modern town and far from the new commercial harbors and fishing wharfs. Most of the tombs in the ancient necropolis had been cut into the rocks and in underground catacombs, allowing them to be hidden for centuries (Chapter 8).

The other part of the ancient city that has survived is what the sea covered centuries ago, which became sunken relics and monuments lying on the ocean floor. Not far from the city's beaches, the waves, the sometimes strong currents, and underwater moving sands all contributed to the preservation of these dilapidated relics and remains of the ancient stone buildings. Most important, the original lighthouse that remains underwater acts as a living witness to one of the greatest buildings that once stood on earth. Many surprises of ancient Alexandria awaited explorers from a new era to reveal the city's secrets and sunken glory.

Discovering the Sunken City—Early Beginning

In 1910, the city of Alexandria enjoyed a wonderful construction and architectural renaissance that had begun in the days of Khedive Ismail in the 1860s. Rapid development attracted a large number of people to the city from all over Egypt for work and living, due particularly to the exceptional rise of maritime activities in Alexandria ports. The ports needed a lot of new working platforms, piers and service buildings to serve an increasing number of larger ships. The Egyptian government hired the French engineer Gaston Jondet to start expanding the old Port of Alexandria to the west, converting it into a large modern port. While surveying the west side of the town and its waterfront areas to determine the size and the length of the new port, Gaston Jondet noticed huge blocks of differing stone types beneath the water not far from the beach of Ras El Teen. Just a few kilometers away, west of the old city harbor, he examined the stones and made a surprising discovery. The stones were the remains of an ancient wall that had been built 400 meters away from the harbor to protect it from waves and currents. The stone wall was at least 15 meters thick and its length was at least 2,000 meters. Jondet also discovered another similar underwater sea wall in front of the old harbor and its bay in the area now called El Anfoshi. These walls were crescent shaped with only one gate to permit ships to enter or depart the bay.

These two old underwater stone walls, discovered in the 1860s, were the early signs of ancient Alexandria's ports that dated back several centuries.

Later, in the 1930s, when Captain Cool, a Royal British Air Force pilot, was flying low above the Bay of Abu Kir, one of the far eastern bays of Alexandria, he noticed an underwater stone structure that took the shape of a horseshoe. The pilot was fascinated with this sunken mystery and talked about it to everyone he met in Alexandria.

Luckily, Prince Omar Tusson, a prince from Muhammad Ali Pasha's line, heard Captain Cool's stories and showed particular interest in exploring such ancient underwater sunken mysteries. He was well known in Egypt for his passion for culture, exploration, enlightenment and his generous contributions to education. Preserving old relics and monuments was his remarkable gift. Additionally, he was fascinated with geography and hand-drawn maps of Egypt and its western desert.

Prince Omar Tusson owned a large farm not far from the Bay of Abu Kir. Being so close to the bay during his summer vacation inspired him to further explore the underwater sunken structure that Captain Cool had so enthusiastically talked about. The prince hired a number of open water divers and launched his own private expedition on May 5, 1933. That day, the divers collected a beautiful marble head, identified later as Alexander the Great. The head was discovered on a five-meter marble pillar about 450 meters from the beach, just east of an old military fort in the area known as the "sand fort."

Prince Omar's efforts of did not stop at this point. He continued exploring the sunken buildings and stone walls in the Bay of Abu Kir with several more finds recorded from his expedition:

- The remains of an ancient temple with 12 large pillars discovered 240 meters from the shore
- An ancient harbor with a large marina and pier
- Seven large piers, sunken in the bay, their length between 100 meters and 250 meters with average width 4 to 6 meters, height about one meter, all made of hard stones except one built of red bricks
- Several huge broken granite and marble pillars scattered on the sea floor, remaining from old religious or palatial structures near where the head of Alexander the Great was found

Prince Omar Tusson linked all the archeological finds he recorded in the waters of Abu Kir Bay with the ancient site of Menutis, which had been described several times by Roman-era, Alexandrian historians and travelers' books. He also was able to link his discoveries to another ancient site of Heraklion. In 1934, the prince published his finds and research with maps and illustrations of all the locations under water.

From the 1960s up to present day, Alexandria's sunken treasures experienced another round of research and exploration through the efforts of Kamal Hussain Abul Saadat, 1933–1984. The Alexandrian hero, born in the same year as Prince Omar, made his discoveries in the far eastern bays. The destiny of Kamal, the urban diver and treasure hunter, was to meet face-to-face with the statues and sphinxes that had decorated the ancient lighthouse some 2,000 years ago, not far from the Citadel of Qaitbay in the central part of Alexandria, where the ancient lighthouse originally stood.

Discovery Story

In the summer of 1961, Kamal Abul Saadat was diving near the Citadel of Qaitbay, close to the bay and harbor (now close to the central part of the modern city). Abul Saadat was a young and enthusiastic diver, known in the city as the best free diver in town. That day, the current was not too strong and the clarity of the water was exceptional, which helped him observe pieces of stones in large quantities and various sizes. His experience in the offshore waters of Alexandria let him know the stones might be the remains of sunken, ancient buildings. The place he discovered first was known on the old maps as Ras Lochias. Abul Saadat reported his observations to the antiquities authorities of Alexandria, and they called the Egyptian Marine Force for help.

Under Kamal's guidance, a small expedition to explore and retrieve some of the sunken treasures was made in June 1961. This first, official mission to explore and collect the remains of sunken treasures of ancient Alexandria began with the discovery of a life-sized granite stone statue of an unknown male figure. Five months later, Abul Saadat and the same team found another statue identified as the Goddess *"Isis faria"* in the deep water close to the

Citadel of Qaitbay. It was a colossal seven meters long in red granite, the largest piece to be collected from the area, perhaps promising that more colossal statues might be found in the future beneath the water.

Abul Saadat's individual dives and underwater surveys also yielded small objects that he collected and delivered to the Antiquities Department: a large number of pottery amphora dating back to the Hellenistic period and several gold coins from the Byzantium period. All were deposited and displayed later in the Graeco-Roman Museum of Alexandria.

The efforts and contributions of Kamal Abul Saadat did not stop here. In 1964, he drew an accurate map of the shores of Alexandria from the eastern Abu Kir to the western Ras El Teen with exacting detail on all the sunken treasures, landmarks and monuments. His map is still a respectable source for all underwater archeology and excavation in Alexandria. His map included many important archeological locations that needed to be researched, such as:

- The original floor of the ancient lighthouse foundations beneath the standing Citadel of Qaitbay
- The remains of the ancient eastern harbor Antirudos and its piers
- The remains of the ancient stone walls of the El Shatbi area, with the harbor and funeral remains and coffins, all under water

In 1965, Kamal Abul Saadat made another detailed map of the Bay of Abu Kir. The map was used in a great expedition to explore in the bay for Napoleon Bonaparte's sunken ships. He was hired as a professional diver to lead the team, and they successfully located three of the seven ships, L'Orient, Airtimes and La Serior. He suggested two other possible locations where Napoleon's ships might be located on his new 1965 maps. He included all the locations surveyed by Prince Omar Tusson, which made his maps a reliable reference for all underwater locations throughout Alexandria. He also worked as a diver guide to the UNESCO expedition, under the leadership of Hanor Frost, to explore the sunken monuments of Alexandria in 1968, near the Citadel of Qaitbay.

His efforts and observations did not stop with guiding important missions to the underwater sites. He explored on his own from time to time, and he discovered other great things, such as the underwater ancient stone walls in front of the beaches of El Mamoura, the remains of a 250-meter long pier and several small marinas next to it. He also dived near the island of Nelson, not far from Abu Kir Bay where he found a 300-meter long underwater pier.

For more than 20 years, Kamal Abul Saadat dedicated much of his life and experience to exploring the sunken treasures of his beloved town, offering his notes, maps and service to anyone who asked. He was more than willing to reveal the sunken glory of Alexandria, but it was Abul Saadat's sad twist of fate to dive with a group of sponge collectors in the deep waters off Alexandria's shores when he died under mysterious circumstances in the summer of 1984. Rumors suggest it was possibly his free diving and knowledge of Napoleon's sunken ships that may have been the reason why he "had to disappear." Egypt suddenly lost one of its dedicated and pioneering sons who had not yet fulfilled his dreams of mapping and scientifically recording all the underwater sites along the coast of Alexandria (some 50 km. long). Using his limited personal resources to finance some of his research dives and then generously offering everything he knew to the authorities, by many standards, he was the hero of this great find. Only after his suspicious death did the world start to hear about the old Alexandrian sunken treasures.

In 1983, a joint venture of Egyptian Marines and French Marines with Egypt's Department of Antiquities collaborated to find the sunken ships of Napoleon Bonaparte's fleet in Abu Kir Bay. They found the flagship L'Orient some 11 meters under water, about 8 km. from the shores of Abu Kir Bay. The famous French marine scientist Jacques Daumas led this scientific mission, and the work in the bay continued for two seasons. They located three other ships wrecked on the sea floor that had been previously located and noted by Abul Saadat. The team was meant to work again in 1985. However, work was postponed by the sudden and mysterious death of Jacques Daumas in Morocco a few weeks before he was to again lead the mission in Alexandria. In addition, very suspiciously, all his maps and documents regarding the underwater research in Alexandria and other places in the world disappeared.

Another team came in 1986 to search the waters west of Alexandria where the French troops had first landed, and at least one ship was thought to have been sunk during the great invasion and landing. They found the wreckage of the ship La Patriate four meters deep near the beach at El Agami. In 1995 and 1996, the area around the Citadel of Qaitbay was researched and examined yet again, and the remains of Old Alexandria's royal quarters were revealed along with parts of royal buildings still underwater. This research and these discoveries prompted the Egyptian government to finally establish a new Department of Underwater Archeology in 1996.

The news of the discoveries in the waters around the Citadel of Qaitbay in Old Alexandria Bay attracted many institutes and professionals related to underwater archeology and exploration, especially from France, a leading country in this field. Right away, we witnessed two French teams start working in Alexandria under the leadership of two well-known and highly acclaimed Frenchmen in the field.

The first team was under the leadership of Frank Goddio, a person of notoriety with much argument surrounding his qualifications, experience and his true goals for such research. He was a Frenchman born in Morocco, a professional urban diver and adventurer. His specialty was exploring ancient relics sunken underwater, and he had surveyed many waters and explored several ancient treasures worldwide. He came to Alexandria to find his new treasure.

Frank Goddio and his team discovered an important ancient city from the Greek period in Egypt, Heraklion, which was very close to Abu Kir Bay. No doubt, he used Abul Saadat's old maps that indicated the sunken ancient city. Goddio furthered his explorations and examined the area around the Citadel of Qaitbay. He photographed and recorded all of the pieces still lying on the sea floor. Goddio's finds and photographs were the main topic of several international exhibitions on the sunken treasures of Alexandria, the most important and famous one in Berlin in 2007; 2.7 million visitors visited the exhibit. The second most famous exhibit, in Los Angeles in 2010, focused on Queen Cleopatra and Goddio's underwater finds made during his ten years of research. This very clever diver Goddio brought to the forefront the legacy of the true hero Kamal Abul Sadaat, his years of work and eventually his sad, mysterious end.

The other French team came with Jean Yves Empereur, who was born in France 1956. He graduated from the well-known Sorbonne in Paris with a degree in archeology. He had made extensive explorations in Greece at some of its underwater sites. The classical professor came to Alexandria in the late 1980s and began his research focusing on the ancient site of the Pharos Lighthouse. His concentration centered mainly on the underwater monuments near the Citadel of Qaitbay and their connection to the dilapidated Pharos Lighthouse, one of the Seven Wonders of the Ancient World. Through his meticulous academic research, he was able to precisely locate approximately 500 stone objects originally from the ancient lighthouse building. Pharos had finally been rediscovered. Empereur published several books and papers about his finds, mainly in French and some in English.

This great scholar contributed beautifully to the modern archeology of Alexandria in later years when he led several teams to rescue old mosaic artworks that had been accidently discovered during the construction of modern-day buildings in the older neighborhoods of the city. He worked with teams of art historians and restorers to move all the found artifacts to the labs for restoration and conservation before sending them to the new Alexandria National Museum. Among the artifacts were the famous mosaic of Medusa, an Alexandrian portrait of a woman and a large number of Greek and Roman coins.

I met and worked closely with Empereur between 2003 and 2010. Generously, he would lecture tourist groups I led in Alexandria. We discussed the city and its hidden treasures that lured explorers and treasure hunters. Amusing and informative, his lectures on Alexandria and his work in the city were always beguiling regardless of the number of times I attended.

Finally, and before we leave this chapter, I would like to return to the hero Abul Saadat, the man whose efforts and dedication to Alexandria opened the door to explore its sunken treasures. Many people and missions have followed his maps and have been guided by his observations, especially in the area near the Citadel of Qaitbay and the old bay, the ancient site of the Pharos

Lighthouse and the royal quarters of Alexandria's Greek and Roman times. Recently, with the aid of Abul Saadat's hand-drawn maps, about 35 stone objects were collected from the water. Some of the granite pieces were of large size and weight. They were the remains of colossal statues that decorated the gates of the Pharos Lighthouse. A small obelisk from the 19th Dynasty, during the time of Pharaoh Seti I, was found broken into several pieces. It has been restored and displayed with other pieces in the open-air museum and garden of the Roman Amphitheatre in the heart of modern Alexandria. The statues date to the Ptolemaic period's kings and queens.

It is interesting to know that thousands of other pieces still lie on the sea floor, waiting to be collected, cleaned and displayed. It is a very complicated issue to dive and lift such heavy blocks of stone considering the strong currents in the area combined with unclear waters most of the year. Consequently, many of the stone objects that weigh less than six tons are constantly shifting and moving underwater, so their precise locations cannot be discerned with GPS systems.

It looks like the pursuit of exploring and discovering the secrets of Alexandria with its legendary treasures shall continue. The lost tombs of the Ptolemys, the lost Tomb of Cleopatra, the mysterious Tomb of Alexander the Great, the site of the lost ancient library and more are still under water. The city's sunken treasures will continue to entice professionals and treasure hunters. The dream is big and worth the effort. Every archeologist in the world dreams of finding the tomb of the most famous queen in the history of humankind, Cleopatra. That dream caused Zahi Hawass to launch an excavation mission at a site southwest of the modern town Tabosiris Magna where a large, Ptolemaic-period cemetery was found near a large religious building still standing today. Excavation in the area is ongoing and we are waiting for a new discovery.

CHAPTER 17

Colossus of Queen Meritamun

No voice rises above the voice of war; this was the most famous slogan in Egypt during the period from the 1960s through the early 1970s, an era known for vicious confrontations and constant atrocities with Israel. The Sinai Desert was the theater of military operations and the battleground of war. At that time, most people in Egypt saw it as a war for pride and national dignity. It was a time when Egyptian society was saturated with anti-Western socialist political thoughts against capitalism and western imperialism, ideas that still echoed from the Suez Crisis of 1956.

As for the field of Egyptology and archeology in Egypt, research and exploration was running very slowly during these heavy war years. Because of the charged political situation, we began to see new foreign missions that had never before worked in Egyptian archeology, missions from Poland, Czechoslovakia, Russia and Hungary. This was also the era of the sudden disappearance of American, English and French missions. In a way, we can say profoundly the archeological movement and activities became a true reflection of the general political compass of the Egyptian state. So, when state politics leaned toward the East (socialism), Antiquities Department permissions leaned, too, toward the eastern European countries. This was very clear in Egypt during the 1960s and the beginning of the 1970s.

(The only exception of this general frame was the international campaign to save the Nubian temples and heritage that was orchestrated by UNESCO. Fifty-two countries collaborated and generously contributed to the salvage rescue campaign despite political disputes with Egypt at the time. USA, France, Germany and all western European countries took a major part in the expedition that lasted from 1960 to 1980.)

The Sinai Peninsula had its share of hot political and military events. In wartime, the Israeli army periodically occupied Sinai, and all its well-known archeological sites scattered on its vast desert were under Israeli control: the Temple of Serabit El Khadem, El Farma forts, the Citadel of Salah El Din and El Maghara Mountain. All these sites and many more that dated back to the historic times of Ancient Egypt were carefully excavated by several Israeli archeologists, some of them military generals such as Moshe Dayan. All the finds and artifacts were collected and taken to Israeli museums and universities between 1967 and 1982. When the Peace Agreement between Egypt and Israel was signed in 1979 at Camp David, the Israeli occupation of Sinai came to an end and the two countries agreed on the return of all Egyptian relics and artifacts that had been collected from Sinai's archeological sites during the occupation years.

The return of all artifacts from Sinai was, and still is, a painful matter, since Egyptian archeologists had to check all the suspected sites and prepare detailed lists with all missing objects to ask for their return through official channels on both sides, Egypt and Israel.

At this time, Egypt has managed to retrieve many artifacts from Sinai and is still negotiating and waiting for the rest of the collection.

The fact is that in this period Egypt never saw a major discovery at any site in the country. For more than ten years, we had no news of any discoveries in Egypt, perhaps because the country's efforts were focused on the war and Egypt's economy had been diverted mainly toward the war effort of buying weapons and military supplies. Gradually, money for archeological surveys and conservation of monuments disappeared despite there being an obvious, desperate need for protection and restoration. However, taking care of Egyptian antiquities requires time and money, and this was clearly a time when the country sadly did not have either time or money.

The principal event in Egypt toward the end of this period was the signing of the Peace Agreement with Israel in 1979. This very brave peace initiative and the visit by President Sadat to Jerusalem in 1977 precipitated the opening of the door for peace negotiations and the subsequent signing of the agreement. This peace opened a new horizon in Egypt, culturally and politically. Shortly after the peace, Egypt's political relationships with the United States and western European countries began anew, and with this change, the field of archeological research and excavations changed accordingly. Egypt again welcomed the large western universities, museums and research institutes that still held a genuine interest in Egyptology and could support excavations on the ground with people and finances.

With this agreement and the peace that came with it, the atmosphere in Egypt was joyfully ready to resume activities once again. Fresh enthusiasm to dig again at archeological excavation sites was shown by several major universities and museums in Europe and North America. By the beginning of the 1980s, Egypt was no longer affiliated with eastern European missions and no longer coordinating with Russian politics. Egypt took rapid steps toward Western culture (as it had before 1952), and became more affiliated with United States politics and economic aid. President Sadat became close to American President Jimmy Carter and was awarded the Nobel Prize for his efforts to achieve peace in the troubled Middle East. Large American and western European tourist groups returned to Egypt in great numbers, bringing with them a new appreciation for an all-new Egypt.

The efforts of Egyptizing the field of archeology and exploration of Egypt had reached a high level during the 1950s, 1960s and 1970s. A new generation of young, well-trained Egyptian archeologists now took charge of the Antiquities Department and were leading all the digs on the ground. The story of this chapter focuses on the fruits of such changes and the spirit of the new age. We can name this period "discovering and exploring Egypt by Egyptians." It is a true story and all the heroes are young, motivated Egyptian archeologists who were educated and trained in the 1960s and by the 1980s were ready to lead all missions and write a new chapter in the book of exploration of Ancient Egypt. The story of the next discovery happened in the first year of President Mubarak's tenure in 1981.

It is the story of the discovery of the largest queen statue from Ancient Egypt.

Akhmim

Akhmim is one of the important towns in Upper Egypt, acclaimed for its great history dating back to the earliest times of Pharaonic Egypt, and for the vital roles the ancient city played from the days of the pharaohs up to the early Christian period. The city sits now on the eastern bank of the Nile facing the capital city, Sohag, the main town in the region that carries the same name, north of Luxor about 200 km. Akhmim is one of the busiest and has the highest population density of all of Upper Egypt's towns. In 1907, the population of Akhmim was already counted as 23,795 (it is difficult now to know the population of the large modern town precisely).

Ancient Akhmim was recorded many times in Ancient Egypt by the name "*ipw*" and in other records "*wnmnw*" which means the place of God Min. During the El Amarna period, it was recorded in texts as "*hntmnw*," which means the town that belongs to Min. In the later years of the Graeco-Roman period, the town was mentioned in the texts as "*khemmis*" and "*khemmw.*" The more recent names have basically been derived from the ancient names of the town.

Surviving Ancient Egyptian geographical texts mention Akhmim as the capital of the Ninth Nome (province) in Upper Egypt, which stretched for almost 70 km. and carried the same name of the ancient town, from the area of El Shiekh Hareedi north to the town Maragha south. During the Graeco-Roman period, the local God Min united with another god called Pan. For this reason, the province during Roman times became known as Panopolis and its capital was "*xemmes.*" In Coptic texts, the town was written as "*xemn-nymin,*" which is the origin of the modern Arabic name of the town Akhmim.

Nothing has been found in the actual ruins of the Akhmim archeological sites that date back to the New Kingdom period, but there were a few indications of its importance at an earlier time, confirmed by the discovery of a large number of tombs and burial graves from the Old and Middle Kingdom eras. Specifically, the great necropolis of Hawawish, just north of Akhmim, and the necropolis of Salamoni which lay northwest of the modern town, revealed a number of tombs dating back to the Graeco-Roman period.

During the New Kingdom, ancient Akhmim played a vital role in shaping the royal dynasty lineage during the mid-18th Dynasty, when Yuya and Tuya, an important priest and priestess who originally came from Akhmim, became the two most famous nobles in all of Egypt. Their daughter Tyi married (in very suspicious circumstances) the young Pharaoh Amunhotep III and ruled for more than 38 years as Queen of Egypt and Mother of Akhenaten, the revolutionary king who would rule after his father. This was the period when Queen Tyi's parents, Yuya and Tuya, were upgraded to carry honorary titles as Father and Mother to Pharaoh of Egypt.

In the time of Tyi, Akhmim witnessed the building of a number of temples and religious centers dedicated to the local deities. Records show that King Aye, the High Priest of Amun at Karnak Temple, who briefly ruled Egypt after the suspicious death of the boy king Tutankhamen, started building a temple dedicated to the local God Min, Lord of Akhmim and Master of

Fertility on the eastern hills of the ancient town. The New Kingdom temple was a cave cut into the eastern hills overlooking Akhmim. In addition, large stone blocks were found during excavations in the heart of the modern town that included Amarna art that probably dated back to the times of Akhenaten, a clue that may indicate that temples existed in the area from his era.

During the 19th Dynasty, Ramses II built, or at least completed, a large temple dedicated to the local God Min. Its ruins now are located in the heart of the ancient town, in the area now called El Berba. The ancient temple gate was decorated with two gigantic colossi representing Ramses II. The remains of one of the two statues has been discovered in a recent excavation in Akhmim.

During the era of Ptolemy II, a large temple was built for the local God Min next to Ramses II's Temple. It was completed and enlarged by Ptolemy III. The famous Arabic traveler Ibn Gebier has beautifully described remains of this temple, during his visit to Egypt and its famous monuments. He visited the ruins of Akhmim Temple in 1350 and described its magnificence and glory. After that, locals deconstructed the temple to use its stones for building the modern town.

It is important to know that Min was the God of Fertility and Reproduction and the Master of Time. He was the patron deity of the region and was worshipped mainly in his eastern rock cave above the ancient town. His cult spread around this region and settled in the modern town Qift. The cave at the modern village El Shiekh Hareedi that was built by King Aye from the New Kingdom perhaps represents the mythical cave, home of God Min, Lord of the Eastern Hills and all desert trade roads from the prehistoric times before the pharaohs.

Goddess Repiet-Triphis, always depicted in the shape of a lioness, was the partner and consort of the God Min, and together they ruled this region of Upper Egypt. A temple, known as the Moon Temple, was constructed for her just north of the modern town.

Min, Triphis and Kolanthes formed the holy triad of deities worshipped in ancient Akhmim. Notably, God Kolanthes/Qarenga in Ancient Egypt was considered a form and local manifestation of God Horus, son of Goddess Isis and God Osiris, always depicted as a child or falcon. His name in Egyptian means the great child. He was the infant in the holy triad of Akhmim whose cult was popular in Upper Egypt until the 2nd century BC.

When we return to the Arabic traveler Ibn Gebier who described the temple of the three gods of ancient Akhmim, we learn that the huge temple had an imposing façade and gate, followed by a large open court that led to a large hall of pillars with about 40 columns in four rows. Recent excavation in the temple ruins revealed stone blocks with the name of the Roman Emperor Trajan carved on them and thus serves to prove that some restoration had been made to the temple during Roman times.

The Damascene traveler Ibn Gebier also mentioned another temple nearby the main one. He wrote about its large pylon that was decorated with military scenes and battle pictures. Scholars think this description fits and qualifies perfectly for the entrance and gates of Ramses II's Temple that was decorated with several colossi of the pharaoh and his queen. The fantastic Colossus of Queen Meritamun that was discovered in the area in 1981 was probably one of these colossi.

The discovery of this wonderful statue in the ruins of Akhmim is the story of this chapter. It all happened by accident in the summer of 1981.

Discovery Story

In 1981, because of the great population growth in the modern city of Akhmim, the city decided to build more schools on land central to the town. One school's purpose was to be dedicated to Islamic religious studies under Egypt's famous Azhar Authority. The selected land was northwest of the city's heart, and it was adjacent to the newly begun Islamic cemetery, on what had been government land. The land and its mysterious mounds clearly suggested ancient history with indications of certain archeological ruins dating back to Ancient Egyptian times. No one really had paid attention to such an insignificant location, a place with dirt, mud and a large number of palm trees growing on it, a place where locals had decided to build a new cemetery made necessary by the constant population increase in town.

Once the local government began to survey the area where the new Islamic school was to be built, the news spread through town and reached the Chief Inspector of Archeology in the area, Zein Zaki Deyab (who went on to become the Manager of Antiquities in Middle Egypt in 2007). He went to the proposed school area but rejected the new project, claiming the historical importance of the site and asserting the need for protection of the land for archeological excavation. He supervised the digging at the site to determine if the foundation work of the new school would reveal something about the ancient site. His suspicions turned out to be correct, and many artifacts were collected during the first few days of foundation work. Because the operation was fruitful, he insisted on recording and preserving everything that came out of this new construction site. He wrote to Egypt's Antiquities Department requesting a support team of archeologists to follow up with excavation and preservation of the site and its relics. (There is a debate about the nature of the new building. Some records mention it was the new post office and others affirm it was the Azhar religious school, but my story is dependent on Zein Zaki himself, who made the discovery later.)

Archeologist Yehia El Masri was the team leader of the new excavations at Akhmim. On September 28th, the team was removing the debris for the new school. Zein Zaki noticed a smooth white limestone block that was likely part of something much larger but still hidden under the ground. The team excavated all around the stone to find it was the base of a giant colossus statue of a pharaoh. The team continued excavating the area to find, a few days later, part of another colossus statue for a queen or a goddess. The large statue lay on its side and the huge head was decorated with a crown adorned with cobras (a royal protection symbol), with remains of its original pigment on the head and face. Considered altogether, this implied a wonderful royal object of high quality and status. The workers continued to explore the rest of the huge sunken statue of the queen/goddess. After a few more days of work, the team determined the figure of the statue was Queen Meritamun, daughter of Ramses II, who ruled Egypt next to her father for some time after the death of the great Queen Nefertari. Both royal names of the king and the queen had been carved on the back of the statue.

Not until 1984 was the statue completely revealed and cleaned, a wonderful large limestone statue with a trace of its original colors still well preserved on the face and crowns. The statue's legs were missing, showing it to be 11 meters high, but had it had its original missing legs, it would have been as tall as 14 meters, the largest existing queen statue ever discovered in Egypt (possibly the largest stone statue ever made for a queen from Ancient Egypt). The head of the queen was adorned with two large feather plumes thought to have been covered with gold. The place where the feathers should have been fixed into the head still exists and is a witness to how it was used in ancient time. The statue would have stood at the temple of her own father, Ramses II, holding the lotus flower in her left hand as a sign of nobility and royalty.

The excavators continued to explore the area and found the remains of an ancient gate, probably the one used to enter the Ramses II Temple, and a number of statues that dated back to the Graeco-Roman period, one of which was a statue to Goddess Isis in the form of Venus. Later, the government decided to prepare an area to house all the discovered finds and statues, the open-air Museum of Akhmim. The statue of Meritamun was restored in 1988 by the famous Egyptian artist Mahmoud Mabrouk and subsequently moved to its new site at the open-air museum in 1991 by Ali Kassab, the chief of the workers from Luxor.

The great discovery of the Queen Meritamun statue in Akhmim compelled Yehia El Masri and his team to spend seven seasons excavating the ruins of ancient Akhmim, and they made other interesting discoveries over the seasons, such as:

- The basalt statue of the High Priest of Min, *Minnakht* (According to research published by Zahi Hawass later in the journal *Kmt*, the high priest was probably related to prince *Nakhtmin*, the son of King Aye, from the end of the 18th Dynasty.)
- A limestone statue of Pharaoh Amunhotep III, thought to be reused in the days of Ramses II
- Many broken pillars and pottery shards

The news of these new great discoveries in Akhmim encouraged the locals to dig enthusiastically, before it was too late, around the ancient mound close to the protected archeological site. Very close to the Islamic cemetery, an unknown family discovered a large stone head thought to be part of another royal colossus statue. The family tried to hide their secret discovery but concealment is almost impossible in a country like Egypt and a town like Akhmim. The news of the secret discovery soon spread in the village. The authorities rushed to the area and antiquities officials took over the site where the head of the statue had been found.

This happened in 2002, when Zahi Hawass was the Secretary General of the Antiquities Department. He visited the site and instructed a team comprised of his best archeologists to survey the site and explore its ruins. The mission was very sensitive in nature because the site was inside the local village's Islamic cemetery, and in order to fully excavate the area, the cemetery needed to be relocated. It was difficult to convince the locals of the new plans. Zahi Hawass managed to arrange for a special fund from the government to compensate the locals and build a new cemetery for them. It was a complicated matter that required intervention from the Ministry of Culture, then headed by Farouk Hosni, and former President Mubarak himself, with pressure put on them by Zahi Hawass to save the site.

Zahi selected one of his best assistants in Giza, the young archeologist Mansour Boriak, to lead the new mission in Akhmim in 2002 (Mansour was Zahi's right-hand man in most of his excavations in Giza). Other young archeologists also joined the mission, Mohsen Reyad, Gamal Abdel Nasser, Zein Al Abdeen Ali and for scientific documentation, Noha Abdel Hafez.

To determine the true connection between the statue and ancient Temple of God Min, the team excavated the surroundings of the stone head recently discovered by the local family (later proven to be a part of a large Colossus of Ramses II). (Zahi Hawass published an article in the journal *Kmt*, stating that excavation had begun with a layer of debris that dated back to the Islamic period. Beneath it, only one meter deep, they found another layer of debris that dated back to the Coptic period, and deeper yet, the team found Ancient Egyptian deposits. The work concluded with the discovery of a huge stone base of the Ramses II Colossus that weighed about 70 tons. It was indeed the base of the statue where the huge head had been discovered years before.)

The team also discovered the floor of the original Temple of Min, but excavation work was interrupted because of the city's heavy traffic. Road closure was necessary to continue uncovering the rest of the Temple of Min that lay beneath the modern town of Akhmim. The work was suspended until the Islamic cemetery had been completely relocated and proper compensation to locals had been settled (only 5 million Egyptian pounds were allocated to this huge project in the Egyptian Antiquities Department budget).

The discovery of the Meritamun Colossus and other large statues of Ramses II is considered the first true big archeological find in Egypt under Mubarak, Egypt's then new president. The beauty and magnitude of the statue marked a new era in rediscovering Ancient Egypt after the long years of war that had suspended all archeological missions in Egypt. This became a new start with new spirit in the archeology field. Finally, the Egyptian government began to show more interest in preserving monuments throughout the country, and permission was granted once again to all types of foreign missions to excavate in Egypt again. As before and during the 1980s, Egypt welcomed foreign archeological teams again, digging and exploring in every corner of Egypt. Excavation, preservation and conservation missions provided excellent training experiences for the young generation of Egyptian archeologists.

Egypt at the time was slowly heading toward stability after the political storm that had arrived with the sudden murder of President Sadat by an Islamic militant group, and the subsequent rise and rule of the new President Mubarak, who had been Vice-President.

Mubarak's biggest goal was to reunite the country once again and to have people embrace his new administration because most people in Egypt at that time were divided regarding Sadat's 1979 Peace Agreement with Israel. Subsequently, there had been political deterioration in most Arab countries. It was Mubarak's main priority to bring Egypt once again to the forefront of the Arab world as leader and as the biggest Arab country, in order to promote the necessity of such a peace agreement for the benefit of Egypt's economy and future. In the 1980s, the winds of change blew, and the Cold War was coming to an end. Egypt was returning to the Arab world. They had negotiated the Peace Agreement with Israel and had developed a special political and military relationship with the United States as a result of America's mediation in that agreement. However, this Egyptian-American relationship certainly came with a price, a price the Egyptian society was forced to pay. Serious challenges had to be faced as the price for peace.

But that is another story.

CHAPTER 18

Luxor Temple Cache

THE 1980S WERE HARD AND heavy years in Egypt with many challenges on various fronts all at the same time. Politically, Egypt made a major shift in its foreign policy by focusing its relationships mainly on the United States and Western Europe. Egypt gambled, relying solely on the generous and constant financial aid promised by the American government as part of an aid and economic stimulus package designed to encourage Egypt to proceed with the

Peace Agreement plans with Israel. This new strategy propelled Sadat's policy changes, and his successor Mubarak walked the same path.

Regionally, Egypt successfully managed to maintain the Peace Agreement with Israel, thus returning the Sinai Peninsula to Egyptian control. A large number of the artifacts that had been collected in the Sinai Desert archeological sites were eventually returned to Egypt.

On the Arab world front, Egypt scored many goals in a short time, first and foremost convincing most Arab countries of the importance of the Peace Agreement not only for Egypt but for the Palestinians, too, pointing out that this agreement would secure communication channels between the Arabs, the Americans and the Israelis. It was to be a vital, positive element that could help rectify the historic conflict and resolve the Israeli-Arab conflict through peaceful negotiation rather than through war.

Mubarak's challenge was to create a critical political balance between keeping the Peace Agreement on one hand and restoring political and economic relations with all Arab countries on the other hand. At the same time, he also wanted to develop special, strategic, economic and military ties with the United States government. Altogether, it was a fine, tangible achievement for Mubarak and his government through the hard years of the 1980s. We saw the Arab League headquarters returning to Cairo along with foreign and Arab investment pouring into Egypt. The rapid growth in tourism and the movement of Egyptian workers into most Arab countries was considered a positive sign of where the country's economy was heading. It was clear that general conditions of life were improving in Egypt.

Internationally, Egypt began to gradually participate in the world market economy and connect itself with numerous international activities and institutions, particularly in the banking and financial sector. The Peace Agreement and exceptional braveness of President Sadat had clearly given Egypt a positive image worldwide.

At the other end of the spectrum, in Egypt and its surroundings, there was another movement counter to the above-mentioned positive changes. This movement took on an obstructionist role; it was essentially political opposition with an Islamic flavor. This began the rise of what we call "the political

Islam." This religious and political movement viewed the Peace Agreement with Israel and the new political and economic ties with the Western world as a reason to attack the government. Angry voices in Egypt and throughout the Arab world protested against the idea of peace with Israel. This politically motivated and religiously seasoned opposition attracted many people in Egypt: conservative Muslims, radical circles, the uneducated, families of war victims, pan-Arab believers, socialists, communists, anyone with anti-Western sentiment.

Egyptian society began a complicated, social, political and religious tug-of-war. Media was caught up in a power struggle between the state-controlled media on one side and on the other side, religious organizations and institutions that deeply penetrated the villages and poorer areas of the country. The historic poverty of Egypt, especially in Middle and Upper Egypt, was in effect a stage where Islamic charity and educational institutions found a welcoming atmosphere in which to spread their beliefs and radical political insight about the country, its political leadership and the world.

The brutal confrontation between the Egyptian government and various types of Islamic organizations (carrying different names, following different doctrines but always sharing the same goals) had taken Egypt to catastrophic but expected results. When an Islamic organization automatically created its own armed militia wing, which took the responsibility of facing police brutality and wrong practices, it often felt like a war of revenge, with Egyptian society taken as hostage. Political reforms, economic growth and true democracy would have to wait a few more years or decades.

Egyptians had to endure the consequences for three decades: dramatic political and social changes in the 1960s under President Nasser to the great shift in the late 1970s under President Sadat and the confrontation of the 1980s and 1990s under Mubarak.

I am not attempting to explain what happened in Egypt during these difficult years, or even trying to rewrite this period in history. My personal concern is to emphasize the social and political development in Egypt, its relationship to cultural and intellectual movements generally, and explore Ancient Egypt in particular. Personally, I see this situation as a battle within

Egyptian society between the so-called secular state and the political, religious Islamic organization, and this standoff will continue for more decades. It will certainly affect Egypt's modern culture and our view toward our own ancient history and the heritage of the pharaohs. As long as we have continual debate about our own lifestyle, doctrine, cultural principals and foundations, confusion will continue and grow. Egyptian society will pay a heavy price for such cultural distraction until we all answer the big question. What do we want for ourselves? Do we want a country ruled by clergy and radical minds (we know exactly where that can lead)? Or, do we want a police state with constant security paranoia ruled by generals (we also know exactly where that can lead)? Or, will we choose to build a modern, civil and educated system that can accept everyone regardless of religion or political faction, respecting true Egyptian culture, ideology and heritage throughout its long history? This is the conundrum. How can we get to an answer that makes sense?

Amidst these political storms, in the city of Luxor in 1989, one of the biggest and most interesting discoveries in modern Egypt occurred. Ironically, it was found inside one of the most well-known monuments in Egypt, Luxor Temple. Egypt once again had an appointment with good fortune, when accidentally, a large underground cache was discovered in the inner open courtyard of the temple. It happened after the breathtaking opera Aida had been performed in the front of the temple in 1986. The spectacular show used the temple façade and gateway as backdrop to the large stage built in the heart of the ancient site. With the imposing statues of Ramses II and giant obelisks decorating the area, it was a dream for opera lovers.

After Aida, a large conservation and preservation mission started working in the temple to save its foundation from decay due to the continuing rise of the underground water table. It was during this preservation work inside the open courtyard of the Amunhotep III pillars that the unthinkable happened.

However, before I tell the story of this fascinating discovery, I would like to take you back in time to the days of Luxor Temple.

When was it built and why?

Historic Background

When Ancient Egypt's 18th Dynasty rulers successfully expelled the Hyksos, circa 1580 BC, the Asian invaders had been ruling the northern part of Egypt for a long period, according to most scholars, around 140 years. The New Kingdom began in the area of Thebes with a series of nationalistic pharaohs who were actively rebuilding the country, its ancient glory and territorial power by expanding its military presence in all directions. The pharaohs wanted not only to expand the kingdom but also to increase and exploit the country's resources. The victorious pharaohs of the New Kingdom brought Egypt to a high level of strength, stability and growth in many fields never before witnessed.

Thanks to the exceptional efforts of the early 18th Dynasty rulers, who fought bravely beyond the Egyptian desert, they not only secured Egypt's borders against invaders like the Hyksos but also capitalized on their battlefield victories to expand their power and dominion over Egyptian society. They created a ruling system that would last for nearly 400 years. The royal lineage of Thebes had dedicated all their triumphs over enemies to their local, beloved God Amun, who later merged with the old and powerful deity Re to become Amun-re, the famous Lord of Thebes, the ruling city of the pharaohs. The divine god lived in his holy shrines at the Karnak complex.

Amun-re was venerated at the time as Lord of all Egyptian Deities, Master of the Two Lands (Upper and Lower Egypt) and Protector of Egyptian Unity and the Throne. Victorious pharaohs attributed their glory and victory to Amun-re. They fought their enemies under his name; so naturally, they generously offered all their riches and exploits of wars to the Lord of Wars, Amun-re, and his religious institutions, temples and priests.

Large edifices, shrines and golden statues were consecrated to Amun-re along the Nile from far north in the Delta to the deep south of Nubia. Thebes (now Luxor) reserved for itself a major part of the great construction that was spreading widely, and a substantial portion of the spoils of war. Exploits and gifts from foreign lands were being funneled into the great Temple of Amun-re at the Karnak complex (*Wasit* in ancient times). Lands, farms, state barns and endowments were assigned to this powerful religious center. During the 18th

Dynasty, Egypt was very wealthy, and Thebes was the capital, the residence of royal families and their associates, where the most powerful people lived together. Thus, Amun-re and his temple became a symbol of national pride, and business was strong for the many groups of people who could benefit directly from the temple institution.

The ancient city of Wasit/Thebes/Luxor was the capital of the Fourth Nome (province) of Upper Egypt and stretched from the area of Tod in the south to the area of El Medamod in the north, along the eastern side of the Nile. On the western side, the ancient province stretched from the area of Gebalain in the south to the area of El Tarrif in the north.

As early as the Middle Kingdom, the ancient city of Wasit was the largest city of the Nome and served as capital for all of Egypt, united under the powerful pharaohs of the 11th Dynasty circa 2050 BC. Following that, it became a major religious center during the powerful 12th Dynasty. Despite Thebes no longer being the political capital because that had moved again to the north, to "*ithet tawi,*" the local god of the town, Amun, became the focus of every pharaoh's building activities. We began to see chapels, shrines and temples being built in and around Karnak, which became the nucleus for one of the greatest building projects in Egypt that would last for nearly 23 centuries.

The rituals, ceremonies and festivals of Amun were established in Karnak, and Amun was celebrated as the Founder of Divine Kingship among gods, and through his power to pharaohs on earth. To rule Egyptians in his own name and image, Pharaoh simply claimed himself to be the human manifestation of Amun on earth. Gradually, during the New Kingdom (1580 BC–1045 BC), Amun-re became the ultimate source of life and afterlife. He brought the flood to Egypt every summer. He renewed life. He rejuvenated and nourished the land, the fields, humans, plants and animals. He rose on his holy mound in the area of Karnak at "*Ipt*" where he had lived since the time of the Middle Kingdom.

Amun-re lived in Karnak Temple and was worshipped as the divine symbol of godly kingship that he alone created, established and then protected. But that godliness had to be renewed every year and so, not far from this temple, we have another form of Amun. It is his image as creator of life who lived on his mound of genesis in what is today Luxor Temple, south of the Karnak complex by only 3 km. Amun of Luxor was responsible for the annual flood of the Nile. He was the symbol of life cycles and recreation of everything in Egypt, and therefore, during the annual flooding of the Nile, the ancient city celebrated the national feast called *"Opet."* During this celebration, God Amun-re of Karnak had to leave his own house and shrine and travel to the southern shrine and the house of his other form, Amun the Creator. The summer celebration lasted several weeks and it was the most important feast par excellence in all of Ancient Egypt.

As early as the Middle Kingdom, and later in the New Kingdom, the two temples of ancient Luxor, Karnak and Luxor, received great care and attention from all ruling families. Statues for Amun and the pharaohs were erected inside the temples, shrines and galleries, and they decorated the courtyards. Many of the statues in the ancient temples denoted the symbolic immortality of the divine god, represented in the form of the king himself, and so we find a large number of these statues inside all temples, ready to receive petitions and daily offerings.

Due to the excessive number of statues inside the temples' galleries and courtyards, the priests' tasks included collecting certain of the statues and burying them with respect in a place inside the temple (it was sacred ground anyway). In particular, this happened to statues of pharaohs who had died a long time ago and were no longer receiving any offerings to provide maintenance service for them. The priests performed this ceremony after several decades when they found it difficult to walk about the temple corridors and pillared halls due to overcrowding. Since the statues were divine images for gods, goddesses, pharaohs and queens, it was not possible to simply get rid of them by breaking them up and throwing them away. This brought about the need for a special ceremony of decent burial within the holy temple ground. We call these clusters of buried statues a cache.

Millennia later, the Aswan High Dam was constructed between 1960 and 1970. It was to be Egypt's main defense against severe droughts and high floods. It was a necessity for the rapidly growing population of Egypt in the second half of the twentieth century and, no doubt, the dam was a great national project with undeniable advantages of water regulation and irrigation. That said, the dam also came with unmistakable disadvantages, such as the increasing rise of the underground water table in Egypt, which directly destabilized the foundation of monuments along the Nile. Where once the annual flooding washed away fertilizers and salts to the Mediterranean, the dam prevented flooding and allowed salt accumulation in the water table.

Before the dam was built, the underground water table measured 1 cubic meter of water to each 1 square meter of land per year. After the dam was built, the ratio soared to become 25 cubic meters of water to every 1 square meter of land per year. This increase was responsible for damaging the soil, deteriorating its solidity and causing it to become waterlogged. This complicated situation has had a negative effect on most archeological sites in Egypt, especially those close to the Nile in Upper Egypt and those built from limestone and sandstone blocks. The stones suck the salty moisture from the earth leading to severe damage of the pillars and stone walls of the temples. Luxor Temple is a perfect example of such recent problems; as the nearest Egyptian temple to the river Nile, Luxor Temple is literally floating on the underground water table, which has destabilized the pillars of Amunhotep III around the inner courtyard.

After the opera Aida was performed inside Luxor Temple, the restoration of Luxor Temple's pillars began. The Antiquities Department raised a special fund to prepare a meticulous engineering survey to determine the best way to prevent the temple pillars of Amunhotep III from falling apart. They decided to deconstruct all pillars, dig under their foundations, treat the damaged bases and underground pillar foundations, support the weak soil and finally rebuild the pillars on top. In 1988, the mission began in the inner open courtyard of the temple with digging near the western pillars to check the surrounding condition of soil and stability of the earth. The mission moved very slowly in that area of the weakly standing western pillars, carefully digging deeper into the earth to reveal the true ancient foundation of the pillars, where the restoration had to begin.

Discovery Story

On the morning of January 22, 1989, the head of workers in Luxor Temple, Ali Fekry, gathered his men and his assistant Farouk Sharid at the "big hole," as the workers called it. The big shaft, four meters deep, was very close to the western row of pillars in the inner open courtyard of the temple. It was another sunny Luxor winter day and the Luxor Temple was always crowded in the morning. Many tourist groups filled the temple courtyards and pillared halls. Fadia Hanna, the Luxor Temple Inspector, was supervising the workers collecting dirt and debris from the big hole. It was tedious work to remove dirt and debris in small buckets made from old rubber materials from the big hole and transport it to another place inside the temple where all the dirt could be meticulously examined. It was slow work and the weather was becoming unusually cold in Luxor. Toward the middle of the day, the workers shouted:

"We found hard stone in strange colors!"

Around noon, as the workers had been digging inside the big hole, and the chief worker, Rayes Fekry, and his assistant, Rayes Farouk, had been watching over the hole, one worker hit something hard with his mattock. It sounded like stone in a place they had been expecting only dirt and wet debris. The sound of rocks under their mattocks was remarkable and awakened a sudden sense of enthusiasm inside the workers to find out exactly what it was.

The inspector in charge of the digs, Fadia Hanna, was standing very close to the hole, and she immediately rushed to see what had caused the commotion. After a careful hand brushing around the discovered piece of rock, it showed itself to be a rectangular base of stone that looked like a big base for a royal statue made of unusual purple quartzite. Inspector Hanna and Rayes Fekry rushed to report the discovery of the unusual colored stone base to the mission manager, Mohamed El Sagher. At first, he was not happy about their deep digs so close to the western pillars thinking it to be a very dangerous operation to find nothing more than a piece of rock. However, Rayes Fekry convinced El Sagher to give him a chance to clear around the strange stone and support him with 15 workers for 24 hours. He wanted to raise the stone and hopefully a large statue still hidden in the wet dirt.

Mohamed El Sagher finally agreed and the chief of workers and his assistants immediately began clearing around the purple stone, and in a few hours, they were able to completely free the statue of a pharaoh. El Sagher quickly read the name of Pharaoh Amunhotep III. Right next to the statue, the team discovered another three statues of Ancient Egyptian gods, including the famous statue of God Atum.

The wonderful purple quartzite statue of King Amunhotep III represented the pharaoh standing on a small base, a sled-like pedestal. The king wore the double crowns of Upper and Lower Egypt and held the sign "ankh–life" in both hands. The statue appeared to have been decorated with precious stones and clearly reflected the highest level of sculpture from the New Kingdom.

At this point, El Sagher realized the nature of this wonderful accidental discovery, and he quickly understood that the team was about to make a resounding archeological discovery right in the heart of Luxor Temple. Most probably, there would be more statues to be found inside this hole. It was a certainly a cache. He wrote to the Head of the Antiquities Department, Sayed Tawfik, and Head of the Supreme Council of Antiquities of Egypt, Ali Hassan, to guarantee special and immediate funding for continuing the search for new finds within Luxor Temple. Soon, a special team was prepared to start digging deeper in the area where the great statue had been discovered, assuming many statues would be found nearby. To everyone's surprise, after the hole was expanded to almost four meters in depth and four meters wide, nothing was found at all. El Sagher and his team were confused. Where was the cache?

On February 9, 1986, the Egyptian Minister of Culture, Farouk Hosni, Head of the Department of Antiquities, Sayed Tawfik, and the Governor of Qena State (to which the city of Luxor belonged) all visited the temple, and the site of the new discovery. To that date, no great finds had yet been revealed, and it was not until April 20th of that year that El Sagher decided to take the risk of digging deeper in the big hole. This was a critical, sensitive decision because the weak pillars that required restortion were very close. The ground could collapse at any moment, and in that event, the pillars would be destroyed. The digging went on, and at a much deeper level, they found more statues and stone objects buried. Most objects dated back to the later period of Egypt's ancient pharaonic history. This was the clue that helped El Sagher to determine the true age of this cache: the priests must have made it back in the later period.

More than 20 statues and other stone objects were discovered in the Luxor Temple cache in 1989. A special wing inside the Luxor Museum was prepared for the collection, and the most important pieces were to be archived and displayed there:

- The diorite statue of God Atum and Pharaoh Horemhep together on the same pedestal. The king is depicted kneeling in front of the god, a unique fashion in Ancient Egyptian art.
- The first piece found, the purple quartzite statue of Pharaoh Amunhotep III
- A statue of Goddess Hathor with the head of a woman, dating back to the time of Amunhotep III
- A statue of Goddess Iuneat with the head of a woman holding the symbol of an "ankh" in hand
- An alabaster sphinx-like statue of the boy Pharaoh Tutankhamen
- A rare statue of God Amunkamutef, in the form of a snake, dating back to the days of Taharqa, the 25th Nubian Dynasty

The discovery of such a cache actually raises more questions than it answers. Do more of these caches still exist inside Egyptian temples or beneath the ground in the courtyards? Can we find, or will we find, more statues buried in special caches? My answer is, yes, we will -- but when or how?

(A German archeological team had been working in the great Mortuary Temple of King Amunhotep III, an area full of ruins just beyond the two Colossi of Memnon in the western part of Luxor, the ancient necropolis. This German team found a cache of large, black, granite statues of Goddess Sekhmet. There were about 28 statues found in one big hole. The statues were in wonderful condition, and they were found in a place everyone had thought had been raided, destroyed or flooded.)

The 1989 cache discovery within the Luxor Temple was a brilliant discovery, and it was made by Egyptian workers and described in detail by Egyptian experts. This was an indication that more great discoveries could and would occur in Egypt, and the heroes were all local Egyptians archeologists.

Egypt did not need to wait long before the next big accidental discovery took place in the most famous and popular site in Egypt, actually, in the most famous and important archeological site on the face of our planet—near the pyramids of Giza.

CHAPTER 19

Workers Village at Giza

WITH THE RISE OF THE 1990s, Egypt entered an entirely new era in the field of Egyptological discoveries. We may call it, the "Age of Zahi Hawass." His passion for excavation, discoveries and preservation of Egyptian monuments was and is, without any doubt, infectious. During the 1990s, Zahi Hawass became the most popular figure in the field of Egyptology. His iconic presence and television presentations have transformed him into a symbol and a star. He is solely responsible for attracting millions of travelers to Egypt, to visit the places he talks about in his widespread, popular shows aired on well-known and respected television channels. In addition, Zahi is an avid researcher. He has written and presented more papers at Egyptology conferences than any other Egyptian scholar (I believe he researched and presented over 185 papers in the last 20 years). Zahi Hawass simply has become the most famous living Egyptologist.

His career began 40 years ago when he started as a young inspector in the Department of Antiquities. His digging experiences accumulated and became a compelling knowledge base that enabled him ultimately to become the Head of the Department of Antiquities, the most powerful man in charge of Egypt's ancient treasures. He strongly believes in the power of modern communications and media. He has presented his country and its fabulous treasures in a unique and fascinating style. With unmistakable passion and undeniable captivation, with his famous hat and Indiana Jones style of storytelling, he has managed to turn eyes and ears toward Egypt. No doubt, though, because of his charisma, power and influence, it is not hard to imagine his growing enemies in Egypt and abroad. It is in part jealousy, sometimes hate, but most of the time, it is only resentment, the perfect combination of elements that haunt every successful person in every society.

Zahi's infectious interest in Ancient Egypt and its artifacts expanded to include stolen and abducted Egyptian artifacts that now exist almost in every corner of the world. On every continent, one can find Egyptian relics. He has used his power and communication channels to bring these artifacts back to Egypt, sometimes through complicated diplomatic channels, most of the time through UNESCO channels, other times through simple personal contacts. Many pieces have been returned while he was in office, and many other pieces have been highlighted in a media war between him and those who refuse to send the pieces back. (The Egyptian Museum of Berlin refused to send the head of Queen Nefertiti back to Egypt, even though it was an artifact stolen from the Department of Antiquities warehouse at the Amarna site in 1887. The Rosetta Stone has been in the British Museum for more than 200 years, and Britain refuses to send it back, claiming it to be a spoil of war given up by the French army as it was leaving Egypt in 1801.) Nefertiti's head and the Rosetta Stone have both raised a lot of arguments around Zahi Hawass. The media have presented unethical news falsifications in an attempt to assassinate Zahi's character and stop him from asking museums around the world to send back their abducted Egyptian artifacts. It's not easy, but someone had to start this war, and after Zahi, others will have to continue the battle.

It is my personal testimonial to Zahi Hawass that, during his days, the Department of Antiquities became powerful once again and achieved profits instead of constant losses. Egypt's monuments have been better protected, and inspectors' and employees' general working conditions have improved after decades of ignorance and poor management. Most people in my country really don't know the man as I do. He is obsessed with Egypt and Egyptian artifacts and monuments, and has a clear vision about how this treasure should be protected, managed and invested in economically. He is a wonderful combination of employee and manager, the great active archaeologist and most important, an iconic figure in world media.

His recent work and discoveries have helped to reshape our knowledge about Ancient Egyptian life and society. His new groundbreaking discoveries, shared on television with the world, have awakened our senses and excitement to better understand the marvelous ancient days of the pharaohs.

The story of this chapter tells us about an important episode of Ancient Egyptian rediscovery, when Zahi Hawass and his team in Giza began to rewrite the history of the pyramids, their construction and most profoundly, sought to answer the question: Who built the pyramids?

After thousands of years, we have been entertained by theories, hypotheses and fictional stories about aliens or the lost civilization of Atlantis coming to build the enigmatic pyramids, later altered by the pharaohs. Religious books that propound slave labor as the building method have influenced us. Finally, in the late 1990s, Zahi and his team resolved the puzzle and closed the question of the pyramids' builders once and for all. Nowadays, archeologists like Zahi Hawass and Mark Lehner don't like to be asked who built the pyramids. They would prefer to discuss how the pyramids as a national project helped to build society in the times of the pharaohs.

The workers village, near the statue of the Sphinx and not far from the pyramids themselves, has been revealed. After thousands of years, the mystery of Giza has been unlocked finally, and it all happened by accident, again.

Historic Background

When King Senefru, the great founder of the 4th Dynasty, died, his son Khufu succeeded him on the throne, and became King of Upper and Lower Egypt toward the end of the 27th century BC. During the times of both Senefru and his son, Khufu, Egypt enjoyed great stability, and Egyptian society peacefully reached a level of political and religious equilibrium. We can call it the final "accepted shape and model," as pharaohs became the image of God Re on earth, his human form and link with earth. Pharaohs at that time enjoyed immeasurable power and unquestionable status over society and all layers of governmental structure. They were the country, its savior and guardian.

For the mighty pharaohs of the Old Kingdom (3rd, 4th, 5th and 6th dynasties, circa 2750 BC–2200 BC), great stone structures in the shape of pyramids were built to serve as tombs and eternal houses for the embalmed bodies and spirits of deceased kings, an era known in Ancient Egypt as the Pyramid Age. The 4th Dynasty saw true mega-sized pyramid constructions ordered by King Senefru, who built the two huge stone pyramids in Dahshur, just south of the main cemetery of Saqqara, not far from the royal capital at the time, Memphis.

Senefru first built a large pyramid with a very wide angle, but due to obvious construction problems causing instability, his building team was forced to change its angle from 54 degrees to 45 degrees toward the top. Because of its distinctive shape, it has become known as the Bent Pyramid. But the pharaoh was determined to build a real and true pyramid with no engineering mistakes or scars, and Senefru built another pyramid just a mile north of the Bent Pyramid, now called the Red Pyramid. After the Red Pyramid, Egyptian pharaohs initiated more large-scale funeral constructions, having learned that integrity of foundations and soil engineering were the key to stability for megalithic stone funeral buildings. King Senefru had opened the door for his own son Khufu to follow him and start his own marvelous pyramid tomb on the Giza Plateau.

Khufu chose the sacred site of Giza for the home of his grandiose project. He wanted his own pyramid to be larger and greater than those of his father. The excellent quality of limestone in Giza was one reason for his decision to leave the heart of the royal cemetery at Saqqara and avoid building near his own father in Dahshur. Because Giza was far from Memphis, Khufu linked his project site with the Nile by canal, making it easy to travel there from Memphis or any other place in Egypt. A simple boat ride made it possible to comfortably reach the new royal cemetery in Giza during the several months of the annual flood season during the inundation of the river valley. To further support his new large project in Giza, he built a small town for the builders and other workers employed for his project. The workers village was not only a convenient place to eat and sleep but it also comprised administration units and government utility stations for support of the overall project for several years. In addition, the king had a royal palace built at the edge of the desert in the Giza area, so when he visited the construction of his pyramid site, he could rest adjacent to his own pyramid. All this additional construction (the harbor, the workers village, administrative units, pharaoh's palace on site) was considered essential and had to have been fully prepared before the actual building of the pyramid began. It is mindboggling to imagine the many other buildings that accompanied the work process: kitchens, ovens, hospitals, scribes' offices, tool workshops, even a little, humble cemetery for the workers who died while working. Archeologists have just recently found the cemetery.

It took nearly 30 years of King Khufu's reign to construct his exceptionally large and almost perfect tomb and pyramid, his dream come true. It was a miracle in every aspect, the fruit of efforts of thousands of loving and believing Egyptian workers who devoted much of their lives to their pharaoh's biggest achievement. Later Khufu's pyramid would become the nucleus of the great Giza cemetery that would be used by his own sons and grandsons and several more generations of pharaohs and noblemen for thousands of years. His pyramid was the first of the cemetery on the great Giza Plateau, which grew later to include 11 pyramids, 7,000 tombs and mastabas of nobles' families and the one-of-a-kind sculpture, the giant Sphinx.

Paradoxically, with all these wonderful buildings and architectural marvels in Giza, people for centuries have wondered about their origin and the people who were really behind this incredible achievement. Was it truly the work of Ancient Egyptians or another civilization? The large Giza cemetery with its thousands of tombs and rock-cut mastabas that served the royal families of the pharaohs and high-ranking government officials: Who built and decorated these tombs? Scholars and archeologists for generations have been hoping to make a substantial find in Giza that would help them answer this important question.

During the 6th Dynasty, significant administrative reforms were introduced in the great royal cemetery of the Giza Plateau to better organize the tombs, their location and protection against grave robbers. A large wall was built surrounding the royal cemetery, particularly strong on the valley side to separate the cemetery from nearby local villages where farmers lived and worked their land. A stone wall marked the border between the royal cemetery and the tombs of the nobles, many of whom had been buried oddly close to the pharaohs. Reform called for a total rearrangement of the land of the entire cemetery and reallocation of tombs according to social rank. Clear maps were drawn and stone walls were built to separate one class from another. The great, external stone wall was as high as 11 meters, and its width reached four meters.

Thousands of years later, the stone walls of the ancient cemetery are still standing and have become the modern borderline for the local people of the nearby village. We can still see the remains of this great stone wall just south of the Sphinx (where the tourist buses now park), known locally as the Wall of the Crow. It currently separates the Giza monuments from the modern Islamic cemetery of today's Sphinx village. Locals enter the Giza tourist area through the wall every day with camels, donkeys and horses. The area south of the Wall of the Crow has served as a playing field for horse and camel riders. It has also served for football/soccer games every afternoon with a breathtaking view of the Great Pyramid of Khufu. It is a good spot with fine sands and gently sloped hills. No one had really ever thought about what might exist beneath the sands just south of the ancient walls. People came and went, horses ran in all directions and young Egyptians played their favorite sport, football/soccer, every afternoon. More and more, people realized the quality of the sand in the area was good enough for their cheap, modern, local houses that began to be built in the 1970s, and so, the area generously provided tons of sand for construction of homes in the nearby village. No government officials took notice. No one imagined what might exist a few feet beneath the surface, until one day in April, the ancient secrets were accidentally revealed as an unlucky tourist fell off her horse.

Discovery Story

On April 14, 1990, Mohamed Abdel Razik, Chief of Guards in the Giza Inspectorate of Antiquities, was walking toward the southern side of the ancient Wall of the Crow. His job was to check on the tombs, mastabas and other burial shafts that lay south of the Sphinx. He always concentrated his walks near the Wall of the Crow knowing that it was the daily playground for the locals, with horses, donkeys and camels. Mohamed also noticed the significant increase in sand being removed by villagers who wanted it for construction. Apparently, so much sand had been collected in a few months that it had changed the ground surface density and the pack of the sand. The experienced antiquities guard also noticed the change of color of the sand in the area.

Then, a small accident occurred. An American tourist was riding a horse in the area and fell. As people were helping her, they noticed mud brick deposited beneath the soft sandy surface. The locals, especially the horse and camel people, never recalled seeing mud brick beneath the sand before. It had to be a mud brick structure or an ancient mud brick wall. All were intrigued and pondered the mystery. Razik went to the offices of the inspectors and managers for Giza Plateau (close to the Mena House Hotel) to describe the details of his observations over the past few weeks to Zahi Hawass. He told Zahi about the American tourist's accident and the mud brick the locals had found under the soft surface of the sand. A revelation, it all made perfect sense to Zahi.

In 1987 in his PhD dissertation, Zahi Hawass had written that the area located south of the Wall of the Crow was the most likely location of the workers village that dated back to the pyramid days and suggested that excavations should be launched. However, from 1987 to 1990, nothing happened. No excavation or even a basic survey took place until the American tourist's accident occurred.

Zahi rushed to the area of the accident. He was certain from the apparent clues on the ground that the place might hide the lost secrets of the Great Pyramid workers village. He gathered his team of archeologists and surveyors in Giza under the leadership of his assistant, Mansour Boriak, the chief archeologist. As general manager of Giza Plateau, Mansour and his team began surveying the site south of the ancient wall and examined the recently discovered mud brick wall to find it was part of a round structure, looking very much like a mud brick oven. With his broad experience in digging archeological sites, Mansour came to a firm conclusion about the paramount importance of this place, even anticipating wonderful discoveries that might follow. Zahi and Mansour together were excited about the potential for a new project in Giza and enthusiastically ordered the removal of a huge amount of sand to reveal what was beneath.

Zahi's mission in the newly discovered workers village of the pyramids' builders ultimately revealed to the world the true nature of ancient builders of the great pyramids, and dismissed all previous theories regarding the origin of this community of builders. Finding the tombs of the workers adjacent to the workers village allowed Zahi to discover the names of many of the pyramid workers. In addition, he was able to establish their titles and the roles they played in the pyramids' construction. We now know the origin of the families that participated in these massive and important projects. They were Egyptians; no foreigners, slaves, Israelites or aliens had participated in the construction of these marvelous monuments. With this important discovery, mysteries, debates and arguments have been allayed. The question has been answered: Ancient Egyptians built the pyramids.

In the first few seasons of excavation in the workers village site, Zahi found wonderful relics and important buildings that revolutionized our knowledge about the community of workers from the pyramids age. He discovered a large cemetery dedicated to the workers' leaders, managers and high administrators. The cemetery was divided into two main sections. The lower section included very poor and humble burials made of mud brick structures, built to look like mini-pyramids. Their dimensions were no more than one meter by one and a half meters. Most of these burials were divided inside into two parts, a room for the burial of the body and a second room for the modest burial accessories that accompanied the deceased in his afterlife journey.

The lower cemetery included about 600 tombs all made of mud brick, and 30 other tombs, bigger in size likely built for the workers' overseers. The odd thing about the 30 larger tombs was that they took various shapes and were not at all like the smaller tombs nearby. Some were square, some rectangular in shape and others perfectly round with a little dome.

In the middle of the lower cemetery, Zahi's team discovered the remains of a causeway used to link the lower and the upper cemeteries together. The causeway was built mainly of mud brick and reinforced with smaller limestone blocks and climbed the hillside all the way to the edge of the plateau where the limestone rock formation was covered with sand and hid more tombs that had been originally cut west of the lower cemetery.

The upper cemetery included 43 tombs, mainly cut into the limestone formation of the upper hill. The tombs were generally of better condition, larger in size and artistically much higher in quality than the lower tombs, which clearly indicated the status of their owners. Certainly, the higher tombs were dedicated to the upper managers of the village and the chief administrators of the royal cemetery of Giza. These tombs were partly built with limestone blocks quarried from the Giza Plateau, and sometimes with sandstone and mud brick as well, in a beautiful imitation of the great tombs of the nobles that exist nearby the pyramids. Other tombs were cut into the hillside, with their walls covered in carved scenes and hieroglyphic texts telling us about the tomb owners, their names and their jobs in the national, royal project and cemetery.

The names of the tomb owners from the lower and upper cemeteries played a major role in understanding more about the workers' community, their relationship with the state and the village's community structure. In the lower cemetery, a tomb was discovered for a person called "*khimnw,*" and his wife named "*hotp rebit*" was buried with him. She worked as a priestess of Goddess Hathor, the Cow Goddess. Another tomb was discovered of someone called "*kay heb*" and his wife "*heban kawis,*" whose small statue was also discovered in the tomb. We learned from these two tombs that wives at the time were buried along with husbands in the same tomb (not necessarily at the same time). There were only two tombs discovered that had been privately prepared for women from the village who were buried alone. One was called "*rebet Hathor,*" who worked as a priestess in the house of Goddess Hathor. The other woman was called "*nubit,*" who worked as priestess in the house of Goddess Niet.

Yet another interesting discovery was made in the lower cemetery. There were two tombs for two dwarf women who lived in the village, one having died while giving birth. This is known because the team discovered the dead fetus inside her body.

Most bodies in the lower cemetery were buried at the bottom of shallow burial shafts, and the embalmed body was protected only by a wooden coffin. But in the upper cemetery tombs we have found the honorary titles of the tomb owners, proof of their special, higher status in the workers village, titles like "Supervisor of Workers at the Side of the Pyramid," "Manager of Craftsmen," "Supervisor of the Sanctuary," "Chief of Workers," and "Craftsmen Inspector." The most interesting title found in the upper cemetery was "Overseer of the King's Work."

The upper cemetery also had a causeway that led up to the top the escarpment and the limestone hill where a large mastaba was discovered cut entirely into the limestone formation, with six burial shafts and a small room with an almost intact and undisturbed burial. A small niche was discovered in the wall; inside it, four small statues in wonderful condition were discovered to be of someone called "*inty sheduo,*" who was the Supervisor of the Sacred Boat/Barque of Goddess Niet. He also carried another important title, found on one of the four statues: "King's Companion." This statue clearly reflects his power and high status in the workers village and is the largest of the four statues. While it is only 19 cm. high, it shows him sitting in a chair, wearing a wig and the traditional short skirt, in typical Old Kingdom style.

Another important discovery made in the upper cemetery in 1996 was the tomb of someone called "*nfr tit*" and his wife "*nfr hotp es*." The tomb walls were covered with very interesting carved scenes about food and bread making in the workers village, a powerful clue to his job as the food supplier to the workers village. His wife's titles on the walls are "The Well-known to the King," and "Textile Maker."

The final example from the upper cemetery is the tomb of someone called "*bi tit*" and his wife "*nisi sokar.*" Their tomb is of particular importance. On its walls and next to the entrance, we found some written curses, warnings to anyone who entered the tomb with the intention of looting or raiding its content. The curse promises that the intruder is to be slaughtered by crocodiles, hippopotamuses and lions. It is considered the oldest example of a curse text from Ancient Egypt.

The general examination of discovered bodies and bones in the two cemeteries at the workers village site proves clearly that those who were buried in the tombs of the upper cemetery lived better, longer lives than those buried in the lower cemetery, who suffered from obvious bone and spine fractures, general deterioration of bones and injuries. In the lower cemetery, one skeleton was discovered in a tomb with a lethal injury, a crushed the skull that led to inevitable death. Many other burials in the lower cemetery show cases of amputation of various body parts, such as arms or feet, as the result of serious trauma and injuries during the construction of the pyramids. When a large, heavy stone crushed a worker's hand or foot by mistake, it would have been amputated in a quick surgery at the field hospital or medical center at the workers village. Sometimes, only amputations saved the life of the worker.

Regardless of the poor artistic and material value of the workers village discoveries, its historic and scientific value is unprecedented and undeniable. The news of its discoveries rapidly spread worldwide and attracted many scholars and tourists to Egypt and the village. Several missions were assigned to work in the workers village in all fields of Egyptology and supporting fields (medicine, anthropology, architecture), and the workers village of Giza became a hot topic of discussion for everyone visiting Egypt in the late 1990s.

Work is still in progress and there is still more sand yet to be removed from the south side of the Wall of the Crow to reveal the true size of the ancient workers village. Expectations are that more tombs and mastabas will be found in both the lower and upper cemeteries. Up to now, the local government in Giza has not relocated people who live above the archeological site, and at least part of the modern village must be relocated before being able to continue excavations. The football field is likely only the beginning because the true size and dimension of the ancient workers village seems much bigger than originally thought. It may have held 10,000 workers concurrently, all involved in the construction of pharaoh's tombs and pyramids.

The results stemming from this discovery are far more important than the actual discovery because it answers the question and has nicely put to rest historic arguments about:

Who built the pyramids?

CHAPTER 20

Valley of the Golden Mummies at Bahariya

THIS STORY AND ITS ENTIRE chapter have made me a little uncertain. I was confused about the best way to present the story of the amazing, accidental discovery of the Valley of the Golden Mummies at Bahariya Oasis. Without a doubt, the discovery includes fun and plenty of excitement, enough to entertain readers; but at the same time, it also has more than one version of the truth about the moment of the discovery. How it came to the authorities'

awareness and how it came to be excavated both remain uncertain. I therefore decided to be cautious in my research as I collected information about the discovery and the people involved.

This story goes back to 1999 when Zahi Hawass began publishing the results of his excavation work in the quiet, remote Oasis of Bahariya after several seasons of digging there, the place he then called the Valley of the Golden Mummies.

In the late 1990s, Zahi Hawass was the General Manager of the Giza Plateau Archeological Inspectorate, but despite its being far away, Bahariya Oasis administratively belonged to Giza. It was therefore part of his inspectorate and under his authority. The story of this great discovery started in 1996, according to Zahi Hawass' book *Valley of the Golden Mummies*, when the Chief Inspector of the Bahariya Oasis, Ashry Shaker, visited him in his office at Giza to report to him that something big had occurred in his oasis, not far from the Temple of Alexander the Great.

However, before we learn about what happened in the oasis that made Ashry Shaker travel 400 km. to Giza to meet with his manager Hawass, I would like to take you straight to this quiet oasis to understand why it is so important. Who was living there in the ancient times of the pharaohs?

Historic Background

Bahariya Oasis is one of the most important Egyptian western desert oases. Geographically, it is about 400 km. southwest of the city of Giza. It is a large, natural depression in the heart of the western desert about 128 meters above sea level. The oasis naturally takes a triangular shape with a total size of 2,000 square km. The triangle's base is toward the north and is the widest part of the oasis reaching 42 km. from east to west. The top points to the south with a distance of 94 km. between its furthest points from north to south.

Small hills and rocky escarpments surround the edge of the depression on all sides, most pronouncedly on the north. The indigenous people of Bahariya call these hills "The Mountains," and they gave each one an interesting name, the most famous of which are El Dist, El Magharafa, Mandisha, Maysara and El Zabou. These little mountains have an important geological quality. The rock formation and fossils that have been found there provide wonderful information about the early geological ages of Egypt's western desert. The oasis' northern hills and escarpments were the perfect habitat for a special type of giant dinosaur thought to be living in the area about 70 million years ago. In 1914, the German geologist Ernst Stramer unearthed the remains of four giant dinosaur fossils from the mountains north of Bahariya. He classified the dinosaur as "Paralitian Stomeri." He found it on El Dist Mountain and moved it to the geological museum of Munich. Sadly, the fossils were completely destroyed in one of the Second World War airstrikes on that city. Providentially, in 2000, the University of Pennsylvania geological mission at Bahariya Oasis found another dinosaur fossil from the same type of dinosaur, close to the area where the other four had been found. The university mission took that fossil to their own university museum.

On the northern and northwestern edges of the oasis, remains of early Stone Age men have been discovered, proving the earliest human settlement in the oasis. At the beginning of the first recorded Egyptian period, the pharaohs' recorded history, we find nothing inside the oasis to affirm human activities. The reason for this may be that development and human activities of later centuries have totally erased all traces of this early Egyptian period, perhaps through recycling and remodeling of materials. However, during the Middle Kingdom, the oasis has been definitively mentioned in state records. It used to be called "*dsds*," and records refer to the oasis' good quality of wine, vineyards and grapes. In addition, the oasis has been mentioned in records in association with the desert Bedouin warriors who would raid the Nile Valley periodically. The western desert oases, including Bahariya, were always targets of such attacks. The oasis is centrally located on main trade and caravan routes in the desert, connecting it with the Nile Valley. Bahariya furthermore held a vital position in the middle of the desert between the southern oases of Farafra, Dakhla, and Kharga and the northern oases of Fayoum, Qattara and Siwa.

During the New Kingdom, several records indicate that Bahariya Oasis was part of the Eighth Nome (province) in Upper Egypt (now the province of *tawr*-Abydos). In wall scenes within Minister Rakhmere's Tomb in western

Thebes, we see the minister meeting a delegation from Bahariya Oasis who had come to Thebes to offer their gifts and tributes to Pharaoh Thotmosis III. The gifts comprised a wide variety of native products from the oasis, jars full of wine and olive oil. The wall paintings in the tomb clearly portray the people of the oasis in their exotic, desert-style, colorful attire with long, fuzzy beards.

Inside the oasis, right in the heart of the modern town, we have an area called Qarat El Helwa where we can visit the oasis' only remaining monument still in existence dating to the New Kingdom, the Tomb of Prince Amunhotep Hua, Governor of the oasis, who lived during the time of Pharaoh Amunhotep III.

Later pharaohs of the 22nd to 26th dynasties showed genuine interest in the western desert oases and in particular, in Bahariya Oasis, for both economic and military purposes. This is clearly reflected in Bahariya by the many temples built during the New Kingdom and the later period, for example, the small Temple of Ein El Meftela from the time of Pharaoh Ahmose II. In the area of Qaret El Helwa, we can see the marvelous, underground cut and painted tombs of *"Jedamunefank"* and *"Panintu,"* the governors of the oasis from the later period of the 26th Dynasty.

During the Greek and Ptolemaic periods, on his way back to Memphis, Alexander the Great was thought to have visited the oasis during his visit to Siwa Oasis and its Temple of Amen, the famous Temple of the Oracles. A small temple dedicated to Alexander the Great and his brief visit is still located today in the area of Qasr El Meqesba. It is the only monument in the Egyptian desert oases with the name of Alexander the Great recorded.

The Ptolemys of Alexandria considered Bahariya Oasis an immensely important desert oasis. They saw it as the geographical and political border of the Nile Valley on the western side. It was the western frontier that supported the central government along the Nile with important crops like wheat, barley, olives and wine. The Ptolemys administratively joined the Bahariya and Farafra oases together under one governor. They called them Oasis Minora and Oasis Parva. The region's headquarters and governorship was in Bahariya in its small military garrison.

During the Roman period, records from 213 AD indicated a 7,000-soldier Roman garrison called Apriana settled in Bahariya Oasis, farming its lands and producing wheat to be exported to Alexandria and then on to Rome. Other Roman records confirmed that Bahariya had six Roman garrisons living there all the time for security and farming purposes. Bahariya's high level of wealth and economic prosperity depended on the high quality of its wine and olive oil. The oasis had the most highly desired wine in the Roman world; in fact, its wine was considered one of the finest in the entire ancient world. A large winery was discovered in the area of Qasr Masaoud, close to the Ancient Roman fort located on the ancient trade and caravan routes to the south toward Farafra Oasis. The wine factory was discovered in 1999 by Zahi Hawass' team in Bahariya.

Later on, during the Christian period, the oasis was known as Oxirinychus, or El Bahnasa Oasis, because it then belonged administratively to the city of El Bahnasa in Middle Egypt. The province itself was known in the later Roman period and early Christianity as Oxirinychus. Its relative proximity to the Nile Valley made it well connected with trade and caravan roads, and many of the early Christian fathers who sought to escape the brutal Roman persecution along the Nile were attracted to Bahariya Oasis. St. Bartholomew, one of Jesus' disciples, who traveled the Egyptian desert to preach about Christianity and elude Roman hands, made records of the journey to Bahariya. Coptic records in Egypt claim that he was finally martyred in Bahariya, and in early Christianity, an annual, religious feast was established to celebrate the memory of the martyred saint, occurring on September 7th, (the Coptic month of Tout). Later, when Islam entered Egypt in 641 AD, Bahariya was soon introduced to the new religion and culture, and the Arabs called it El Bahnasa Oasis or Mendisha Oasis.

In modern times, the oasis attracted the attention of Muhammed Ali Pasha for economic reasons and enticed European explorers with the possibility of finding artifacts, lost tombs and treasures. Giovani Belzoni visited the oasis in 1819. In his records, he called it El Bahnasa Oasis or Mendisha Oasis, just like the Arabs before him. He spent a few weeks exploring tombs and monuments, recorded everything he witnessed and left. The next person to follow Belzoni had clear orders and a mission assigned to him by Muhammad Ali. He was Fredrick Chiliad, who traveled to the oasis in 1819, searching for natural resources, gold or any other minerals of worth. Later, during the First World War, Captain Claud Williams, the British commander in Egypt's western desert, came to the oasis chasing the followers of El Senousi and his rebels, who had incited trouble throughout the western desert all the way from Libya to the five oases of Egypt. They stormed the Kharga and Dakhla oases and defeated all the desert's rebel troops who surrendered in Bahariya Oasis to Captain Claud Williams.

The true beginning of modern scientific exploration in Bahariya Oasis took place in the days of the great Ahmed Fakhry. Between 1934 and 1937, Fakhry made several visits to the oasis and recorded all its surviving monuments. His excavation in Bahariya was the first true archeological mission ever accomplished in the remote oasis. His finds, exploration and results were published widely. His books about Egypt's western desert oasis (*The Egyptian Oases*) still continue as the most respectable source of information. Ahmed Fakhry was the founder of a new field in Egyptology. He called it "the science of the oasis monuments." The oasis did not host any true, scientifically organized excavation missions after Fakhy until Zahi Hawass' team arrived in the late 1990s. The 60-year gap in exploration is testimony to the ignorance and disregard of Bahariya and its monuments in modern times.

Now, Bahariya consists of six large villages and Managem, a small town of iron ore mineworkers' homes, just outside the oasis. The oasis' total population now is nearly 30,000, most working in farming with about 3,000 to 4,000 workers in Managem.

Discovery Story

Early mornings in Egyptian deserts can feature temperature drops to below freezing, and people of the oasis normally avoid such early winter mornings. They prefer to let time pass until a few hours after sunrise when the air gets warmer and the sky is always clear blue. On one of these winter days in 1995, just before the break of dawn, something happened outside the oasis, 6 km.

south of the modern town center of Bawiti, on the main road leading to the southern Farafra Oasis. The locals call this place, located near a small military police unit, Kilometer 6. A small group of local tomb-robbers was digging in the desert area, toward the west, not far from the asphalt road that leads to the small village called El Hez. They were searching for buried antiquities (many people of Bahariya Oasis, who live on the outskirts of the town center, dig privately under and around their homes and farms, believing they might find some ancient treasure within an ancient tomb). Certainly, many people before them had found numerous tombs or humble burials, and finding a big cache of gold and marvelous treasures was the dream that lured these ambitious locals.

In the area where the robbers were digging, people had found human bones and skeletal remains close to the ground surface, indicating that tombs and burials might be just a few meters underground. The scattered bones in the desert area had lain under the sun for so many years, for centuries or at least decades, that the bones' color had been bleached to a true white. The bones naturally attracted treasure hunters from the nearby villages with thoughts of finding gold or precious stone amulets. Only about 2 km. away to the west of the site was the Temple of Alexander the Great at Ein Qeseba, and between the temple and the white bone field was nothing but flat, sandy land, a little valley with natural dunes and desert plants.

Shortly after sunrise, the night watch guard at the Temple of Alexander the Great, Abdel Mawgoud, noticed the small party of men digging in the desert area, at a far distant point but close to the main road, where a number of scattered white bones lay on the ground. It had been an archeological protected area since the time Ahmed Fakhry had examined it in his Bahariya excavations in the 1930s. Fakhry had written about the site and indicated the possible existence of a large cemetery dating from Roman times, but he had not excavated the place.

The guard, Abdel Mawgoud, suspected shifty activity on the part of this small group of men, especially at such an early hour of the day in the middle of winter. They must be tomb raiders. The brave guard decided to walk all the way to them and find out what they were really doing. It was a 2-km. walk, and the gang noticed his approach. They ran away to the main road, took the truck that was waiting for them and fled the site.

Abdel Mawgoud went to the Bahariya Inspectorate of the Antiquities Office (where the local museum is now located) to make his report to Ashry Shaker, the chief inspector and archeologist. After listening carefully to the guard's story, Ashry Shaker took a small group of young archeologists and inspectors to check the site and examine the suspected digging area. Serendipity led them to the hole made by the grave robbers, small but very deep and leading to an underground cave. Everyone realized it was certainly an entrance to an ancient tomb. When he looked carefully into the hole, Ashry Shaker held his breath. He found a golden mask looking straight up at him.

This shocking image compelled Ashry Shaker to rush 400 km. to the Giza Inspectorate of Antiquities, to meet with Zahi Hawass and report his new find in the desert area just south of Baharaiya Oasis. This is one version of the truth.

Another story about how we came to know the tombs of Bahariya with their mummies and golden masks, we read in Zahi Hawass' book about his discoveries. He said that the true hero behind the discovery of these ancient tombs was none other than the guard's smart donkey! According to Abdel Mawgoud's own story, he told Zahi Hawass that the donkey he used as private transport to commute between the village where he lived and the Temple of Alexander the Great where he worked as a guard, had somehow become untied one morning. The loose donkey roamed freely toward the desert flatland, away from the temple, but Abdel Mawgoud did not follow the donkey. He felt it prudent to wait for the next shift guard to arrive first, and then go fetch his loose donkey.

The little donkey had returned to the temple before Abdel Mawgoud had left to find him, and the guard realized that his donkey was not acting normally. The two guards thought the donkey might be trying to give them a message. They needed to find out why the donkey had walked away into the desert. The two guards followed him anxiously and reached the place in the desert where white bones lay scattered on the ground. The donkey acted strangely once again and kicked the ground with its legs. The donkey tried to attract Abdel Mawgoud to something under the ground. Finally, it grabbed

By Way of Accident

his galabia in its mouth and took him to the hole. The two guards peaked into the hole and found themselves staring incredulously at a golden mask looking back into their faces.

The two stories are both intriguing and there is no definitive clue as to which to believe, but I think the world is committed to thanking Abdel Mawgoud, the guard and his very smart, lucky donkey, who a few years later had become the most famous donkey on the face of the earth. In truth, the guard and the donkey had helped find the second most interesting archeological discovery in Egypt after the discovery of Tutankhamun's Tomb in 1922.

In March 1996, special funds were raised by the Department of Antiquities to start surveying the location and prepare for the first excavation season under the leadership of Zahi Hawass. Hawass' mission started with the area mentioned in the guard's story. Zahi and his team first surveyed the huge site, realizing they were about to make a big discovery, an ancient cemetery that covered a large area of desert land. Zahi Hawass' mission to Bahariya included some of his best team and assistants, Ashry Shaker, Mahmoud Afifi, Mansour Boriak, Tarek El Awadi and Ayman Wahbi. Later, Nasser Iskandar joined the team, as did Mustafa Abdel Kader and Noha Abdel Hafez.

During the initial digs, the team found a large tomb under the ground. It contained several mummies together (perhaps one family), with a stairway cut into the mother rock of the land. The tomb had a central rectangular room, with several alcoves carved into the rock on both sides. Within the first season of excavation, the mission uncovered several human mummies buried in these side alcoves. Most of the mummies' heads were covered with limestone masks that had been coated with gold leaf, but six mummies still wore their original gold masks. Unfortunately, no writing or texts were found inside this tomb to help us determine the true names or ages of these burials.

Zahi's interest in Bahariya Oasis grew daily with the promising excavation of the newly discovered cemetery. It was a paradise for an avid archeologist like Hawass. The team recovered over 100 mummies in the first season alone, igniting the entire team's enthusiasm. They began to widen their surveys and digging areas to include other potential locations in the Bahariya Oasis. Sometimes the crew had to excavate under people's private homes, where the existence of ancient tombs had been confirmed, but this made for quite complicated issues and required much money to be paid as compensation to families before being able to declare the right of eminent domain.

By the end of the second season of the mission, the team had found 134 mummies, six of which had golden masks. All the mummies dated back to the early Roman period in Egypt, the 1st and 2nd centuries AD. The finds confirmed previous knowledge of the high level of wealth and prosperity of Bahariya, and showed that its nobles, traders and landowners still followed the Ancient Egyptian funeral traditions of embalming and mummification.

General remarks about the finds:

- Poor burials were also found in the tombs, but those were in pottery coffins.
- A few bronze coins were discovered dating back the times of Queen Cleopatra VII.
- All discovered mummies are still inside the tombs where they were found, except those of the six gilded-mask mummies. They were moved to the small museum at the Bahariya town center to accommodate the influx of visitors, journalists and tourists to the oasis who all had wanted to see the mummies but could not be accommodated inside the tombs.
- Zahi Hawass' mission in Bahariya between 1996 and 1999 found several other tombs in other areas of the oasis and rediscovered many tombs and other structures, previously recorded by Ahmed Fakhry in the 1930 that were now covered with sand or had houses built above them. These included the wine factory and the small Temple of God Bes from Roman times.
- The most exciting discovery outside the Valley of the Golden Mummies was the rediscovery of three tombs that Ahmed Fakhry had noted in his records but had been lost without a trace. Rediscovered by Zahi Hawass under modern houses of several families were the tombs of:
    - The High Priest "*jedashtar*," the great grandson of the ancient Governor of the Oasis "*jedkhonsuefank*" from the 26th Dynasty

- The priest *"thani"*
- The wife of the priest *"thani,"* named *"tanfrtpastit"*

The rediscovery of these last tombs by Zahi Hawass was another amazing accidental discovery in itself. Ahmed Fakhry's original records indicated that the painted room was the last room in the tomb of the governor, and Fakhry therefore had stopped exploration at that room. However, more recently, when Zahi Hawass stood in that room and examined its walls, rechecking Ahmed Fakhry's notes and observations, his intuition told him it was not the true end of the tomb. There had to be another room hidden somewhere or perhaps a secret tunnel.

After a few days of searching, Zahi and his team realized that the painted wall scenes at the end of the tomb had been made only as a decoy for tomb robbers, to fool them into stopping at that point. Actually, the wall was hiding the inner part of the tomb behind it, the interior burial chambers at the bottom of the very deep shaft. To explore the burial shaft of the tomb that lay beneath several houses, the team needed to negotiate with the villagers to remove the ten houses located above the tomb. The families were compensated with other land allowing the mission to proceed in exploring the tomb.

With this great discovery, Egypt entered the third millennium with a golden find, full of mummies with golden masks, fueling the romance of timeless Egypt around the world. More visitors have been coming to Egypt to see the new finds and learn about the new discoveries. As a result of such discoveries, the remote, quiet Bahariya Oasis now has several small hotels, lodges and tourist camps. Life there is blossoming with the recent, great discoveries.

That said, to see the tombs of the Valley of the Golden Mummies, special permission must be obtained from the Antiquities Department Inspectorate in Giza before hitting the road to the oasis.

In the end, it seems clear now that many villages in Bahariya and its outskirts are situated literally on top of underground rock-cut tombs dating back to the 26th Dynasty and the later period, and I am certain we will soon hear about more discoveries in the peaceful Bahariya Oasis.

Its ancient cemeteries may hold up to 10,000 mummies!

Epilogue

THE BIRTH OF THE THIRD millennium, with the internet and telecommunications revolution, always puts Egyptian archeological discoveries in the international news, regardless of how big or small, important or insignificant. News of finding something new in the Egyptian desert or in one of the famous archeological sites usually hits the front pages of popular newspapers, internet news and social network pages. Even Egyptians hear about new discoveries from outside sources and international media.

In the last 15 years several important discoveries have occurred in Egypt and filled many pages in well-known international media. Today, the sweet accident still generously occurs and plays a vital role in finding the hidden secrets of Ancient Egypt, helping lucky archaeologists meet their dream discovery.

In the heart of the Valley of the Kings, where until recently no one dared to think about finding new tombs since the discovery of Tutankhamen's, a team from the University of Memphis in Tennessee, under the leadership of Otto Shadene, made a wonderful discovery in 2006. The location was almost unimaginable as it was very close to the entrance of Tutankhamen's tomb. The new tomb was called KV63, the tomb next in succession to Tutankhamen's KV62.

It is never too late to dig in Egypt, never too hopeless and never time to stop looking. These are three guiding bits of advice for every ambitious archeologist and they are what drove a team of Egyptian archeologists to unearth a new pyramid in north Saqqara when it was thought there were no more pyramids to find. Not an archeological season takes place in Egypt without some new discovery. News about new discoveries comes from all over Egypt and dates back to almost every historic period in Egypt.

Lately, on the west side of Luxor, the ancient Theban necropolis, new discoveries have been recorded, found cut into rock in cave-like style beneath the village of Qurna. The tombs were revealed only after the Egyptian government started relocating the village to a different place, away from the protected archeological site. For several centuries, the village houses had sat atop the tombs which dated back to the New Kingdom. Many of the tombs had been partially explored, primarily by the locals, a very long time ago. Now, under some houses, surveyors and archeologists have found a number of tunnels running for long distances and reaching the heart of the ancient Theban cemetery of Dra Abul Naga with its many nobles' tombs. Archeologists remain still in Qurna village leading the relocation mission, expecting to find a large number of tombs hidden beneath the houses. At this time, revealing the new tombs will have to wait until the relocation of all families to the new village is completed. Next will come the demolition of all the village houses, removing all mud and dirt, followed by clearing and surveying the site in preparation for exploration. When the preservation and conservation teams commence their work, the hope is to find as many as 900 new tombs as yet never recorded which will be added to the great cemetery of ancient Thebes. We must ready ourselves for the great news to start trickling from the Luxor area soon.

According to Egypt's Department of Antiquities, there are over 250 foreign missions working in Egypt annually. They all belong to respectable universities and educational institutes which share a special interest in Egyptian archeology and are willing to cooperate with the Department of Antiquities on new projects. A quick look at the nationalities of all the foreign missions shows them coming from all over the world, the majority from Western museums, universities and other cultural institutions. Only the richest educational and cultural institutions in the world can finance the costly excavation and preservation missions in Egypt that often extend into several seasons.

The unspoken word in such regard and unwritten contract is: if you want to dig in Egypt and look for new discoveries, you must be fully prepared financially. Hiring local workers, transporting them to the worksite and digging locations, supplying accommodations for staff, covering expenses for inspectors and hired archaeologists are all things the mission must pay for. The laws of Egypt prohibit a mission from retaining any of the found artifacts. Under the law they can only experience excavating in Egypt with the right to scientific publication. Certain publications are large with annual circulation while other articles can be found in smaller professional journals and bulletins that are read by small circles of people interested in Egyptology as a science. The grand prize after all, is the assumed glory of an Egyptian archeological discovery.

This is the operational atmosphere in the field of Egyptian archeology in recent years, certainly since the beginning of the new millennium. There has been a rise of a new generation of Egyptian archeologists, Zahi Hawass and others, who have begun taking brave initiatives to establish a new school of Egyptology based on Egyptian works, discoveries and doctrine and with generous contributions from the working foreign missions on the ground.

On another front, the stories I selected to share with you in this book are about the great discoveries which occurred *by way of accident* in the last 200 years. But these are not all the stories that Egypt can offer. There are many more discoveries and stories which include an element of accident and some are really worthy of being told, stories which include much fun and excitement, too. That said, I must explain my decision to omit certain stories. First, I think the research in some stories can be too cumbersome for light reading in Egyptology; and second, I selected only the stories that are well documented in multiple references and/or supported by living eyewitnesses. I chose to exclude any story that does not have scientific papers, publications or eyewitnesses. The following list of discoveries all include the element of accident within details of their discovery but not enough to make a full story from them. These discoveries occurred in locations throughout Egypt from Alexandria in the north to Aswan in the south:

1. The Roman amphitheater, discovered in Alexandria in the 1960s, during the construction of a large government edifice in the downtown area
2. The tomb of *nfr maat* and *nfrt* from Mydoum

3. The Colossi of Akhenaten from Karnak Temple
4. El Bahnasa Papyrus collection
5. The alabaster statue of Amunhotep III with Sobik from Arment, now in the Luxor Museum
6. The tomb of the sons of Ramses II, Number 5 in the Valley of the Kings
7. The tomb of Psmatik in Saqqara
8. Akhenaten Stelae from Amarna
9. Zenon Papyrus from El Fayoum
10. The sarcophagus of Queen *tak hut* from Tel Atrep, from the 26th Dynasty
11. The Magical Stelae of Matreniekh from Heliopolis, now at the Metropolitan Art Museum
12. Karnak Caches of Statues, discovered in 1903
13. The tomb of *Bedosiris* from Tuna El Jabal
14. The Alexandria Catacombs of El Qabari

This is just a short list of artifacts and relics discovered here and there, by accident. In Egypt we hear about new accidents leading to new finds almost every month, often while building new roads or bridges. The frequent incidents of suddenly finding ancient relics and monuments can easily fill many pages, but I find it hard to trace the stories, as they often hit the news in daily newspapers and then evaporate, never to resurface. I consider this to be insufficient documented information.

Additionally, there are hundreds of daily stories and incidents from all over Egypt about locals who dig randomly and illegally on their own, searching for ancient treasures. The quickest possible way for a poor Egyptian to become rich is to find just the right tomb. Sadly, many of these people pay with their lives for such dangerous digs which are not only illegal but extremely unsafe for unprofessional locals.

The obvious truth remains clear: Egypt is the richest country in the world with archeology and monuments. The pursuit of new discoveries remains an exciting matter. The ancient treasures of the Pharaohs still entice the minds of people. Scientists and archeologists still dream about great discoveries and unrivaled glory, while the poor villagers in Egypt, especially those living near famous monuments and ancient sites, challenge everyone, scientists and government authorities alike, as they enthusiastically dig to find the treasure before it's too late.

Only the accident will occasionally intervene to help them both!

BIBLIOGRAPHY

Chapter one
- W. Budge, Rosetta Stone, London 1892.

Chapter two
- J. Romer, Valley of the Kings, New York 1981.
- B.A. Fagan, the Rape of the Nile 2nd edition, AUC Cairo 1992.
- G.B Belzoni, Narrative of the operations and recent discoveries within the pyramids, temples, tombs and excavations in Egypt and Nubia and a Journey to the cost of the Red Sea in search of the ancient Berenice and another to the Oasis of Jupiter Amon, London 1821.
- A. Siliotti, the Discovery of Ancient Egypt…AUC, Cairo 1998.
- Wilkenson G. Richard & N Reeves, The Complete Valley of the Kings, London 2000.

Chapter three
- A. Rhone, L Egypt a petites Journies, Paris 1877.
- A. Marriette, Le Serapeum de Memphis, part I, Paris 1882.
- E. Uphill, Who is Who in Egyptology, London 1972.
- A. Marriette, Choix de Monuments, Paris 1856.
- J. Malek, CDE, LV III, 1983.

Chapter four
- J. Romer, Valley of the Kings, New York 1981.
- B. Fagan, the rape of the Nile, 2nd edition, AUC Cairo 1992.
- E. Feucht, Cachette … LA.I …Wiesbaden 1975.
- G Maspero, Les Momies Royales de Deir El Bahari, MMAF I, 1889.

Chapter five
- Petrie W F, seventy years in Archaeology, London 1931.
- W. F. Petrie and E A Gardener …Naukratis I, London 1886
- W. F. Petrie, the discovery of Naukratis, JHS 5 1885-1886.

Chapter six
- Maron L., The Amarna Letters, London 1992.
- Budge W., by the Nile and Tigris, London 1920.
- Campbelle E., The Chronology of the Amarna Letters, Baltimore 1964.

Chapter seven
- Reeves N & J Tayler, Howard Carter before Tutankhamun, New York 1993.
- Carter H, report on the tomb of Mentuhotep I at Deir El Bahari, known as bab El Hosan, annales de services des Antiquities de l Egypt …Vol II, 1901.
- J. Romer, valley of the kings, New York 1981.
- Redford D, the Oxford Encyclopedia of Ancient Egypt, Oxford 2000
- James T.G.H, Howard Carter, the path to Tutankhamun, London 1992.

Chapter eight
- D.M. Reid, Whose Pharaohs, University of California Press, 2002.
- A.K. Bowman, Egypt After the Pharaohs.
- M. Saad El Din, Alexandria, the site and the History, Cairo 1992.
- J Empereur, Alexandria rediscovered, Paris 1998.
- A. Rowe, Kom El Shukafa, Alexandria 1942.

Chapter nine
- B Grenfell & A Hunt & Smyly, The Tebtunis Papyrus, London 1902.
- The American Discovery of Ancient Egypt, Los Angeles 1995.

Chapter ten
- E Naville, The XIth Dynasty Temples at Deir El Bahari, Vol I, London 1907.
- D Arnold, Deir El Bahari, LA I, 1975.
- J Lipinska, the temple of Thutmosis III, Deir El Bahari II, Warsaw 1977.

Chapter eleven
- **Hawass Zahi**, Tutankhamun and the Golden Age of the Pharaohs. National Geographic DC, 2005.
- Carter H., The tomb of Tutankhamun, London 1972.
- Paterson J., The Murder of King Tut, New York 2009.
- Reeves N., The Great Discoveries, London 2000.

Chapter twelve
- C.A Reisner, A History of the Giza Necropolis Vol II, The tomb of Hetebheres, Cambridge, 1955.
- M. Lehener, the Pyramid Tomb of Hetebheres and the Satellite Pyramid of Khufo, Meinz 1985.
- J. Shaw & P Nicholson, The British Museum Dictionary of Ancient Egypt, Cairo 2002.
- Hawass Z., The Treasures of the Pyramids, the Mystery of Hetebheres, London 2008.

Chapter thirteen
- Monter P., The Royal Tombs of Tanis, Paris?
- Ritchard H Wilkinson, *the complete temples of ancient Egypt*. London 2000.
- A to Z of Ancient Egypt, Cox Simon & Davies Susan, Edinburgh 2006.

Chapter fourteen
- J. M. Robinson, The Nag Hammadi library, New York, 1981.
- Mayer M., The Gnostic Discoveries, the Impact of the Nag Hammadi library, San Francisco 2005.
- Atyia A., Coptic Encyclopedia, New York 1991.
- Hess J., Der Gnostische Papyrus von London, Frieburg 1892.
- Kamel J., Coptic Egypt, History and Guide, Cairo 1987.
- Pagels E., The Gnostic Gospels, New York 1979.

Chapter fifteen
- K Kitchen, Barke, Lexikon der Agyptolologie, Band I, Wiesbaden 1975.
- P Lipka, The Royal Ships of Cheops, Oxford 1984.

Chapter sixteen
- J Empreuor, Alexandria rediscovered, Paris 1998.

Chapter seventeen
- D Arnold, Temples of the lost Pharaohs, London 1992.
- **Hawass Zahi**, a new Colossal Statue of Ramses II from Akhmim, Timeline studies in Honor of Manfred Bietak.

Chapter eighteen
- M Sagher, Das Statuenversteck in Luxor Tempel, Meinz 1990.
- J Berger, those Gods being unearthed, article …Ahram Hebdo 23, 12 1992.

Chapter nineteen
- M Lehner, the complete pyramids, London 1997
- Manley B., the seventy great mysteries of ancient Egypt, London 2003
- Hawass Z,. Lehner M, Builders of the Pyramids, article, Archaeology Vol 50 1997.
- Hawass Z., secrets from the sands, New York 2012.
- **Hawass Zahi**, The Workmen's Community of Giza, The International Symposium in Cairo, April 1992.

Chapter twenty
- C. Vivian, The Western Desert of Egypt, Cairo 2008.
  A. Fakhry, the Oasis of Egypt, Bahariya and Farafra Oasis, Cairo 1973.
- Hawass Z., Valley of the Golden Mummies, Cairo 2000.
- **Hawass Zahi** and **D. Grossman**, Recent Discoveries in Al Haiz, Baharia Oasis, Bulletin de la Societe d'Archeologie Copte. 33.
- **Hawass Zahi**, personal account of the Valley of the Golden Mummies, KMT 10/4…1999.

Made in the USA
Middletown, DE
22 November 2016